THE CORY ARCANGEL HACK

LEONARDO

Seán Cubitt, Editor-in-Chief

Voicetracks: Attuning to Voice in Media and the Arts, Norie Neumark, 2017

Ecstatic Worlds: Media, Utopias, Ecologies, Janine Marchessault, 2017

Fred Forest's Utopia: Media Art and Activism, Michael F. Leruth, 2017

Making Sense: Cognition, Computing, Art, and Embodiment, Simon Penny, 2017

Weather as Medium: Toward a Meteorological Art, Janine Randerson, 2018

Laboratory Lifestyles: The Construction of Scientific Fictions, edited by Sandra Kaji-O'Grady, Chris L. Smith, and Russell Hughes, 2018

Invisible Colors: The Arts of the Atomic Age, Gabrielle Decamous, 2018

Virtual Menageries: Animals as Mediators in Network Cultures, Jody Berland, 2019

From Fingers to Digits: An Artificial Aesthetic, Margaret A. Boden and Ernest A. Edmonds, 2019

MATERIAL WITNESS: Media, Forensics, Evidence, Susan Schuppli, 2020

Tactics of Interfacing: Encoding Affect in Art and Technology, Ksenia Fedorova, 2020

Giving Bodies Back to Data: Image Makers, Bricolage, and Reinvention in Magnetic Resonance Technology, Silvia Casini, 2021

A Biography of the Pixel, Alvy Ray Smith, 2021

Living Books: Experiments in the Posthumanities, Janneke Adema, 2021

Art in the Age of Machine Learning, Sofian Audry, 2021

Design in Motion: Film Experiments at the Bauhaus, Laura Frahm, 2022

Northern Sparks: Innovation, Technology Policy, and the Arts in Canada from Expo 67 to the Internet Age, Michael Century, 2022

Christa Sommerer & Laurent Mignonneau: The Artwork as a Living System 1992–2022, edited by Karin Ohlenschläger, Peter Weibel, and Alfred Weidinger, 2023

Computational Formalism: Art History and Machine Learning, Amanda Wasielewski, 2023

Picture Research: The Work of Intermediation from Pre-Photography to Post-Digitization, Nina Lager Vestberg, 2023

Art + DIY Electronics, Garnet Hertz, 2023

Voidopolis, Kat Mustatea, 2023

After Eating: Metabolizing the Arts, Lindsay Kelley, 2023

Tactical Publishing: Using Senses, Software, and Archives in the Twenty-First Century, Alessandro Ludovico, 2023

The Future is Present: Art, Technology, and the Work of Mobile Image, Philip Glahn and Cary Levine, 2024

Living Surfaces: Images, Plants, and Environments of Media, Abelardo Gil-Fournier and Jussi Parikka, 2024

Heartbeat Art, Claudia Arozqueta, 2025

Ecologies of Artistic Practice: Rethinking Cultural Economies through Art and Technology, Ashley Lee Wong, 2025

Proxistant Vision: Motion, Navigation, Scale, Synne Tollerud Bull and Dragan Miletic, 2025

The Cory Arcangel Hack: Digital Culture and Aesthetic Practice, Eivind Røssaak, 2025

See http://mitpress.mit.edu for a complete list of titles in this series.

THE CORY ARCANGEL HACK

DIGITAL CULTURE AND AESTHETIC PRACTICE

EIVIND RØSSAAK
PREFACE BY ALEXANDER R. GALLOWAY

THE MIT PRESS
CAMBRIDGE, MASSACHUSETTS
LONDON, ENGLAND

The MIT Press
Massachusetts Institute of Technology
77 Massachusetts Avenue, Cambridge, MA 02139
mitpress.mit.edu

The MIT Press would like to thank the anonymous peer reviewers who provided comments on drafts of this book. The generous work of academic experts is essential for establishing the authority and quality of our publications. We acknowledge with gratitude the contributions of these otherwise uncredited readers.

This book was set in Arnhem Pro and Frank New by Westchester Publishing Services. Printed and bound in the United States of America.

Library of Congress Cataloging-in-Publication Data

Names: Røssaak, Eivind, author. | Galloway, Alexander R., 1974–writer of preface.
Title: The Cory Arcangel hack : digital culture and aesthetic practice / Eivind Røssaak ; preface by Alexander R. Galloway.
Description: Cambridge, Massachusetts : The MIT Press, [2025] | Series: Leonardo | Includes bibliographical references and index.
Identifiers: LCCN 2024059430 (print) | LCCN 2024059431 (ebook) | ISBN 9780262552547 (paperback) | ISBN 9780262383387 (epub) | ISBN 9780262383394 (pdf)
Subjects: LCSH: Arcangel, Cory, 1978-—Criticism and interpretation.
Classification: LCC N6537.A633 R67 2025 (print) | LCC N6537.A633 (ebook) | DDC 776.092—dc23/eng/20250226
LC record available at https://lccn.loc.gov/2024059430
LC ebook record available at https://lccn.loc.gov/2024059431

10 9 8 7 6 5 4 3 2 1

EU Authorised Representative: Easy Access System Europe, Mustamäe tee 50, 10621 Tallinn, Estonia | Email: gpsr.requests@easproject.com

To Thomas, Marthe, Vilde, and Lia

The MIT Press's publishing mission benefits from the generosity of our donors, including Prabha Kanna and Amar Kendale.

CONTENTS

PREFACE

Alexander R. Galloway

Memory fades. And then it comes rushing back. Images from the past come and go, sometimes remaining clear, sometimes murky, but always somehow reprocessed.

I mean computer memory. Persisting for a while, it mostly disappears. Even in the age of GitHub and cloud backups, computer art often vanishes more quickly than explicitly ephemeral formats like performance or installation art, these frequently immortalized through silkscreened fliers and grainy photographs. Eivind Røssaak does his readers a service by holding on to the computer memories for a bit longer, preserving this history and interpreting it too.

I guess I also mean people memories. I remember a video of rotisserie hot dogs, fleshy and sweating from electrical heat, in a second-floor loft on Broadway below Canal Street in New York City. The video was part of Cory Arcangel's first gallery show, curated by Michele Thursz. And I remember meeting Cory at Rhizome events on the Lower East Side, as Røssaak recounts at the start of the book, although I'm certain the floppy disks were Mark Tribe's idea.

I remember dumpster diving with Cory once behind the Apple headquarters in Cupertino, California, hoping to find something good. No dice. I remember going over to Cory's Brooklyn apartment for a long session of soldering EPROMs onto NES cartridges. In gratitude Cory rewarded me with my very own *Super Mario Clouds* cartridge, which remains one of my prized possessions from that era. (Later, this generated headaches for the registrar at Cory's gallery, who was grumpy that I had obtained a version of the work circumventing the gallery's officially numbered edition.) I remember when Cory wanted to hack the iconic Macintosh Flurry screensaver so that the dazzling and ethereal animation would instead look low-energy and depressed, cowering in the corner of the screen. (It didn't happen; too difficult.) I honestly don't remember writing the 6502 assembly code for Cory's "Space Invader," but if he says so

I'll take it. The creative flow in those years was roughly: get a goofy idea; try to build it within a day or two; get bored and move on. It wasn't always clear who cooked up the goofy idea to begin with. But it was usually Cory who had the best ones, the funniest ones, and the ones that resonated with the most people.

At a certain level, it's all stolen. Plagiarism is necessary; progress demands it. Cory has long been captivated by the pilfered quality of vernacular consumer culture. Images and motifs capture viewers' attention before being recycled and recirculated in a new form. Everyday ephemera appears all over this artwork. You will find neon-colored pool noodles and airplane barf bags, Tetris and blue jeans, JPEG compression and GeForce graphics cards, Fila and Soulcycle, Kim Kardashian and Art Garfunkel, the Photoshop gradient tool and dunkindonuts.com, pumpkin pie Pop-Tarts and prog rock crop tops. Okay, I might have made up those last two, but it's a good bet they're in there somewhere. I suspect this is one reason why Cory's work surged rather than receded during the historical transition from the Net Art of the early 2000s to the Post-Internet art that came a few years later and was a good deal more inspired by everyday consumer culture. In a sense Cory had already been making Post-Internet work before the fact, somehow anticipating and precipitating a new sensibility that would eventually arrive.

If there's a tragic quality to Cory's work, it would be how quickly internet culture has metabolized many of these gestures. Cory's supercut of cats walking on pianos, precisely sequenced to the score for Arnold Schönberg's Drei Klavierstücke, op. 11, is a brilliant and funny video. But today's YouTube is chock-full of nerdy stunts, even if few of them are as wink-wink about the history of modernist music. Many of today's memes are just re-ups of computer art from ten or twenty years ago. Or maybe it all just completes a cycle, as Cory continues to upload his work back into the same cultural froth from which it originally emerged.

As Røssaak describes it, much of this work has a hacker's sensibility. Hacks offer a conspicuous display of skill targeted toward a specific audience primed to admire such technical feats. In other words, hacks are about showing off. But virtuosos can become smug and annoying when overly invested in their own talent. Cory uses humor as a way to downplay an inherent cleverness. The jokes help soften what might otherwise appear gimmicky or merely dexterous. (Cory attended a music conservatory for undergrad where he also took a few programming classes, but he never studied studio art and doesn't have an MFA.) In other words, while the Arcangel Expanded Universe features many instances of technical peacocking, like Eddie Van Halen's "Eruption" or Niccolò Paganini's Caprice No. 5, such displays are always undercut by a healthy admixture of absurdity and wit. Indeed, Cory has made work about both of these musical compositions, and whenever a guitar was nearby was known to spontaneously rehearse the former.

The work is funny, let me stress this. Writing a Perl script that orders a pizza from the command line is funny. Processing Iron Maiden's "The Number of the Beast" through MP3 compression 666 times in a row is funny. Modding *Hogan's Alley* to display the pope and Flavor Flav is funny. Composing a new glockenspiel accompaniment for Bruce Springsteen's *Born to Run* and releasing it on vinyl is funny. Running an iPhone through a printing press is funny.

Reminding people what is funny is not funny, of course, and I never quite had the same knack for the humorous stunt. There was the time when I tried to take out a patent on "net.art," as a cruel joke on all the artists who had actually invented it, before learning to my chagrin that it would entail gobs of lawyer's fees. Cory was better at all this stuff. For example, he came up with the idea for T.A.C. (Total Asshole Compression), a compression tool modeled after StuffIt or Zip that we made together in 2004. T.A.C. made files larger rather than smaller—tag line "it makes files bigger, much bigger"—by bundling them with useless crap like Debbie Gibson ringtones and random binary files spidered from the user's own "/System Folder" directory.

Fans of classic Hollywood will often reference the "Lubitsch touch" as a way to capture the indescribable verve of films made by auteur director Ernst Lubitsch. We might today talk about "the Arcangel touch" as the perfect formula of deadpan comedy and pop-cultural references, mixed with a healthy dose of ironic detachment. Or maybe "Arcangel's alchemy" is a better phrase, as Røssaak will suggest in the pages that follow. Through this special alchemy, this special touch, there emerges a whole image of art and culture that is both trashy and clean, eminently consumable even when it remains blank and dissociated, highly technical and dumb as dirt, unmistakably postmodern yet thoroughly cognizant of the historical avant-garde.

ACKNOWLEDGMENTS

This book contains a thousand voices, but legally, I am the one to blame. I extend my heartfelt thanks to Cory Arcangel for his generous availability for interviews, gallery and studio visits, and for graciously sharing documents and recordings from his private archive. A special thanks to my colleagues and friends—Alexander R. Galloway, Ina Blom, D. N. Rodowick, Wolfgang Ernst, Susanne Østby Sæther, Ivar Håkon Tjelta, Jacob Lund—for reading early versions of chapters. Thank you as well to the excellent anonymous peer reviewers and the editors at the MIT Press, including Gabriela Bueno Gibbs and Elizabeth Agresta. I am also grateful to Knut Ove Eliassen, Øyvind Prytz, and Anne Ogundipe for publishing a short essay on Cory Arcangel in their research volume *Estetiske praksiser i den digitale produksjonens tidsalder* (Fagbokforlaget, 2022), supported by Arts Council Norway. It's fair to say that that process, along with Sean Cubitt's encouragement, drew me into embarking on this book project. The feedback I received on my presentations at the Connect/Cut conference, organized by Frederik Tygstrup at the University of Copenhagen in 2022, and at the Nordic Conference on Aesthetics at Södertörn University in Stockholm that same year, was especially inspirational. I also appreciate the workshop devoted to an early draft at the Media Aesthetics Seminar at the University of Oslo, organized by Aurora A. S. Hoel and her students at the Department of Media and Communication. The conversations I've had on this material with Matthew Fuller, Christiane Paul, Christian Refsum, Patrick Jagoda, Ian Buchanan, Marius Wulfsberg, Kjetil Jakobsen, Harald Østgaard Lund, as well as the programmers and hackers Lars Johnsen, Cato Johnsen, and Audun Wilhelmsen, have been invaluable. Art critic Ed Halter's public conversation with Arcangel was a significant catalyst for me at an early stage. It took place at the launch event of Arcangel's zine *The Source Issue #10* at the Arcangel Flagship Store in Stavanger in 2018. Thanks to Arnhild Sunnanå for recording the conversation. For help with images and illustrations, I am grateful to Arcangel and his assistant, Rute Ventura. Many thanks to Arts Council Norway for the grant. I could not have done this without Betty's and Lia's patience and support.

Oslo, September 11, 2024

INTRODUCTION

The Milieu

"Hackers create the possibility of new things entering the world."
—McKenzie Wark[1]

Around the turn of the century, Rhizome.org organized club nights for new media art called OpenMouse at Fun on the Lower East Side. When the young Cory Arcangel first went to the club night, Alexander R. Galloway, the founder of RSG (Radical Software Group) and now a professor of media studies at NYU, was sitting at the door handing out floppy disks, using them as flyers. The information about the club night was printed on the label of the disks. Arcangel took one home, inserted it into his computer, and discovered that there was nothing on the disk. Later, he approached Galloway and asked him, "Why don't we put an art show on this disk, so the next time you guys hand these out, there will actually be something on it?"[2] This is how Arcangel ended up cocurating an art exhibition on a floppy disk in 2001 with Michele Thursz.[3]

Its title, *1.44 Megs*, simply refers to the amount of space on the floppy disk. The concept? "All works was to be equal to or less than 150k."[4] It featured fifteen artists, many of them major figures from the Net Art scene.[5] Arcangel's contribution to his own show was *Temple Drive*. It consisted of landscape photographs taken from his grandmother's rooftop on Temple Drive, Cheektowaga, New York, a suburb of Buffalo. They were computationally redrawn as four extended ASCII prints. When viewed with

0.1

Cory Arcangel and Michele Thursz, *1.44 Megs*, 2001. Floppy disk exhibition. Photo by Michael Connor, courtesy of the artist and Rhizome.

Arcangel's homemade TrueType font, one could zoom in on the miniscule building blocks, tiny grayscale patterns, squares, characters, and letters. The extended ASCII prints were presented as DIY prints; one could take them to a print shop and have them printed out. At one of the next Fun events, Galloway would hand out Arcangel's and Thursz's floppy disks containing the group show *1.44 Megs*. This was Arcangel's first art exhibition in New York. Alongside Thursz, he had displaced and compressed a center of the art world onto a floppy disk.

Cory Arcangel's artworks from 2001 to today emerged during a pivotal transition in human history. As computers and the internet gradually became a 24/7 obsession, they reshaped the flows and rhythms of life in unprecedented ways. While Arcangel's work may initially appear as an array of absurdity and humor, in retrospect, it reveals itself as a profound experiment and vigilant exploration of our encounter with what we used to call "new media." Understanding his art requires us to explore the technical operation that makes it possible: the hack.

To Arcangel, format, in its most concrete technical sense, matters. What I call "the Cory Arcangel hack" makes format as a mattering matter speak. In my reading, the hack provokes an encounter with the resistance and physicality of matter. Media life relies on hardware and software to direct flows of electricity and electrons, allowing bits and bytes, sounds, and images to move along specific pathways. The Cory Arcangel hack intervenes in these paths, cutting up the flows to produce alternative flow-cut arrangements. This intervention reveals the inframachinic layers of computation—the underlying, often invisible processes that condition and control these flows—while also bringing them into dialogue with cultural expressions. In this confrontation, computational and cultural flows collide, articulating what can be called a schiz-image. In this context, any matter can express itself—whether it's a protruding chip, a malfunction, a technical detail, or a piece of code or software—each becoming an actor capable of altering the situation. This book sets out to uncover these actors and the forces they engage with in the contemporary toxic spaces of an informatic milieu.

Inspired by the slogans of Gilles Deleuze and Félix Guattari ("follow matter") and Bruno Latour ("follow the 'actors'"), I reverse engineer the hacks in two directions, toward their tiniest components (a piece of code or a bot) and toward a larger media ecology (networks and platforms).[6] Furthermore, there is always a relation between the modification of minor actors and matters and larger networks or the social. Where Latour decomposes a tiny fragment of the social—for example, a science experiment in a lab—to render visible the network of the actors, flows, and forces that "reassemble" the social, I decompose the Cory Arcangel hack to reveal the codes and tricks (call them nonhuman actors) that make up its flow-cut arrangement and the forces that reenvision the social. The hack conjures a vision of how society works techno-aesthetically and suggests alternative flows or rhythms. By targeting a special field where, as Latour writes, "forces are made of smaller ties, whose resistance can be tested one by one," the hack has "a chance to modify a given state of affairs."[7] The hack always reflects techno-aesthetic relations that are larger than themselves. Tiny operations make the operationality of larger media ecologies tangible. In this way, Arcangel becomes a critical "mechanologist" reflecting on the technicity of culture.[8] The hack is techno-social philosophy done *with* technology to reenvision the social as constituted not only by humans, institutions, and traditions, as in traditional sociology but by human–thing relations of all kinds, a multiplicity of codes, circuits, microchips, algorithmic tools, and platform affordances.

VIDEO CULTURE

Before examining Arcangel's hacks or flow-cut arrangements, it's helpful to begin with some background. What are the beliefs, desires, and skills that make up the milieus from which Arcangel came? He emerged as an artist in the period 2000–2004, after the 1990s Net Art scene which mostly took place at festivals, and before the Post-Internet artists exploded into the art world after 2010.[9] He combined the hacker-oriented hands-on skills from Net Art with what would be Post-Internet art's fondness for memes and the generic image. He became one of the first artists from a new generation of punk DIY geeks to crack the contemporary art "code" and make new media art interesting in the field of contemporary art, claims Christiane Paul, new media curator and art historian at the Whitney Museum of American Art in New York City.[10] The conundrum is, Arcangel cracked the art "code," while experimenting with computer code. He was a hacker who relatively quickly became a contemporary artist, and not just a new media artist. His contributions, along with those of other young artists, were instrumental in enabling the contemporary art scene to engage with and respond to emerging new media practices, particularly in the realm of digital culture. The new digital infrastructure of desires and expressions (that is, the computational logics of command and control), the real codes of the contemporary condition, could be queried in galleries and museums. Most images, sounds, and texts in his work have been obtained, not by traditional media, but by coding and data processing. He writes code and makes most of the software himself or with the aid of his assistants.

In Arcangel's earliest years as an artist, his hacks and performances were carried out while working and touring with the underground groups Beige, Paper Rad, and Radical Software Group in New York, Chicago, Pittsburgh, and East Hampton, Massachusetts, and to festivals in Europe, before he established his own studio in New York City with several employees and programmers in 2010, and moved to Norway in 2015.[11] These groups were not particularly concerned with the art scene; they had their own networks and channels. In retrospect, Arcangel says, "We were not artists making works, but instead, we were nerds making projects."[12] The title of Arcangel's first big museum solo show, *Nerdzone Version 1*, captured this scene.[13] Some of these early "projects" are important for understanding Arcangel's later works, because both his hacker skills and his talent as a performer were developed during these early apprentice years. However, I would assert, his early projects were not nerdy exercises without connections to the art world, they were experiments in cutting into and connecting to technology and societal flows, without the art world really understanding it at first.

Arcangel was born in Buffalo, New York, in 1978 to Michael and Maureen Arcangel. His father comes from a long line of Italian craftsmen and builders and was a commercial real estate developer, who, in Arcangel's words, "takes raw land, obtains the necessary permits, creates building lots, and puts in the sewers, the water and electric lines, the streets and curbs. Now, he does the opposite, he demolishes old structures like factories."[14] Arcangel's brother introduced him to the guitar hacker Eddie Van Halen, and with his sister, he made rock music videos. His extended Italian family also includes the pop art painter Allan D'Arcangelo (1930–1998), whom he never met. In high school, Arcangel took two different classes in experimental video and one in computer art, learning animation. In an early interview with his future wife, the Norwegian curator Hanne Mugaas, Arcangel talked about growing up with video art in Buffalo:

> I remember watching TV when I was younger and seeing these weirdo minimal color field videos late at night. It is hard to put into words, but by growing up there I never thought it was weird to make a 15 minute [sic] slow motion video. No one ever told me this was strange [. . .] it wasn't until I moved away that I learned that these were "art videos."[15]

Buffalo had a unique video culture. Video artist Tony Conrad had joined the faculty at the Center for Media Study at the University of Buffalo, and became part of a scene that included Paul Sharits, Hollis Frampton, Steina and Woody Vasulka, Peter Weibel, James Blue, Cathy Steffan, and Gerald O'Grady.[16] Arcangel's interest for this generation of artists has only grown. Later in his career, he would befriend Conrad and help him restore and publish online his private cassette collection of piano pieces as *Tony Conrad: Music and the Mind of the World* (2017). A year earlier, he had restored Andy Warhol's Amiga computer, and most recently, he restored Michel Majerus's PowerBook G3 as *Let's Play Majerus G3* (2017–2025).

BEIGE AND RADICAL SOFTWARE GROUP

As many video artists before him, Arcangel went on to study music at Oberlin Conservatory of Music, initially majoring in classical guitar before switching to technology in music and related arts. He also studied composition with Pauline Oliveros. With Joe Beuckman and fellow students Joe Bonn and Paul B. Davis, he co-established the hacker-inspired collective Beige in 1998. Beige was initially only a record label initiated by Beuckman and Davis but gradually became a loosely organized multimedia programming collective and performance group called Beige Programming Ensemble.[17] They experimented with computer art, Net Art, and "video game rock music," and organized programming workshops and "multimedia rags."[18] Their most well-known record is the DJ battle record, *The 8-bit Construction Set*, which they started work on in 1998 and released as an EP in 2001. It contains music, two tracks of software stored as audio data, and a sheet of instructions on how to upload the software. The 8-bit music was made on Commodore home computers on the A-side and Atari home computers on the B-side, downloaded to audiotapes, encoded, and inscribed as sound-bites into vinyl. It received a lot of attention. Reviews included: from Drax, of Bodenständig 2000, "What Joe Satriani is on guitar, The 8-Bit Construction Set are on Atari!"; from drummer Nic Collins (son of Phil Collins), "Says in 8 bits what takes everyone else in the world 16"; from Paul D. Miller/DJ Spooky, "Da bomb! Dope dope dope dope!!!!"; and from the *New York Times*, ". . . a testimony to nerdiness."[19] Writing about it years later, media art historian Domenico Quaranta says, "*The 8-bit Construction Set* reflects the predilection for low-tech and lo-fi aesthetics that is characteristic of a lot of European Net Art; but it also echoes the advent of 8-bit music, which was then emerging in both the US and Europe, with old platforms being used as musical instruments."[20]

In 2001, Beige was invited to the Make World festival in Munich, curated by Olia Lialina and Florian Schneider, where Arcangel met several inspirational figures such as Dragan Espenschied and Dirk Paesmans, the latter from Jodi, and experienced the German electronic music group Bodenständig 2000. Of course his influences didn't come solely from that experience. Beige collaborator Paul B. Davis would also have a significant impact on Arcangel. He introduced hacking Nintendo cartridges to Arcangel.[21] They created works together like *Fat Bits* (2001), with screen prints and television footage of an NHL hockey fight looped as real-time animation in slow motion generated on three reprogrammed Nintendo cartridges. Their hacktivistic and media archaeological self-understanding for the show *Post-Data in the Age of Low Potential* at Deadtech, Chicago, in 2001, reads like a manifesto:

We create computer art which is aesthetically aware of both its own identity and the underlying process which supports it [. . .]. The use of the Nintendo Entertainment System is itself important because it, firstly, signifies an artistic "re-licensing" of proprietary corporate technology and, secondly, refutes Nintendo's forced obsolescence profit structure which defines it as "outdated." [. . .] Our primary foundation of Post Data is then this: the conscious corruption of data, the releasing of bits from their imprisonment within the restrictive, limiting boundaries of corporate software applications, and the exploitation of the extreme complexity of computer systems paired with the extreme intentionality of artist(s) who seek to engage the computing process at a fundamental level. It is at this point that the machine "speaks" to us, revealing a more honest representation of the technological extremity.[22]

In another joint piece, *Untitled Landscape Study* (2002, handmade hacked Nintendo NES cartridge), they erased an NES cartridge and used it to synthesize audio-visuals such as Davis's 8-bit music and Arcangel's pictures from his grandmother's rooftop, again. Members of Beige would also make individual pieces. In 2002, after long nights of experiments with ROM hacking Arcangel would post a work called *Super Mario Clouds* online. It was exhibited at the School of Visual Arts Gallery and Team Gallery in 2003 and would go on to make art history after being chosen to feature at the Whitney Biennial in 2004.

Arcangel had moved to New York City in 2000, where he also did collaborations with the hacker group RSG (Radical Software Group, 2001–2011), established by Alexander R. Galloway, who had made Carnivore (2001), an internet art platform that allowed artists and designers to make real-time visualizations of network data. It was based on the notorious FBI network surveillance software of the same name.[23] It could map a web infrastructure by listening to internet traffic (email, web surfing, etc.) on a specific local network and animate, diagnose, or interpret the network traffic in any way one wished. Galloway invited artists to bring clients to Carnivore. Arcangel wrote a script using Perl to instruct Carnivore to find the number of times out- and inbound internet traffic referred to the gangster rappers Boo-Yaa T.R.I.B.E. Arcangel's spyware work, *Boo-Yaa Counter: Carnivore Client* (2001), would broadcast the result in real time to a TV screen (figure 0.2). With Galloway, he also made an archival video and website documenting hacker culture, *Low Level All-Stars* (2003) (figure 0.3).

It collected eleven demos made by hacker collectives flashing their "awesome hacks" online. They were "the fearless geeks who remove the game's copy protection through brute force."[24] These were documents

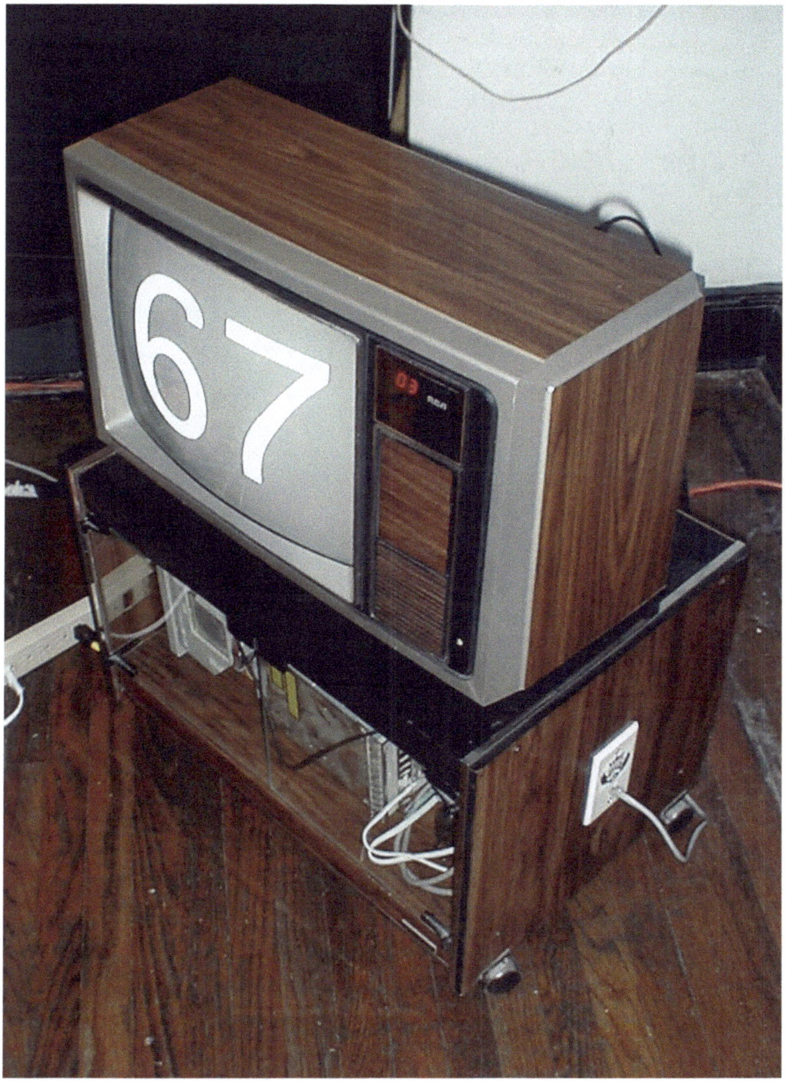

0.2

Cory Arcangel, *The Boo-Yaa Counter: Carnivore Client*, 2001. Power computing Macintosh PC, artist software, CRT TV. Photo by Cory Arcangel, courtesy of the artist.

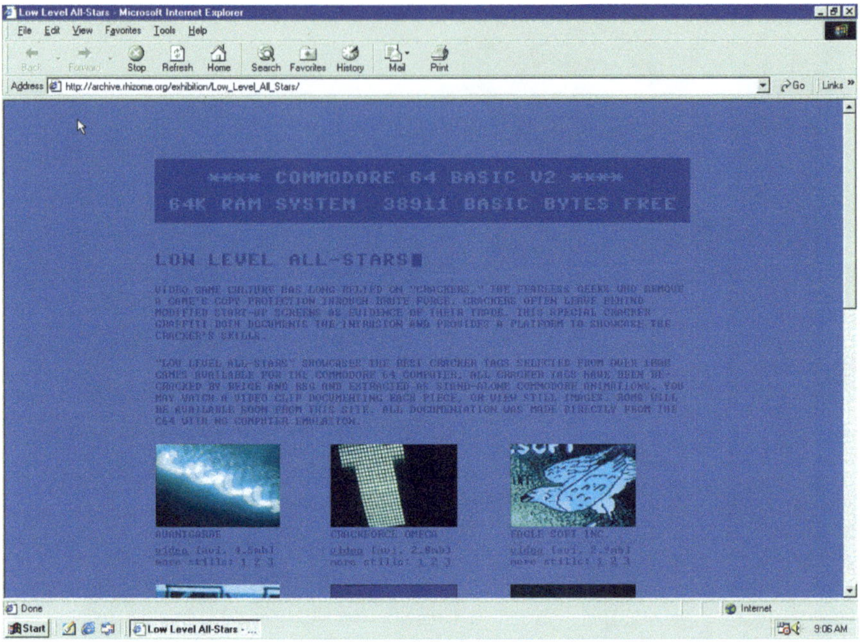

0.3

Cory Arcangel and Alexander R. Galloway (under the auspices of Beige + RSG), *Low Level All Stars*, 2003. Website exhibition. Photo by Cory Arcangel, courtesy of the artists. Historically accurate screenshot created using oldweb.today.

from the so-called game warfare among hackers in the cracker culture scene of the 1980s and 1990s. As soon as video games were released, people would crack them and make videos about the hack, which they shared among collectives of crackers, not over the internet but hand mailed on disks to each other around the country and the world. Arcangel explained the phenomenon in a lecture at UC Berkeley:

> Cracker culture groups were young people who would hack their Commodore 64, Attari, or Apple machines and brag about it online. They would make introductions to their hack which were animated showcases of their programming skills. This was especially big in Europe. Alex [Galloway] and I collected a bunch of these introductions and assembled eleven of these. One group is called NATO, one RAD [Rowdy American Distributer], one is called Avant-Garde, or Mayhem in Monsterland, Game Gone Crazy. At bottom they thank all their friends.[25]

Low Level All-Stars collected what could be called early digital graffiti, lo-fi dirt-style expressions spreading from a margin of art.

One of Arcangel's most curious 8-bit video works from this early period is *Data Diaries* (2003). It is highlighted as among the 100 most "exemplary works" of "Net Art from the 1980s to the 2010s" in Rhizome's Net Art Anthology from 2019.[26] *Data Diaries* (2003) was based on "RAM-phishing," a hacker technique used to spy on what people had been doing on a public computer, like in a lab, classroom, library, or at an internet cafe.[27] "The random-access processor (RAM) of a computer never gets erased; it just gets overwritten until the computer is turned off," Arcangel explains.[28] The computer user's activities, emails, notes, picture, video, or sound edits, would always remain in the computer's temporary storage as ghosts, dead raw material, but nevertheless as encoded strings. Could this be made public as art in another format? Could dead or dormant matter begin to "speak" again? Could the RAM be played as music or a movie?

Arcangel discovered that he could fool a QuickTime player into reading a RAM-file as a movie file if the header indicating format specification got hacked. He decided to make movies with sound generated from his own RAM for every day of the month, thirty-one abstract, glitchy videos with noisy sounds published on a homemade website, where one can choose to play them in either color or black and white. Each movie

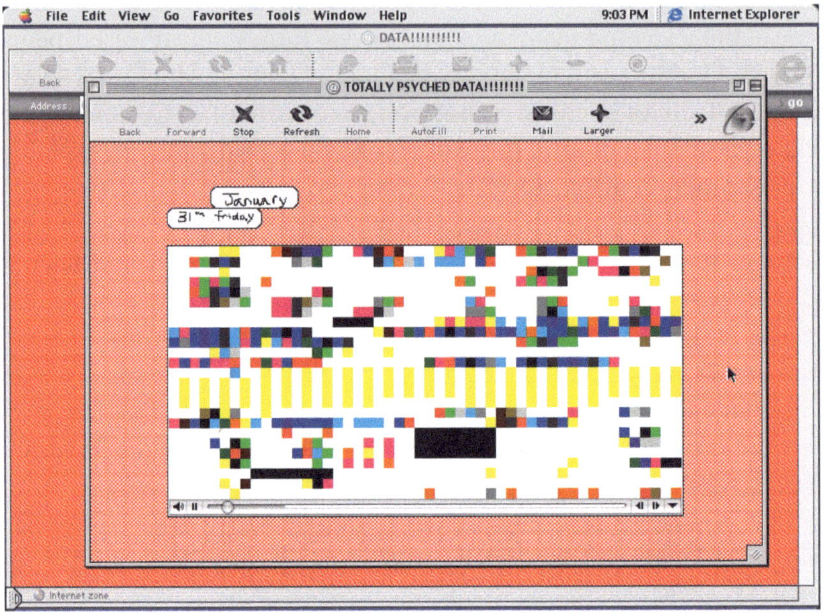

0.4

Cory Arcangel, *Data Diaries*, 2003. Website showing 62 single-channel videos (optional selection). Photo by Cory Arcangel, courtesy of the artist and Rhizome. Historically accurate screenshot created using bwFLA, Emulation as a Service, University of Freiburg. *Data Diaries* is a commission of New Radio and Performing Arts, Inc., dba Ether-Ore, for its Turbulence website. It was made possible with funding from the Jerome Foundation.

contained all 128 MB of Arcangel's computer in up to sixteen colors. Galloway explains the simple but ingenious method this way:

What did Cory Arcangel do in this piece? Next to nothing. The computer did the work, and he just gave it a form. His discovery was this: take a huge data file—in this case his computer's memory file—and fool QuickTime into thinking it's a video file. Then press play. Your computer's memory is now video art. QuickTime plays right through, not knowing that the squiggles and shards on the screen are actually the bits and bytes of the computer's own brain. The data was always right in front of your nose. Now you can watch it.[29]

The computer always relies on several operations that work in the background. Nigel Thrift, a geographer known for his interest in what he calls "the technological unconscious," wanted to address these "backgrounds" in a seminal essay published a year after Arcangel's piece.[30] Thrift writes: "This powerful infrastructural logic which allows the world to show up as confident and in charge is rarely written about in and for itself."[31] However, artists have always been interested in these problems, and Arcangel's way of breaching the background/surface dichotomy of computation goes to the heart of the technological unconscious. To Thrift, the technological unconscious designates complex aspects of human behavior in a technological world. He continues:

Our conventions of *address*, of what will show up where and what will show up next, are often arbitrary, and they rely on knowledges of position and juxtaposition—sometimes tacit, but increasingly systematised—which lie at the base of Euro-American societies. When practice is established and runs smoothly without being perturbed by disruptive events, conventions of address sit there quietly in the background and the fictional nature of organisational knowledges does not surface easily.[32]

Data Diaries is such a disruptive event. It does not accept the order of positions and juxtapositions but explores their conventional order to encounter "the fictional nature of organisational knowledge." Computer science and human-computer interaction (HCI) research has long been involved in making sure that the standards for computer interfaces conform to society's normal ways of making sense, communicating, displaying, and storing. By entering the black box of computation, hacks can penetrate the ordered space of normalcy and become an ally with the hidden layers of computation for other purposes. In this way, Arcangel's artworks are also epistemic objects questioning the logic of infrastructures and the way culture works.

According to Arcangel, it was the artist Seth Price who inspired him to bring more of the hacker projects into art galleries. Price had distributed, as a PDF file, the first version of his essay/artwork, *Dispersion* (2002 and later). It carried an epigraph by Marcel Broodthaers: "The definition of artistic creativity occurs, first of all, in the field of distribution."[33] Seth writes:

> Some of the most interesting recent artistic activity has taken place outside the art market and its forums. Collaborative and sometimes anonymous groups work in fashion, music, video, or performance, garnering admiration within the art world while somehow retaining their status as outsiders, perhaps due to their preference for theatrical, distribution-oriented modes. Maybe this is what Duchamp meant by his intriguing throwaway comment, late in life, that the artist of the future will be underground. [. . .] Distribution is a circuit of reading, and there is huge potential for subversion when dealing with the institutions that control definitions of cultural meaning. Duchamp distributed the notion of the fountain in such a way that it became one of art's primal scenes; it transubstantiated from a provocative *objet d'art* into, as Broodthaers defined his Musée des Aigles: "a situation, a system defined by objects, by inscriptions, by various activities."[34]

Seth describes what he saw in the New York underground and put it in a historical context going back to avant-garde art. There were connections between the "various activities" of "collaborative and sometimes anonymous groups," and Duchamp's way of changing art from outside-art. Seth conjures forth what could be called a "minor history" in art. The minor is not inferior to major trends; it is rather nonstandard, what Gilles Deleuze and Félix Guattari would call a "subsystem or outsystem" (*hors-système*).[35] No wonder Seth was interested in collectives such as Beige and Paper Rad where Arcangel was active. Arcangel would also present the history of Paper Rad as a kind of minor history; their "refusal to distinguish between hierarchies of distribution [. . .] led to their work slipping out of the art historical discourse," he writes.[36] Arcangel and Seth's common "preference for theatrical, distribution-oriented modes" as art was demonstrated at a joint hybrid screening event at the New York Underground Film Festival in 2003 called *Beige and Seth Price Collective: Psyche Out 2k3*, programmed by Ed Halter.[37]

> *Super Mario Clouds*, Price's PDF "Dispersion," and paperrad.org crystallized the multi-platform approach to internet art that became the dominant paradigm in the '00s, mobilizing online audiences and traveling through the contemporary art world in the form of established disciplines like video installations, performance, photography, or sculpture.[38]

If art historian Branden W. Joseph writes the minor history of Conrad's generation, Seth and Halter envision how a minor history could be written for Arcangel and his generation.[39] Furthermore, the Cory Arcangel hack can be viewed as a form of machine art, which at its arrival always appear as a minor history. Arcangel extends the machine art of the twentieth century into the twenty-first century.

MACHINE ART

Machine art riddled the entire twentieth century.[40] Art has reacted to, simulated, or built machines—both creative and dysfunctional machines. However, only recently, and especially after the emergence of first, apparatus theory with its focus on social machines, and then media archaeology with its focus on technical machines, have art historians cared to go deeper into the workings of various artmachines from sound recorders to film, video, and the computer. Art historian Caroline Jones's fascinating study, *Machine in the Studio: Constructing the Postwar American Artist* (1996), analyzes the moments when "the machine" entered and transformed the artist's studio in the 1960s. The "machine in the studio" supplanted notions of originality by practices of appropriation and the readymade. The artist became a recorder, a curator, and an editor of available culture. Jones sees a radical break in studio practices from "the romance of the studio" of painters like Jackson Pollock who contended, "I am nature," to the pop art Factory of Andy Warhol and his slogan, "I want to be machine." Warhol's Factory represents a move from the isolated sanctuary of the abstract expressionist who created works "from a deeply private inner source to achieve an individuating sublimity" to the industrial aesthetic of the latter. The machines connected Warhol to the world in an uncontestably mediated way, Jones asserts.[41] Machines left their traces. They became not surrogates but new artificial limbs and senses for interacting with the world. The "1960s technological sublime" of Warhol relied on "assembly-line production techniques."[42] Warhol established the studio as a complex and collaborative site, a mass production facility. Jones's machine-focus highlights devices and reproduction machines like the tape recorder, camera, and film. Warhol's companion machines set up both symbolic relations and actual modes of production: the machines' need for collaborators, their contemporaneity, their anti-humanist qualities, and their productivity, were all elements that allowed Warhol's studio to be recoded as the Factory, Jones concludes.

However, Jones's *Machine in the Studio* does not address television, video, and computers. According to my former research project colleague, art historian Ina Blom, the emergence of video art ushers in "the electronic studio" where machines and materials are no longer serving "mainly as means for human artistic creativity"; they take on "multiple nonhuman agencies" that machines did not possess earlier.[43] Nonstandard uses of video equipment "articulate an intra-machinic redefinition of the workplace," Blom stresses. The video artists' experiments in art and engineering "bring out latent properties of electronic tools that figure as distinct creative personae." They become "object-comrades or coworkers of an emergent social order of human–thing relationality," and reveal unused potentials of televisual culture. Video could produce, record, and store television. It was "television's archive." Yet, "the event-like technicity" of "videotaped television was also, in a sense, a living vision of television, another way of 'watching' television." Counteractualizations of television technology prefigure Arcangel's counteractualizations of computational technology. Nonstandard uses of technology may produce not only an alternative to how technologies can be used in society but what Blom calls new social ontologies.[44] This resonates with the microsociology of Gabriel Tarde, Bruno Latour, and Maurizio Lazzarato, and the techno-aesthetics of Gilbert Simondon, and the memory studies tradition from Maurice Halbwachs, where society *is* memory.[45]

Blom's model is a new way of writing art history, not an art- or artist-centered history, but rather a "technocentric" account, which follows the agency of various technologies.[46] She attempts "to trace the effectuating powers of a memory technology—analog video—that *used* artistic frameworks and art-related materials, personnel, and skills as part of an exploration of its own capacity for memory."[47] According to this model, memory is "simply a force of retention at work in all perception and sensation." The social is produced by the "differentiating forces at work in all [types of] memory." Therefore, as Lazzarato has shown, time technologies become key to understanding contemporary social organization. Video technologies are time machines assembling memory and the social differently (i.e., they produce interdependent collectives of agents that are both human and nonhuman, transforming perceptions of time and the social).[48] Video experiments with "the *technicity* of memory" through "new compositions of time and sensation," open "onto a new realm of social invention."[49] Consequently, the events of video art partake in the production of the social, because the social is never a given but "must be explained *in terms of* the events that constantly produce them."[50] Video art is an experiment in "social ontology," to Blom.[51]

Blom's "technocentric" account of video history is not technocentric in a narrow media archaeological sense, but uses insights from media archaeology, such as the focus on the microtemporal events conditioning the levels of perception and sensation available in televisual technology, to redefine what produces the social. Her account—polemically entitled, *The Autobiography of Video*—has been important to this book's assessment of Arcangel's work. However, the prolific heterogeneity of his work makes it much more than and much less than "the autobiography of the computer." Regardless, its time-critical operations and flow-cuts produce arrangements that speak to the infurious memory of the early twenty-first century, yet to be conceptualized.

FROM TELEVISION TO COMPUTER

The history of video art holds a special position for Arcangel. "I actually looked at myself as a TV artist for a while," he says.[52] He continued the "intra-machinic redefinition of the workplace" started by video artists, but the machines Arcangel connected to his TV were not video synthesizers but hacked digital video games like *Super Mario Clouds*. Despite video being the outcome for both, the networks the artists operate in and the visions they carry are very different. All technological shifts seem to produce both mainstream and various subcultures; however, the standards and protocols of today's Big Tech are more dominant and ubiquitous than a TV company could ever have dreamt of. A quick look at some of the visions of early video artists and the later digital artists speaks to this.

The first journal for experimental video art, *Radical Software*, established in 1970, is an interesting source for understanding both the visions of early video artists, and the counter-visions of Radical Software Group (RSG, 2001–2011, made up of Galloway and various collaborators such as Arcangel) some thirty years later. Indeed, in 2003 Arcangel was part of a team at Harvestworks that digitized the entire *Radical Software* journal and made it available online.[53] The two key writers of the journal were the experimental video artist Frank Gillette and Marshall McLuhan's assistant Paul Ryan. They considered *Radical Software* an alternative media think tank and saw it as "The Alternate Television Movement" inspired by radical cybernetics and systems theory.[54] Some of the journal's contributors were visionary utopians. They published pieces like "Expanded Education for the Paper-less Society" by Nam June Paik, "The Videosphere" by Gene Youngblood, and a talk with Richard Buckminster Fuller about how video can become "the great educational system." "If information is our environment, why isn't our environment considered information?" the editors asked in their first editorial, noting that they "felt that thrusting into the public space the concept of practical software design as social tool could not wait."[55] Video could be a tool to challenge and change the media infrastructure.

Significantly, thirty years later, Radical Software Group highlights a less visionary worldview and more pessimism, perhaps due to a different media infrastructure. The name, RSG, was both a homage to the original journal community and a reminder to the video artists that "software" now had taken on a new meaning primarily relating to computers, programming, and code, and the RSG followers were the hacker community.[56] Indeed, video artists had experimented with computer programming to manipulate the video signal, but as the dominance of television was replaced by computation and the internet, media culture had changed. The challenges, the workplace, and the concerns of the RSG generation were different. In an unexpected way, Paik's and many video artists' dream of "self-cybernation" (i.e., being able to produce content from your own television production site and involving the public in an endless feedback loop) was now realized in a perverted way by corporate culture and Big Tech. The cybernetization of culture took on a rather apocalyptic tone. Feedback, participation, and interactivity were no longer utopian ideals for many video artists but became regarded with an air of disfavor by many. These techno-cultural transformations are useful backdrops for understanding the fact that the aesthetic, humor, and machinic milieu at play in Arcangel's art are very different from the early video artists' utopian accent and at times literal ambition of transforming the media infrastructure into a liberated videosphere.

Nevertheless, early video art and contemporary new media art are often displayed together because they both entertain a complicity with technical machines. This was addressed in the Guggenheim show *Seeing Double: Emulation in Theory and Practice* (2004), in which Arcangel's video game work, *I Shot Andy Warhol* (2004) was exhibited alongside works by Grahame Weinbren, Paik, and others. Video art, computer art, and artist-made video games used TV screens for display. While Paik turned TV technology into a video painting machine using an analogue video synthesizer from 1969, Arcangel created TV art using programmable systems. Where Paik had manipulated the electronic image-scans of TV screens physically with magnets and analog video equipment, Arcangel's manipulations went via programming language or chip modulations. Paik was interested in new forms of electronically assisted interactivity and an almost cybernetic symbiosis with image technologies; Paik's Buddhist-inspired notion that everything could be connected via an "electronic superhighway" was experimentally explored with broadcast and video technologies in works such as *Participation TV* (1963), *TV Garden* (1974), *Wrap around the World* (1984), and *Internet Dream* (1994).

Arcangel's experiments with disrupting and displacing interactivity foreground the failures rather than the utopias of new technology. Paik and Arcangel are situated in two different techno-historical eras. Paik worked and dreamed before and at the beginning of the internet's spread, Arcangel after. Especially after the dot-com crash in 2000–2001, experiments in new media were looked upon with suspicion in business and art alike.[57] However, there are also parallels between Paik and Arcangel; their dismantling of instrumental reason and the belief in subcultural networks of sharing. After all, Paik's trust in interactivity was rooted in a confidence in a different form of interactivity outside the hegemony of the television industry of his day.

Video art was for a long time considered a bastardized component in the art world. It was somehow too connected to commercial technologies or "popular imagery." That was a topic when *ArtForum* invited Dara Birnbaum to meet Arcangel for a conversation in 2009. Birnbaum represented a video artist of the older generation who had worked with "popular imagery" from the 1970s and 1980s, and Arcangel, one who works with "popular imagery" forty years later. In her early career, Birnbaum used other venues than the art gallery to show video art. Gradually, as the art world began to understand how video art had broken the code of television, it became interesting also for the art gallery. A similar trajectory happened with Arcangel. For a long time, game mods were considered too "low art" to be accepted in art galleries, but as Arcangel's game mods became too artsy and too abstract to work online for the hacker audience, as with *Super Mario Clouds*, that is when he transitioned into the art world. The game mods began to resonate with video art, which was now an accepted art. An abstract game mod could bring "to mind the history of landscape and video installation," Arcangel tells *ArtForum*.[58]

Birnbaum recounts the story of Arcangel's success in the art world, by recalling what happened when he performed *The Bruce Springsteen "Born to Run" Glockenspiel Addendum* (2006) at one of MoMA's "pop nights." Arcangel, onstage, plays a simple melodic addendum on glockenspiel on top of a playback of *Born to Run*. "I mean, it's ridiculous. I use a spotlight

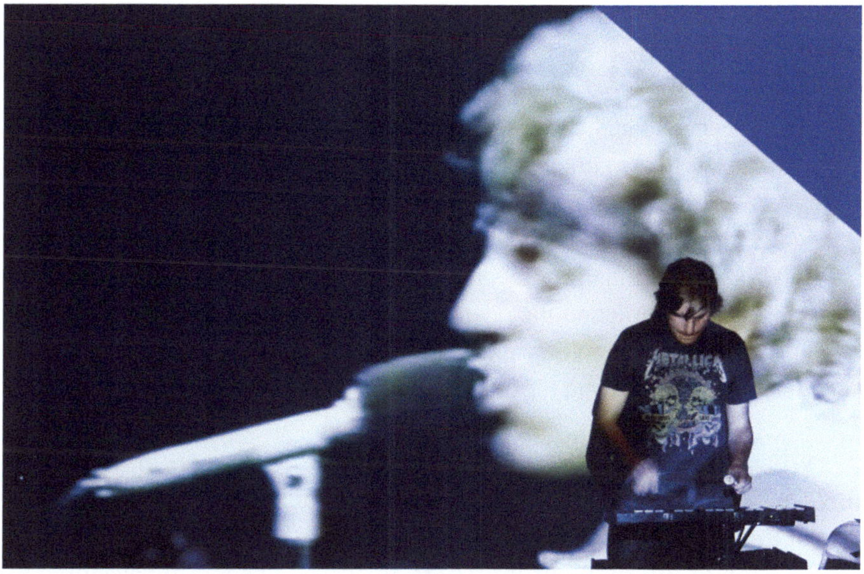

0.5

Cory Arcangel, *The Bruce Springsteen "Born to Run" Glockenspiel Addendum*, 2006. Performance for solo glockenspiel and optional electronics. (Performance view: Content Producer, Light Industry, Brooklyn, New York, August 8, 2008.) Photo by Damien Crisp, courtesy of the artist and Light Industry.

sometimes. I dress all heavy metal. I create a cultural mixture that doesn't make any sense," Arcangel interrupts. "But my point is," Birnbaum retorts,

> that the audience is screaming before you even start playing. I asked myself, 'What the fuck is this, where an art audience is cheering like that, giving you star status?' It made me think about how odd it is, when the arts seem to demand that someone's got to 'crack the code' of popular culture [after digitization]. I remember feeling like people in the '80s wanted me to crack the code of television. I did that, but then I never found the next model. I thought a generation was clearly looking for that in you—waiting for a superhero to crack the codes of newer mediums, like video games and the internet.[59]

What does it imply to have cracked the code of contemporary culture? Yes, there is a definite way to crack the code of a CD or DVD, but I do not think there is a definite or a once-and-for-all way to crack the code of television or internet culture. There are ways of becoming accepted as an artist, but a much more complex thing to assess, I think, is, what is at stake when *trying* to crack the code of contemporary culture? I am not asserting that Arcangel has succeeded, but I think he is trying, and it is the forces at play in this attempt, in the Cory Arcangel hack, that intrigue me a lot, and that is what I set out to explore in this book.

INVENTORY OF PARTS

This book's arrangement is simple. The introduction delineates a biographical milieu as well as a short history of machine art. In chapter 1, "Flow-Cut Arrangements," I discuss key terms and concepts such as the hack, games and cybernetics, flow and arrangement, the schiz-image, the gimmick, and transcoding. Theoretically, it draws inspiration from the momentum of critical media theory that emerged prominently during the first decade of Arcangel's career. It seems as if perspectives in theory and thinking underwent a shift to better understand especially media art's new entanglements with society. I discuss Deleuze and Guattari's "generalized theory of flows" to underscore the urgency of these perspectives and develop two new concepts—the flow-cut arrangement and the schiz-image—to prepare for an exploration that addresses the conundrums and paradoxes inherent in the Cory Arcangel hack, which both participates in and critiques the culture it simultaneously loves and despises. The method is based on the reverse engineering of specific hacks, a method inspired by media archaeology and software studies, which effectively supplements, for instance, the abstract theory of Deleuze and Guattari. Media archaeology is used throughout to grasp how a hack generates and turns artworks into agents or machines that can gather and cut into the computational and cultural flows of our current media ecology.

The three readings will detail these processes through tracing the different inframachinic actors that mutate flows in key artworks. The flow-mutations are divided into flow-breaks (chapter 2), flow-remixes (chapter 3), and flow-parodies (chapter 4). Each reading reverse engineers specific hacks to analyze how code and digital tools mutate or liberate expressions, impacting our understanding of agency, technology, and the social.

Arcangel has made close to one thousand clever hacks exhibited throughout the world during the first two decades of the twenty-first century. Since they exist in different media and frequently reference or resemble each other across various periods, my selection of fewer than sixty mentioned works, with even fewer analyzed in depth, represents only a preliminary attempt to discuss his relevance for understanding our times in monograph-form. The periodization into an early, mid, and late period and the reduction of the hacks into three basic hack types presented in this book serve primarily analytical and pedagogical purposes, aiming to help the reader understand the rationale behind my argument. Nonetheless, it is worth noting that one could challenge the logic of this periodization, as game- and sound-based works appear across all periods, while his sculptural works, lecture-performances, musical compositions, and print-based works are mentioned only briefly. However, I would argue that my periodization facilitates the identification of significant trends in his oeuvre, and most importantly, key differences with regards to hacks and how flows are mutated. Ultimately, the selection of works in the three readings is intended to highlight the connections between hacks, flow-mutations, and media systems.

Therefore, the selection criterium for this book is technocentric or machinic rather than genre- and medium-based as in traditional art history. It follows the flow-cut operations set up by a specific hack. The hack bends, fragments, and isolates a flow by messing with the hardware and/or the software. Arcangel tends to use plug-ins—a programming twist or a homemade tool—to initiate modifications. The modded work become a node in a larger ecology often governed by a platform, but it is a node, usually, detached and displaced from the platform circuit it once operated in. This perspective highlights the engineering quality of the hacks, typical of media archaeological approaches. However, I go beyond a strict media archaeological approach and analyze the artworks' connections to complex networks of powers and forces (i.e., the hacks entertain an ironic and critical relationships to Big Tech platforms and the way they impact desires and beliefs). This highlights the artworks' media ecological entanglements and is closer to an assemblage theoretical approach, mixing, say, Deleuze and Guattari's machine theory with Wolfgang Ernst's media archaeology.[60] Furthermore, this forwards attention to how the artworks' eco-operational relationship to larger networks always murmurs as a sense- or nonsense-making machine, as in the relationship between the artwork *Super Mario Clouds* and its source, the Nintendo Entertainment System.[61] Therefore, also some of Arcangel's "analog" works are significant, such as the experimental novel *Working on My Novel* (2014) or prints like the *Inspos* series (2020), as these works also draw attention to how historically "determined" platform pressures play a specific role in the atmosphere and sense-making of several works.

What are the various elements within the contemporary media landscape that are exerting pressure on us? There seems to be an interest in how people's expressions take place "inside" shifting force fields dominated by large corporations and Big Tech, constituting a media ecology of standards affecting what media and people can do. Arcangel's hack are like cuts into these force fields. His art seems to trace the disciplinary and facilitating social aspects of technology, and he goes under the hood of new media to commit hacks to turn techno-social pressures into a variety of hilarious blocks of sensation. The sociopolitical pressures from shifting platforms, affecting users, affordances, and design, invite a historical and chronological perspective on the hacks as they are extremely sensitive to changes in their eco-operational environment.

It may seem as if Arcangel's art engages with fun but trivial details in the media landscape, but on closer inspection, each intervention is minimal and precise, targeting aspects of the emerging and free-floating cybernetic organization of society in computers, games, platforms, and networks. The hacks attack soft spots where the pressure from various techno-organizational modes of domesticating forces seems most innocent, but it is perhaps where its power is most efficacious. The growing cybernetization of society implicitly addressed, can be delineated into three relatively distinct techno-historical periods in the digital economy: 1) the rise of interactive entertainment, such as digital video games; 2) the emergence of early Big Tech social media cultures; and 3) the advent of platform capitalism.

Arcangel engages with these significant shifts and trends through small yet precise interventions. He may catch, arrest, and re-execute in odd ways a sliver of flow from games or social media. These catches may seem odd, trivial, or, as he calls them, "dumb" or "stupid"; they are like hieroglyphs or ciphers in need of interpretation. As most of them are based on detaching and subtracting elements from large corporate and commercial media to make them work in a new machine, I read them according to the way the machine works and how the material is treated, defamiliarized, and changed. It is my hypothesis that these interventions are micropolitical, in that they often redirect and repurpose a seemingly trivial speck of major flows for new purposes. Gradually, it reveals a deeper engagement with core tenets of the digital regime, its flow-paths, affordances, and the ideal of error-free operational control. I have organized the hacks' various flow-cut arrangements into three different flow-mutations or hack types that characterize the way the artist cuts or intervenes differently into the techno-historical "periods" mentioned previously. I tentatively call them: 1) flow-break hacks, which often employ versions of so-called ROM hacking (chapter 2); 2) flow-remix hacks using Arcangel's Gould-Pro software (chapter 3); and 3) flow-parody hacks using monkeyrunner tools and bots (chapter 4).

While all genres and media are increasingly present throughout Arcangel's body of work, I emphasize primarily time-based works for the given periods and hack-types for the purpose of coherence and clarity, as they most effectively demonstrate how the various hacks give form to different aesthetic expression and send different messages to the respective techno-industrial milieus of gaming or social media. Despite the works' apparent similarities, it makes only limited sense to call them post-cinema, video art, or post-internet video art, because I am not interested in how they relate to old media, cinema, or video art, but how they address specific new media milieus through specific operations that technically vary significantly from one period to another. It is through these differences that we can best understand how the Cory Arcangel hack evolves alongside the shifting flow-paradigms of the industry it "observes." Even though this book stresses discontinuities between periods and hack types, lines of continuity are discussed throughout. It is perhaps the "alchemy," style, attitude, sensitivity, touch, and vision behind each hack which unite them, despite their, at times, radical differences in approach.

Each reading has a similar structure working its way from context to analysis. The groups Arcangel is affiliated with and the platforms the groups mine for resources lead into an analysis of exemplary works. From each techno-historical period, I have selected only one or a few paradigmatic artworks for an in-depth analysis, which are methodically reverse engineered through a step-by-step approach to the hacking technique in question, before I interrogate the connections between flows and technical, aesthetic, and social machinations, resonances, and interpretative possibilities. For convenience, each techno-historical period fits with three biographically and stylistically distinct periods in the first half of Arcangel's career from 2001–2021.

The first reading (chapter 2) focuses on *flow-break hacks*, used extensively during his apprenticeship period (roughly 2001–2006), where Arcangel was active in several subcultural hacker groups, such as Beige, which basically operate outside the art world. The chapter focuses on Arcangel's seminal work *Super Mario Clouds*, offering a detailed analysis of his signature flow-break hack, making an unplayable game. This chapter provides the most comprehensive examination of his hacker technique, establishing the origins of his association with the hacker label, the metallurgy involved, the artisanship, and the source code operations. But is *Super Mario Clouds* really a ROM hack? An interesting hacker controversy, sparked by game hacker Patrick LeMieux's critique of *Super Mario Clouds*, highlights the complexity of issues such as media specificity and the difference between hacking and art. Furthermore, a key characteristic of the Cory Arcangel hack is what I call the schiz-image, which reveals a clash between the computational and cultural on the image plane. This image type also participates in the much larger theoretical debate on the ramifications of the digital in culture and aesthetic practice.

The second reading (chapter 3) focuses on *flow-remix hacks*, used extensively during a midperiod (2007–2014). They coincide with the emergence of social media and typically remix the web and social media using, among other things, his own software called Gould Pro. A significant shift of environment takes place. Even though Arcangel did a performance with Paper Rad at MoMA's "PopRally" as late as 2007, he was no longer an active participant in the hacker collectives from his first period. He got an office at Eyebeam and worked on various research projects of entrepreneur Jonah Peretti and for BuzzFeed. Influences from these environments gave his works a distinct new quality characterized by remixing and reblogging content from Web 2.0 platforms such as YouTube and Twitter in particular. He had known Peretti since 2003, but the supercuts from this period did not emerge until later, many of them shown at his solo exhibition *Here Comes Everybody* at the Hamburger Bahnhof—Museum für Gegenwart, Berlin, in 2010. If his first period was dominated by games and computer-based music, the midperiod incorporates references to classical music, Glenn Gould, and rock guitar. Three supercuts will be analyzed, including his funny and complex *Drei Klavierstücke op. 11* where cats play an atonal work by Arnold Schönberg. He mixes flows into expressions invoking notions such as Deleuze and Guattari's "becoming-animal," Sianne Ngai's theory of the gimmick, and contrasting perspectives on "musical material" drawn from Theodor Adorno's music theory and John Cage's experiments with found or readymade sound-material. We will also analyze his experimental novel *Working on My Novel* which remixes tweets into an emerging darkness. As in the first reading, the second follows the way flow-cuts are used to alter the velocity and dimensionality of flows in ways addressing both the digital regime and new territories of becomings and unexpected lines of flight—or devastating cartographies of the networked self.

The third reading (chapter 4) focuses on the tactics of *flow-parody hacks*. They took shape during the final or current period (2015–ongoing) and reached a preliminary culmination point with the solo show *Century 21* at Greene Naftali in New York in 2021. They demonstrate a new technological approach which includes AI, bots, and the monkeyrunner tool to hack various online platforms. This is the only chapter that explores the tactics and strategies employed in one exhibition. Why is *Century 21* dominated by an eerie feeling of apocalypse, and why is it perhaps Arcangel's darkest and most pessimistic exhibition so far, in terms of worldview? Two economic and social shifts may be critical. First, this period epitomizes the rise of platform capitalism, whose negative effects have been highlighted by several scandals and the resulting online discourse (see, for example, the rise of Trumpism). Second, Arcangel has moved to Norway. He no longer participates in hacker collectives or start-ups typical of the New York scene. A combination of reflective distance and subversive affirmation seems to characterize the flow-parody hacks. Furthermore, he runs his New York studio, where programmer-assistant Henry Van Dusen executes many of Arcangel's programming ideas, remotely from Norway. Moving from a former media and entertainment capital, New York, to the oil-industry capital of Norway, Stavanger, seems to have inflicted a growing awareness of the obvious connection between a 24/7 online culture and a 24/7 oil and energy extraction culture, giving the temporal dimension of the flow-parody hack's characteristic loop-aesthetic a different meaning. The three readings reflect on how different types of flow-cut arrangements unfold alongside the evolving techno-cultural landscape surrounding his practice, transitioning from gaming communities in the early period to social media communities and entrepreneurs in the mid-period, and eventually to full-blown platform capitalism in the late period.

The conclusion, "The Hack as Social Invention," discusses whether the Cory Arcangel hack is an ironic withdrawal from society or an experimental attempt at inventing a new lineage in the machinic phylum, pushing the media system from the flow-paths of Big Tech and the entertainment industry and onto a thousand minor ecologies.

1

FLOW-CUT ARRANGEMENTS

"What is given, quite possibly, one could always call a flow . . . and creation consists in dividing, organizing, connecting flows in such a way that a creation is drawn or made around certain singularities extracted from flows."
—Gilles Deleuze[1]

This chapter develops a philosophy and an aesthetics of flow-cut arrangements drawn from my extensive engagements with Cory Arcangel's art and the new media philosophy emerging at the time, often inspired by Gilles Deleuze and Félix Guattari's machine theory. Hopefully, it can be a toolkit to *think* with the Cory Arcangel hack and for understanding contemporary art and vernacular culture more generally. *Flows*, *hacks*, and *arrangements* are the key terms. At this juncture, let us consider *flow* as an ever-evolving matter of expressions circulating in culture and media, setting the stage for a deeper analysis. *Hack* denotes the action of cutting into a specific flow to make a new *flow-arrangement*, basically a *flow-cut arrangement*, because the new flows are rearranged, distorted, detached, and displaced, spatially and temporally, into complex parasitical masquerades. Alchemy or transcoding denote the sense- and nonsense-making processes making up the signature of the hack and the style of the artist.

All art involves a transition from a given flow or flows at one end to an altered flow, or "singularities extracted from the flows," at the other, as Deleuze says in the epigraph to this chapter. Network culture intensifies notions of flows and flow-cuts. "[Our] society is constructed around flows, flows of capital, flows of information, flows of technology, flows of organizational interaction, flows of images, sounds, and symbols. Flows are not just one element of the social organization: they are the expression of processes dominating our economic, political, and symbolic life," Manuel Castells writes in his seminal work, *The Rise of the Network Society*.[2] Tools that can intervene in networked flows are urgently needed to understand and challenge these powerful processes. Furthermore, the cuts triggered by the Cory Arcangel hack do not only intervene in society but rely on tricks and recipes that increase the number of "agents," human and nonhuman, which go into addressing and reassembling what constitutes the social today.

HACKING

Hacking in art designates a practico-empirical attitude to computers, games, and the internet, and a conceptual attitude to hacker culture and art. Therefore, hacking has both a technical and a discursive side. This is confusing because hacking has its origins in computer subculture but has spread to all aspects of culture; any smart solution in any area is now called a hack. For clarity, we must specify. Even within the relevant area of hacker culture and art, a definition of *hack* can become either too broad or too narrow. On one hand, there is the issue of being overly broad. Nowadays, there is a tendency to label any clever solution to a problem in business or daily life as a hack. This broad usage is also reflected in contemporary art history, where some art historians and curators, such as Nicolas Bourriaud, extend the term too liberally. For instance, Bourriaud categorizes most contemporary artists who engage in practices like appropriation art, citation, recycling, *détournement*, and readymades as hackers or programmers.[3] To him, hacking implies "reprogramming social forms" through the reuse and recirculation of images, imaginaries, and cultural discourses.[4] Bourriaud's use of hacking as an extended metaphor for art practices that barely involve or do not involve hacking proper is not helpful in the case of Arcangel. Indeed, his art relies on many of the post-conceptual procedures of appropriation and the readymade dominant among 1990s artists, but for my purpose it is key to highlight the way Arcangel appropriates the actual practice and skills of hacker culture.

On the other hand, there is the issue of defining hacks too narrowly. Some hackers argue that Arcangel's entry into contemporary art represents a departure from hacker culture, as he explores the potential of hacking as a tool in aesthetic and postconceptual art practices. For instance, game hacker Patrick LeMieux reverse engineered Arcangel's most famous hack, *Super Mario Clouds*, and concluded that the Cory Arcangel hack is inauthentic. LeMieux's dissertation in critical code studies proposed to demonstrate how to do "a more authentic or better crafted version of *Super Mario Clouds*."[5] To him, Arcangel's conceptual and aesthetic fuzz prevented him from doing a correct medium-specific hack and makes him an imposter.[6] LeMieux's critique of Arcangel will be examined more fully in chapter 2. Here, it suffices to say that I will argue that Arcangel's self-presentation of his hack is influenced by art discourse lingo such as "the readymade" and the conceptual practice of "erasure" to reframe what hacking does. Consequently, he needs to be scrutinized for the ways in which he not only alters hacking but also reshapes the discourse on what hacking is.

When Arcangel occasionally refers to himself as "a hacker in the traditional definition," it is a blend of honesty, exaggeration, and irony.[7] It is like a signpost, not directed toward hackers but rather toward the art world. It emphasizes that his art represents a postconceptual approach through a different avenue, forging an alliance with coding skills and hacker culture lingo. To writer and hacker historian Bruce Sterling the term hacker "can signify the free-wheeling intellectual exploration of the highest and deepest potential of computer systems."[8] Historically, the term "to hack" found its way into the abodes of hardcore computer users at MIT in 1959. In connection with initiation and graduation ceremonies at MIT, the students had long performed what they called "hacks," then meaning pranks, on new students through stupid and funny rituals. The computer nerds picked up the term as a joke to describe what they were doing late at night in the AI lab: trying to come up with creative and alternative solutions to programming problems on early computers without their professors knowing. "They were such fascinating people," writes Steven Levy. "Beneath their often unimposing exteriors, they were adventurers, visionaries, risk-takers, artists . . . and the ones who most clearly saw why the computer was a truly revolutionary tool."[9] Early hackers are also highlighted as crucial to the PC revolution a couple of decades later. However, after "a combination of public technophobia and aggressive government legislation [like the Computer Fraud and Abuse Act of 1986]," Alexander R. Galloway writes, "the identity of the hacker changed in the US in the mid to late eighties from do-it-yourself hobbyist to digital outlaw."[10]

Today, a distinction is often made between hackers who are considered criminals, even terrorists, so-called black hat hackers, and white hat hackers who use their expertise for high-value purposes such as exposing crime or uncovering weaknesses in a system to help a business.[11] Arcangel could perhaps be in a third category of hackers, who use their expertise for explorative or artistic purposes. His hacks are infrastructural operations in the sense that he goes under the hood to reverse engineer devices; identify structures and logic; read, interpret, write code, create a new software tool or a bot; combine everything together; and then execute, present, and exhibit the hack.

Arcangel's hacker impulse shares three basic characteristics with the original hackers at MIT:

1. An interest in finding alternative and smart (re)programming solutions to computer problems. Arcangel translates this into an effort to solve aesthetic problems, that is, how to make artmachines through hacking.

2. An interest in computer games from *Ping* and *Pong* and on to *Spacewar!*, evident in a series of Arcangel's works from *Super Mario Clouds* to */roʊˈdeɪoʊ/ Let's Play: HOLLYWOOD*.

3. An interest in the sonicity and audiovisual aspects of computation such as making the early computers like the PDP 1 play Bach.[12] Arcangel excels at turning code into music or visuals (8-bit works and ROM hacking) and has extended this interest into cross-fertilizing seemingly incommensurable practices, like remixing the web into playing Bach like in his supercuts, modifying digital toys into playing La Monte Young (*Composition #7*, 2010) or turning data into any sensory form of abstraction (*Data Diaries*, 2003).

Arcangel is also part of a maker culture. He creates his own digital editing, compression, recording, game-playing devices (Gould Pro), bots, and phishing techniques (*Data Diaries*), and combines various tools as well. Sometimes he does not hack in the proper sense of the term but uses commercial tools in a way that resonates with hacking, like when he (mis-) uses Pro Tools, Photoshop, older tools like the pen plotter, or a Sandin Image Processor.[13] These are hacks by proxy. As hacks often are learned and developed collectively, his aesthetics and hacks change slightly according to the collectives or environments he works in. He has extended and developed the ROM hacking practices he learned while in the hacker collective Beige, the website and HTML practices learned while working with Paper Rad, and the data traffic surveillance techniques learned while collaborating with RSG. While working on Jonah Peretti's projects Contagious Media and reBlog, Arcangel moved from ROM hacking to phishing and scraping and into developing postproduction tools. These are all just to name a few of his hacking tools and techniques.

The artist duo Jodi (Joan Heemskerk and Dirk Paesmans) and the net-artist Olia Lialina seem to have been an inspiration throughout Arcangel's career, and he has done dual shows with both Lialina (*Asymmetrical Response*, 2016 and 2017) and Jodi (*404.lissongallery.com*, 2021).[14] Arcangel often talks of his shock at first seeing Jodi's artworks online in the 1990s. It was rumored that Jodi's webpages would destroy computers.[15] Jodi is known for aestheticizing computer errors and technical malfunctions. They attempt to bring the inside of computer systems up to the surface. Lialina's Net Art often has an archival web art impulse that both refashions and documents what she calls the "digital folklore" of the web, like in her work *One Terabyte of Kilobyte Age* (with Dragan Espenschied, 2010—ongoing). It is centered around the preservation and restoration of websites from GeoCities, "the early internet's agora of vernacular design."[16] In 2009 Yahoo shut down GeoCities, destroying "the most amount of history in the shortest amount of time, certainly on purpose, in known memory."[17] It would have been completely deleted from the web if it wasn't for artists and independent archivists outside the corporate world who harvested the content.

GAMES AND CYBERNETICS

Interactivity transformed the computer from a calculator to a machine capable of transforming communication and entertainment. A key factor in the development of interactivity was video games.[18] Games as rule-based systems challenge art and its anthropocentric freedoms, but *computer* games bring in engineering and cybernetics in a new way. To Arcangel, as Galloway has shown, a computer game is never simply a game but is a passage into the secrets of computation, human/machine evolution, and contemporary society.[19] Reviewers think Arcangel loves to play games, but he says: "I don't love the games so much, but I really love the systems."[20] A game is perhaps both a system and an entity that enacts and *plays* the systems surrounding it. It is an agent of connection, coupling, a seemingly simple apparatus linking humans to machines. Furthermore, it is a metasystem because it is used to configure any computer system; games test and demonstrate computing. In human–computer interaction (HCI) research, games are training grounds for understanding interaction with running software. To game historian Claus Pias, the arrival of computer games changed not only the notion of play but also the age-old definition of man as *homo ludens*.[21] From having been surrounded by a metaphysics of freedom and creativity, play—and *homo ludens*—was now implemented into cybernetic machines, circuits of feedback and control, decentering human creativity as a node in a machinic universe. Games now demanded a computer interface.

If cybernetics is defined as "control and message transmission in the living being and the machine," then the computer has a different status than all previous "game tools." If it is about feedback control technology and information processing in both living beings and machines, then the question of play is no more one of fiction, but of simulation. If universal machines simulate the human being and both are conditioned by "metatechnology" [Max Bense's term for cybernetics], then the application of anthropological game theories on computer games is problematic, to say the least. Man (or even that "primal" child) as a reference to "free" and "indeterminate" play becomes an insecure instance simply because man is no longer irreplaceable.[22]

Software, hardware, and circuit diagrams "identify the outline or shape of the player."[23] Games had become miniature cybernetic machines testing the human through simulation, the computer systems through trials and tribulations, and conceptual steps toward more sophisticated "real-time" programming.[24] Games are effective experiments in reaction times, given that the number of interactive steps from task identification to task executions connecting humans and machines can be measured in real time. The loop between stimulus and response can be "tightened into a noose," and it "empowers users by modelling them, and in doing so effects their disappearance, their incorporation into its model," software theorist Matthew Fuller writes.[25]

Contemporary cybernetics manuals view human/machine assemblages as a problem because humans are too slow. Often, HCI is about how to turn the computer's default inclination for high-speed calculation, done as multiple microtemporal processes, into slower human-perceptible forms to be interacted with. Jokes addressing this HCI concern are typical in many of Arcangel's works, such as in his attention to speeds and thresholds of human perception, for example when he produces videos or sounds that are too slow, too fast, or too compressed, or when he juxtaposes too many layers at various speeds using phase-shifting techniques. Cybernetics attempts to support the relatively slow process of communication and control in the human body by making computers more "human-oriented." Cybernetics can be applied to all devices concerned with the exchange relationship (recursion, feedback, and communication) and the interaction between humans and machines. The human being's relative slowness is also what grants computers the ability to harvest, track, and measure elements in this exchange relationship at nonhuman scales in terms of big data, a topic we will return to in chapters 3 and 4.

The hackers at MIT built *Spacewar!* (1962) to test whether the computers worked as they should.[26] At the same time, they tested the user experience. How do graphics, algorithms, and interfaces work in an interactive feedback loop with a human? How seamless and comfortable was the user integrated into the machine universe? The structure of computer games is also a picture of how cybernetics works in society at large. Today's postindustrial machine complex of interconnected platforms, with their infrastructure of recursive tracking technologies and recommendation algorithms, can be viewed as the implementation of cybernetics on large populations. Several curators and media philosophers have commented on this. The curators Diedrich Diederichsen and Oier Etxeberria toured with the art show *Cybernetics of the Poor* in Europe in 2020–2021. They concluded: "the public . . . has fallen under the control of social-engineering cybernetics . . . a cybernetic totality."[27] The French collective Tiqqun and Galloway discuss what they call the "cybernetic hypothesis." It "refers to a specific epistemological regime in which systems or networks combine both human and nonhuman agents in mutual communication and command."[28] Tiqqun writes, "the image of steering [after the Greek term *kybernetes*], that is to say management, has become the primary metaphor to describe not only politics but all of human activity as well."[29] The German media philosopher Erich Hörl talks about a general *cybernetization* of society led by states, corporations, Big Tech, social media, and search engines.[30] Now, command and control through communication take place seamlessly and flawlessly as entertainment. "The cybernetic hypothesis . . . proposes that we conceive of biological, physical, and social behavior as both fully programmed and also re-programmable," Tiqqun comments.[31] The hunt for fun, friends, and news, and the will to share has become financialized and gamified. The radical MIT hackers could never have envisioned that their struggle for smoothness in interactivity would end up like this. This is "the political tragedy of interactivity," Alexander R. Galloway and Eugene Thacker conclude in *The Exploit*.[32] Arcangel's sabotage of interactivity in games for other purposes, becomes even more urgent when seen in this light. However, Arcangel's art is not as explicitly critical as works by CAE or Yes-Men; rather he experiments with the capacities of tiny devices—a code or a chip—to alter, cut, and connect flows in new ways to redirect, misuse, or reassemble a certain social flow in miniature, micropolitically. The works ask, as I see it, what can a body of components do? Can their ability to affect and be affected be altered?

CODE AND INFRASTRUCTURE

"All I do is steal and recycle code," Arcangel likes to say.[33] It is a mixed statement. It references both contemporary art and hacker culture. On the one hand, it aligns itself with appropriation art; on the other, it translates art lingo to the more specific ethos of open-source culture where it refers to a collaborative and transparent approach to creating, sharing, and improving software and other intellectual products. Open-source culture is in many ways at odds with a commercialized art world based on copyright, secrecy, and the romanticism of the genius. In addition to sharing tricks and source code on his website and at github.com, Arcangel produces his own zine, *The Source* (2006–ongoing), where he has released some of the software programs he created as code printed with archival toner on acid-free archival paper with corresponding pictures, an essay on how compression conditions communication, conversations about hacking, instructions, and explanations of artworks.

This is not merely an archival project but has a social and utopian dimension as well. "Flooding the world with as many versions of an artifact as possible, in all possible formats, increases its cultural circulation and keeps it in use instead of in remembrance," Dragan Espenschied writes in the preface to a collection of Arcangel's zines, *The Source Digest*, published as a paperback in 2016.[34] Furthermore, printed source code "could stand next to the [art]work itself on equal footing. But that's just me as an artist talking, and an artist doesn't have to make sense," Arcangel says in an interview on the status of code in his oeuvre.[35]

More than in art culture, hacker culture is built around an infrastructure and an ethos of sharing. It emphasizes recycling, mixing, coupling, and grafting scripts and ideas. Unlike the tactics of modernist art, codes and scripts are always potential collaborative objects. The willingness to share, spread, and reference infrastructures of sharing is often an implicit theme in Arcangel's work. He finds similar sharing cultures in popular music online. The electric guitar with its fretboard even invites a player to think in coded patterns across the guitar neck. Hackers, and especially electric guitar players—Arcangel plays rock guitar himself—share a common interest in patterns, scores, scripts, collaborative objects, repetitions, and loops. Code, technical manuals, and musical scores are silent displays that vibrate with the promise to be executed, to sound, to act. This also resonates with Deleuze's idea that the actual always vibrates with the virtual, and that as far as affects and memory are concerned, the virtual is never less real than the actual; it is rather the "embryonic" element of the real.[36]

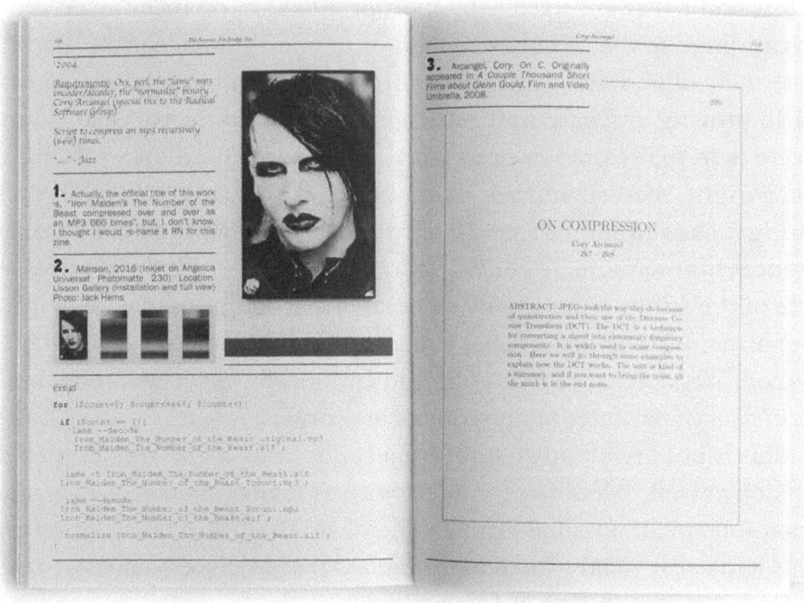

Another topic in Arcangel's art is the errors, weaknesses, and failures in computational systems.[37] We have all experienced that certain data flows can be flawed, but flaws can be turned into opportunities. Knowledge of how the computer relies on a precise set of processes or interactions between different layers of software and memory enables a hacker to trick the computer into making errors as in the aforementioned *Data Diaries*. The hacker's knowledge of code and the logic and architecture of the computer prepares for direct access to some of the hidden layers, the nerves and veins, of the computer. Hacks are "investigative tools" that put "in play the capacity to experiment with reality formation more broadly."[38] As a lurker of games, platforms, and computers, Arcangel can capture aspects of societal flow, isolate it, and accelerate and decelerate it—"to

1.1

Cory Arcangel×Arcangel Surfware, *The Source Digest*, 2016. Paperback book. Photo by Cory Arcangel, courtesy of the artist and Arcangel Surfware.

uncover the real, we must make the real."[39] He uses his skills to crack and capture the audiovisual resources and flows at their seemingly safe and protected hidden abodes, under the surface or inside the machine governing devices and platforms. He collects visible evidence of culture at its microcritical infrastructure.

The standard definition of infrastructure as simply fixed equipment organizing mobility and storage in society no longer holds. With digitization, and even more so with the implementation of smart technologies, infrastructure is not only tunnels, cables, and satellites but lurks behind the blip of every interface. Media and communication infrastructures promise 24/7, always-on connectivity. The macroregimes of storage, production, distribution, communication, mobility, platforms, and flow rely on the rhythms and flow-paths set by the inframachinic microregimes of specific software programming, RAM, ROM, chips, algorithms, code, and the seemingly innocent surface layers of OS and GUI that are in our faces. The micropolitics of infrastructure take on a new meaning—with digitization new layers of infrastructure become programmable. Computation relies on modularity of scale.[40] "The small always holds the big" and the small is "always the more complex."[41] This logic calls for awareness of details. Reprogramming a tiny segment of code on the backend can have wide-ranging consequences on the front end. Code becomes a techno-cultural superagency. It governs flows of inputs and outputs—and has optics of its own, a kind of seeing from below or inside the machine.

Media criticism contends that code and algorithms have significantly changed not only games and digital products but the economy, politics, corporations, defense, policing, and military intelligence.[42] Hacks, for Arcangel, were from the start a counter-space for freezing, rerouting, and hijacking computer-assisted flows. His artworks have a timestamp quality; they are precise operations capturing striking aspects of human/machine entanglements at specific moments in our coevolution with Big Tech. His hacks freeze or loop traces of life detached from the infrastructures of Big Tech. They are minor interventions in big infrastructural operations that "make sense-able" certain aspects of how media and communication infrastructures work.[43] Invisible mechanisms, seemingly immaterial infrastructures, are made visible, and Arcangel always highlights how code and formats are among the tools of these mechanisms. Indeed, the hacks make mechanisms sense-able, but they also liberate matters of expression for other purposes. They respond to the command-and-control level of flows and dissect and redirect them. In this way, hacks operate on specific environmental flows to invent new composites that envision the social otherwise. The hacks enter the technical abode of an environment to ally themselves with a modded apparatus, a new agent, and in this way reassemble or reinvent the social. There is both a new member and a new flow. The hacks instantiate a version of what Mauricio Lazzarato and Tiziana Terranova call "invention" or "social production": "the capacity of free social cooperation to produce new forms of life" where human and non-human actants are positioned and juxtaposed differently, "connecting to other kinds of knowledge."[44]

Code is infrastructural, but not like roads and tunnels, more like air, the omnipresent. It constitutes a language, many different languages at many different computational levels, but unlike ordinary language, they are executable. "I've never seen a hacker using so many different programming languages," a hacker friend of mine told me, while flipping through Arcangel's journal *The Source Digest*, which documents his work. The more languages one knows, the more one can modify, manipulate, distill, and transform.

Arcangel taught himself the art of hacking while a student at Oberlin Conservatory of Music. That was also where he, together with fellow students, established the hacker collective Beige, which will be presented more fully in chapter 2. It is significant that he learned computer skills before Web 2.0 arrived. Web 2.0 made people lazy. Suddenly anyone could publish online without needing any programming skills. Coding became superfluous. In other words, Arcangel learned the language of computers before this knowledge became obsolete among common users, before the "protected mode" which "guards the operating system from users" became the standard operating procedure of Big Tech.[45] Big Tech remade the user-subject to ignore the fact that computational devices are programmable systems. States, the entertainment industry, and tech companies prefer to underplay their formatting power to operate more invisibly and efficiently as part of the human's "natural" habitat, as if it was unchangeable, not reprogrammable. Design guru Don Norman's imperative—"The computer of the future should be invisible"—is now the norm of computer design.[46]

As Lialina has observed, tech-companies have gradually erased the good old term for the computer as a general purpose "programmable system" and replaced it with terms such as "experience" and "technology," as if to hide the fact these machines *are* programmable.[47] This also speaks to the transition Raymond Williams saw, when an experimental technology establishes itself and is perceived as a fixed "cultural form" and no longer as a process amendable by the public.[48] This can happen to such a radical extent that many young people think of the internet and its services as simply standardized "forms" with a specific flow-form and as nothing else. Instead, Arcangel breaks down the forms and flaunts programmability. He emphasizes alterability and the whimsical randomness of affordances, constraints, and flows. Standards, platforms, and formats can be modified and mixed. The given, in computation, is ephemeral, intermittent, and up for grabs, but, nevertheless, hails individual and collective expressions in specific ways. But it can be undone. It is programmable. All Arcangel's hacks demonstrate this. Implicitly, his audience becomes a potential task force equipped with the means to joke around and mess up. His hacks are not evil, but rather joyful yearnings for play and other forms of conviviality. In this way, hacks are micropolitics; they can reassemble the social and ease the paralysis of habitual instrumentality and the perception that devices cannot be changed. He works at miniature scales with information society's basic exchange logic: command, control, instruction, code, action, and change.[49] Control can be sublated, and media remodulated. A quote from McKenzie Wark's *A Hacker Manifesto* serves as the epigraph to this book's introduction: "Hackers create the possibility of new things entering the world."[50] I have always thought that the Cory Arcangel hack inspires a belief in this possibility. For Wark—and for everybody else, I think—it is important that someone outside of tech has the insight needed to be able to change data structures.

ASSEMBLAGE THEORY AFTER DIGITIZATION

The emergence of large-scale new media systems in the early twenty-first century—coinciding with the first decade of Arcangel's career—led to significant advancements in media aesthetics and critical analysis. This period saw a renewed and updated examination of how new media shapes aesthetics, thought, critique, and the production of new societal arrangements and subjects. It was evident in book titles—*The Language of New Media* by Lev Manovich, or *New Philosophy for New Media* by Mark B. N. Hansen.[51] I am not advocating for outdated theories; rather, I argue that we still live within the realm of these once-emerging inquiries. To understand Arcangel's work, we need to reclaim the critical and creative force of some of the most ambitious moments in early twenty-first-century theory. Its playful and visionary energy has, in a sense, been lost with the current enshittification of the web and the turn to new public management in art and education institutions. Most relevant to my book are Matthew Fuller and McKenzie Wark's investigations of pirating and hacking, Alexander R. Galloway's study of gaming and counter-gaming, Wolfgang Ernst's analysis of art as radical media archaeology, Ina Blom's art historical stylistics of the life-environment, Maurizio Lazzarato and Tiziana Terranova's explorations of technical "invention" as a political force reshaping social ontologies, and Bruno Latour's notion of computational "plug-ins" as "actors" that can "reassemble the social."[52] I will return to their insights and terminology throughout this book. A common thread in their investigations was the revival of assemblage theory—the study of the redistribution of agency and meaning in the digital age—an interest that is also evident in Arcangel's art. However, in my view, the notion of "flow" remains undertheorized and must be further explored to complete the picture.

I endeavor in this book to understand the Cory Arcangel hack as an intervention in technical and cultural flows. To develop a useful notion of flow for this purpose, it is necessary to return to the early stages of assemblage theory—specifically, the one articulated in Gilles Deleuze and Félix Guattari's seminal two-volume work *Capitalism and Schizophrenia*. Volume 1, *Anti-Oedipus*, was published in 1972, and volume 2, *A Thousand Plateaus*, in 1980.[53] A general theory of society must be "a generalized theory of flows," Deleuze and Guattari claim.[54] Their inspiration can be traced back to pre-Socratic philosophy. The Greek term *rythmós* (rhythm) is intimately connected to the Greek term *rein* (flux), used to understand the world as a dynamic configuration—a continuous unfolding and enfolding of meaning.[55] Similarly, Deleuze and Guattari systematically follow flows and rhythms as mattering matter, exploring how they give rise to patterns, arrangements, assemblages—what they, in an expanded sense, call "machines"—in societies and beyond. Entities—people, tools, and institutions—emerge through the ways they shape, machinate, capacitate, disseminate, and produce flows or vice versa, through the ways they are shaped by them. Thus, these entities—and art—constitute what I call flow or flow-cut arrangements. These arrangements, and some artworks in particular, set in motion a process that couples, strengthens, bends, folds, or ridicules certain social forces or flows. Art can map a potential and instigate alternative flows for the imagination and for social action.[56] Deleuze and Guattari were themselves keen on exploring how art—and especially the "artmachines" of Dadaists, surrealists, Charlie Chaplin, Buster Keaton, Franz Kafka, and the cartoonist Rube Goldberg—exemplify counter-actualizations of societal and psychical flows.[57] They saw "minor," and often useless, artmachines as urgent diagrams of how the world works actually, potentially, and critically. Arcangel continues this tradition of making minor and useless machines as a reflection on the world. More precisely, his works are minor operations constructing minor media or minor machines that mirror, reflect, incise, or disfigure the ordered and functional flows of major or hegemonic media.

Flows can be any matter in motion from money to people and merchandise, but also desires, beliefs, thoughts, ideas, utterances, expressions, images—including art styles, clichés, and prejudices. All these phenomena can be decoded and recoded through various forces and powers. In *A Thousand Plateaus* Deleuze and Guattari expand the notion of "flow," "code," and "coding" to include "the machinic phylum."[58] *Phylum*, a biological term for evolutionary flows, is provocatively connected to technological lineages. The machinic phylum is exemplified by the art of metallurgy, which taps into the energies of basic matter flows. Metallurgy domesticates the forces of the earth (metals) using fire, water, and air to create tools, instruments, and technologies, illustrating a technological lineage from earth to computers and screens.[59] Artisans and metallurgists follow "the singularities in the machinic phylum, selecting a few of these 'virtual machines' to actualize, creating new phyla, new lineages of technological objects."[60] To Deleuze, "each kind of society corresponds to a particular kind of machine—with simple mechanical machines corresponding to sovereign societies, thermo-dynamic machines to disciplinary societies, cybernetic machines and computers to control societies."[61] Furthermore, each machine regime seems to invoke specific forms of resistance. When the machinic phylum reaches a stage where "cybernetic machines and computers" are used to control information and communication, Deleuze predicts that hacking—"computer piracy and viruses"—may be a way "to create vacuoles of noncommunication, circuit breakers, so we can elude control."[62] Hackers follow the machinic phylum in reverse. They take the phyla or flows apart technically to make new operations possible. They work at a level where encoded technology is decoded and recoded again. Deleuze and Guattari view their approach as an infrastructural analysis in an expanded sense.[63] They were interested in how flows are building blocks that can both construct and dismantle aspects of infrastructure. The flows are decoded and encoded through cuts, connections, disconnections, and rearticulations by a multiplicity of competing machines following certain patterns, strata, and velocities.

Their work is usually characterized as a starting point for a very influential but "incomplete" assemblage theory.[64] An assemblage is not reducible to a technological machine but refers to a dynamic, heterogeneous collection of interacting elements that come together temporarily to form a functional whole. Unlike traditional concepts of structure or system, an assemblage is not a stable or fixed entity. Instead, it is fluid, contingent, and constantly evolving, depending on the relationships and connections between its parts. Many things can be read as assemblages: epochs, nations, states, regimes, communities, companies, institutions, platforms, sciences, artists, an artwork, or a book. Assemblages develop as territories spreading standards and styles; their attitudes can be disciplinary, confrontational, oppositional, and/or parasitical to other assemblages, inviting complex critical infrastructural and relational analysis.

A flow is not reducible to media flows but is used to investigate the evolutionary emergence and comingling of natural and cultural flows as they merge in various machinations or assemblages through human history from industrialization to computation. More than ever, Deleuze and Guattari's materialist approach to flow can be applied to understand flows through evolutionary and political lenses. Flows—from the elemental and geological to the computational and cultural—are continuous yet cut. They are cut and mashed—melted, reshaped, and programmed—as they move from the natural world to the technological and cultural domains.

Different strata of reality (geologic, metallurgic, cultural) are interconnected and influence one another, creating complex networks of interactions that shape both the natural and cultural worlds. To clarify, natural flows are elemental, geological, and chemical. With the development of the computer, metallurgy is used to harness the natural flows of metals into processors, chips, motherboards, gates, and screens, and vice versa, cultural flows and significantly, *logos*, initially tied to language and reason, evolve into programming language and machine code to direct the functions of technological components. *Logos* can address metals operating in the computer.[65] *Geos* and *logos* converge. In sum, both elemental flows and *logos* evolve to drive the informatization of the world.

The Cory Arcangel hack effectively captures the intricate relationship between natural and cultural flows as they intersect in the realm of computation. The synthesis between biological (bodies), geological (metals), and noological (thought and programming) strata is elegantly reflected in *Super Mario Clouds*. Its making intervenes in both elemental and cultural flows. In the process, flesh meets metal. The hack combines the hands-on physicality of DIY and maker culture with the intellectual ingenuity of hacker culture. Arcangel dismantled the game cartridge with a screwdriver to access the microchips and the metallic conductive pathways on the motherboard. To replace or modify chips, he heated the existing joints with a soldering iron, melting the solder to release the components (figure 1.2).

When adding new components, he applies fresh solder—a fusible metal alloy with a lower melting point than the base metals—to create a strong electrical connection between the chip's leads and the motherboard's circuitry. This metallurgic process alters the hardware, ultimately adjusting the elemental flow-paths of electricity. Furthermore, the hack modifies the software, using code to detach and loop audiovisual flows. Programming details will be explained in the next chapter. In this way, the Cory Arcangel hack commits cuts in the flows of both electricity, metals, and logos. The process of the hack is more akin to the physicality and cuts at play in the Deleuzoguattarian materialistic notion of flow than the psycho-immersive processes at play in the infamous flow theory of Mihaly Csikszentmihalyi. A few words are needed to clarify this difference, as Csikszentmihalyi's theory has been immensely influential in game theory.

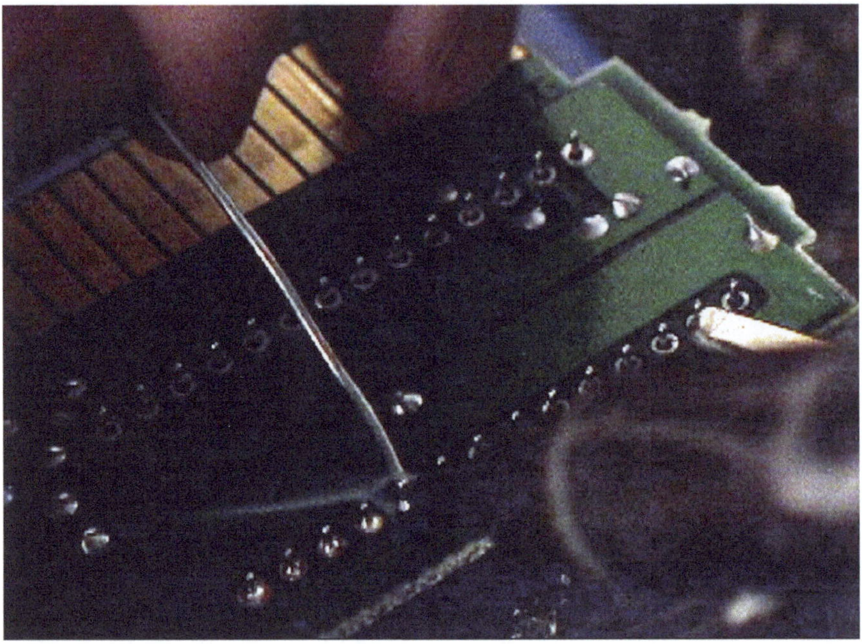

1.2

Cory Arcangel, "The Making of *Super Mario Clouds*," 2005. Text and image tutorial from Migros Museum's exhibition catalog (image B-roll). Photo by Cory Arcangel, courtesy of the artist.

Developed in the 1970s and popularized in his 1990 book, *Flow: The Psychology of Optimal Experience*, Csikszentmihalyi's flow theory has had a profound impact on the game design industry, cognitive psychology, business management, and the self-help industry. The latter has come up with, in this context, the malignant term "flow-hack," designated as a smart way to find "your personal flow."[66] Terms in this book *must not* be confused with the flow-hack of the self-help scene!

Indeed, Arcangel's hack plays a prank on and even at times unmakes the possibility of a flow in Csikszentmihalyi's sense. Csikszentmihalyi describes flow as pleasurable experiences and absorption: "A state in which people are so involved in an activity that nothing else seems to matter; the experience is so enjoyable that people will continue to do it even at great cost, for the sheer sake of doing it."[67] A flow state of mind is attained by intensely focusing on an activity—it can be games, sports, entertainment, sex, etc.—often leading to "loss of self-consciousness." This can have both negative and positive effects. He is most interested in the positive effects because they "can lead to self-transcendence, to a feeling that the boundaries of our being have been pushed forward."[68] Furthermore, Csikszentmihalyi seems to indicate that human beings have an innate tendency to seek out flow-experiences to survive or seek bliss. He refers to how imprisoned authors and intellectuals during Stalinism could transform the most degrading situation into flow experiences by recalling or seeking out in the noise around them potential rhymes, rhythms, and images they could disappear into.[69]

Csikszentmihalyi's psychological flow theory has been aptly criticized in Braxton Soderman's *Against Flow: Video Games and the Flowing Subject*, as an "ideology of flow":

> [It] privileges individuality over social collectives, growth and accumulation over equilibrium and sustainability, self-determination over the idea that external forces shape human consciousness, and action over critical examination. [. . .] Flowing subjects are not simply game players experiencing the psychological state of flow; they are being positioned as media consumers in a way that promotes flow's ideology.[70]

Soderman explores instead critical approaches to flow. Many of these are helpful and already available in critical game studies, but in his search for a "critical flow," it is perhaps surprising that Soderman only mentions Deleuze and Guattari in a footnote.

Contrary to the neoliberal psychologism, individualism, and egoism of Csikszentmihalyi's flow-theory, Deleuze and Guattari's notion of flow is materialistic and collective, or pre- or transindividual. They write, "An assemblage, in its multiplicity, necessarily acts on semiotic flows, material flows, and social flows simultaneously."[71] That is, it acts on flows of signs (e.g., discourses, regimes of meanings), flows of matter and energy (e.g., electricity, electrons, metals), and flows of capital, people, desire, labor, belief systems, affects, and institutions. Through powers of invention, assemblages (e.g., states, institutions, communities, science, or artists) actualize, stratify, and modulate flows into technologies and representations—both signifying and a-signifying.[72]

Actualized flows are usually coded with a more or less clear instrumental purpose and are then called *molar flows* constituting *striated spaces*, meaning spaces that are measurable, organized, structured, and segmented, characterized by rigid boundaries, grids, and hierarchical arrangements, and associated with stability, control, and regimentation. They are often found in urban environments, institutions, and systems of governance.[73] A computational platform milieu may look smooth on the surface, but it is deeply striated at the backend through surveillance mechanisms. When users are drawn to or connect to these flow-spaces they *become* with them. In this way, striated flows discipline and facilitate subject formations. Striated flows are control infrastructures.

There are also certain matter-flows or aspects of matter-flows that evade an easy integration into representation, molar flows, and striated spaces. These flows are called *molecular flows* and produce *smooth spaces*, or spaces dominated by fluctuations, ambiguities, and a lack of fixed boundaries or divisions, often associated with art and aesthetics.[74] While social flows tend to be molar and striated, many artistic flows (or what are called desiring-machines) tend to be molecular and smooth. Jackson Pollock's drip-painting produces a typical smooth space, in Deleuze's sense. Arcangel's art introduces complexity differently, as it often simulates the structured nature of striated spaces yet disrupts them through skewed and comical gestures, thereby challenging the control and rigidity inherent in such spaces.

The distinction between smooth and striated spaces is not strictly binary but rather exists on a continuum. Many spaces exhibit both smooth and striated characteristics to varying degrees, highlighting the dynamic interplay between openness and constraint in the organization of space and experience. In the same way, molar and molecular flows are always mixed in assemblages. Molecular flows, although rarely dominant, play along as contingencies, potentialities, remains, and forces inside and between assemblages, and are important in acts of decoding and freeing matters of expression through the comical and critical.

Yet, molecular flows are not necessarily liberating; they can be a trap. Deleuze and Guattari developed a historical analysis where they viewed capitalism as a break from earlier formations. Capitalism, in contrast to earlier formations, is notorious at decoding all flows for profit leading to a dissolution of values and a radical fragmentation of ties and traditions. However, just around the next corner, this radical capitalist "deterritorialization" is met with an equally forceful reactionary "reterritorialization," where all flows are recoded into stereotypical values centered around the family, the state, and patriarchal authority. This reactionary response manifests today in the form of a blend of neoliberalism and ethnonationalism, marked by hostility toward experimental art and critical discourse. Capitalism is, in other words, a complex play between decoding and recoding. These processes have been seen in the development of social media as well. They started with an outburst of creative user-generated content (UGC) flows but reached a tipping point leading into enshittification. The Cory Arcangel hack seems to evolve alongside these developments in the machinic milieu.

"Machines," according to Deleuze and Guattari, encompass not only mechanical or technical machines but dynamic arrangements of humans and the nonhuman—flows connected by desires, beliefs, forces, and powers. Their preferred term, "machine" from *Anti-Oedipus*, was replaced by the term *agencement*, or "assemblage" in its English translation, in *A Thousand Plateaus*. They analyze how an *agencement* assembles (*s'agencent*) actors and becomes a social machine by "taking men and women into its gears, or, rather, having men and women as part of its gears along with things, structures, metals, materials."[75] Éric Alliez and Andrew Goffey underscore how the French term *agencement* "conveys an active sense of agency as being what some or other entity does, a precious indicator of the constructivist horizon within which it operates." It produces "sense"; it would "refer not just to the syntactic and semantic ordering of terms [or codes or images] but to the way that it generates sense, as well."[76] Secondly, at the level of culture or society, the level of actualization, flows, as expressions, are always the result of forces in conflict and rupture (i.e., flows and expressions are always machinic somehow). This implies that flows are always already connected to other flows—for example, a media flow is always connected to another flow within or between assemblages or machinic milieus where other flows, other knowledges or forms of power, reside.

Ian Buchanan suggests "arrangement" as a better English translation of *agencement*.[77] I agree, and it works better with the perspective developed in this book. All arrangements and *agencements* work on, with, and from flows. When I explicitly connect "flow-cut" and "arrangement" in the term *flow-cut arrangement*, I emphasize the "flow" and the various cuts involved, such as the physical "cuts" of metallurgic, electronic, and audiovisual flows in the Cory Arcangel hack, and the alternative arrangements and rhythms it makes. The hack extracts a sliver of flow from a hegemonic arrangement, transforming it into a different type of arrangement, thus constituting a flow-cut arrangement. A *flow-cut* arrangement is always disjunctly related to another flow arrangement that was hacked. It mutates aspects or flows from a large or dominant arrangement (a specific media system) to make them operate differently in a smaller arrangement (an artwork).

Flows and rhythms are orchestrated differently in the transition from the majoritarian to the minoritarian. Typically, the minoritarian mode, which is parasitical and oppositional, cuts and detaches a flow from a major system—say, streams of clichés—and mixes it with other flow types—say, audiovisuals, tricks, and styles from hacker culture and the avant-garde—to create a minor flow-cut arrangement following a different set of standards or standards that are emerging.[78] The minor flow-cut arrangement is open. Its mix of cuts, flows, and rhythms follows an aesthetic, or laws and standards, yet to be determined. This book explores the Cory Arcangel hack by focusing on the techniques used to alter and modify flows. How does the hack modify and transcode the flows' dimensions, velocity, connective patterns, and sense-making affordances? The modifications may appear fuzzy or nonsensical in relation to the "original," dominant flow arrangement that has been hacked. I will argue that it is in these (non)sense-making displacements that the hack becomes inventive and opens for new meanings and connections to other societal forms and collectives.

Furthermore, Arcangel's transcodings use the hack conceptually and transversally to incorporate tricks from art and the avant-garde as a "vector" in the new arrangement it conjures forth.[79] Functional flow arrangements are disrupted to become socially "dysfunctional," yet, gain aesthetic functionality by revealing aspects of flows that are usually hidden in their "original" or "proper" contexts. These flow potentials or breakthroughs modify sense-making processes by establishing new connections to artistic flows as one of their many tangents. Thus, Arcangel's flow-cut arrangements bring out the machinic as a concatenation of forces between the elemental (or technological), the social, and the aesthetic. The Cory Arcangel hack combined with the machinic flow theory allows for a social and political *thinking with* the multiple flows at play. The hack transports, transforms, or deterritorializes, as Deleuze and Guattari would say, various flows from the coded spaces of gaming, early social media, and platform capitalism into an experimental art space for sensations and reflections on machinic milieus, their making and unmaking.

TO SURGICALLY REMOVE A FLOW-SAMPLE

The hack commits an act of penetration into a flow which leads to a physical transformation of the flow it operates on. The brutality when two assemblages collide can be compared to the chopping up of meat in a butcher's shop. The crash implies a series of flow-cuts but also analysis and tests. Deleuze and Guattari describe the cuts taking place as *des prélèvements*, a term taken from medicine, indicating the surgical removal of tissue to be used as laboratory samples that can be explored microscopically, chemically, or otherwise.[80] This is critical theory as critical practice, an intervention and a physical action deployed on flows through flow-cuts. The Cory Arcangel hack surgically removes a flow-sample to observe it in the laboratory of a specific artmachine and the art world.

The hack produces not only a snapshot of a situation but an analysis of how an operation works in a larger ecology. In this way, the Cory Arcangel hack is eco-operational; it implicitly maps the workings of a territory through various flow-cuts in the form of audiovisuals, electrons, and affects. The Cory Arcangel hack is not only art but a lab scene or a lab report enumerating the tasks and tests being undertaken during specific clashes and interventions. I view the artworks and all the paraphernalia accompanying them—the pictures, interviews, lectures, and lecture-performances by the artist, and of course, the release of the hack's source code or instructions on the artist's website, as well as the instructional videos (e.g., "The Making of *Super Mario Clouds*")—as a part of the paperwork coming out of the lab experiment.

When Deleuze and Guattari analyzed the author Franz Kafka, they were not simply interested in his major novels or a short story or two; no, they set out to analyze what they called "the Kafka machine."[81] "Machine" was their term for assemblage at the time. To understand this machine, they decided to read all texts left behind by Kafka, not only novels and short stories but, more importantly, his letters and diaries. This constituted the paperwork from the lab, as I see it. However, to understand the Cory Arcangel machine or hack, it no longer suffices to limit the paperwork to texts or images, because the Cory Arcangel hack is not constituted by ideas, texts, and images alone but by every trick and skill that goes into making a digital machine work, from hardware to software, machine language and programming code, computers and screens, cables, Wi-Fi-connection, if needed, and electricity. The Cory Arcangel hack can work directly on physical and elemental flows and thus operates in the belly of the communicative apparatus, at the level of electricity and electrons. These are flow-levels not reachable with literature, as in Deleuze and Guattari's analysis of the Kafka machine, but are of key importance to the Cory Arcangel hack.

When encountering the Cory Arcangel hack in the gallery, what is shown is only the tip of an iceberg. So much is going on under the surface. The hack attacks the contemporary media system from below, at the level of computation. It engages with the inframachinic, as in *Super Mario Clouds* where specific flow-paths in the coded space of a tiny Nintendo cartridge are interrupted to reduce the game's flow-arrangement to a minimal flow-cut arrangement—a sky with moving clouds. The interruption is not done by analog means outside the medium (i.e., by other media such as photography, film, or painting) but by medium-specific operators such as programming code. In this way, the Cory Arcangel hack operates on media flows infrastructurally. Using the building blocks of code, it rebuilds—or, rather, displaces—its operations cine-sculpturally from the inside. Computer art can be viewed as sculptural since it uses code to shape and move around audiovisuals.[82] Code works as knives and hammers cutting through the flows of a media landscape. Despite the transformations, the reworked flows retain some of their material and physical qualities intact as indices of a larger ecology. Hacking in art, while distinct from traditional practices like mixing or creating paint from scratch, shares a fundamental similarity: Both involve manipulating materials to produce a creative outcome. However, the "materiality" in hacking is different—it's not about physical substances like paint or clay but about modulating the building blocks of digital technology through cuts, code, algorithms, and electronic components. Just as an artist might blend colors or shape a sculpture, the hacker-artist reconfigures digital systems, repurposing the tools and techniques of Big Tech to craft new forms of expression. This process may reveal the underlying conditions of our digital world, making the invisible visible and challenging conventional uses of technology. In this way, hacking in art is as physical as traditional artistic methods but operates within the digital realm, where the materials are the very infrastructures that shape our contemporary experience.

The basic operation of the Deleuzoguattarian machine is to cut a flow. "A machine may be defined as a *system of interruptions* or breaks (*coupures*)," Deleuze and Guattari write.[83] All flows are actualized through cuts. In the Deleuzian world, this must be understood at two levels. First, according to Deleuzian metaphysics, any machine, any perception, is the result of a physical confronting with the flow-event of the given. Perception is cutting and delaying a flow before it is sent off in some other form through an action.[84] Second, at the level of social machines, any engagement with a flow which tries to wrest it out of its zone of comfort for either philosophical, artistic, or scientific purposes implies a cut, a delay, and a dispatchment inducing other dimensions and velocities of the flow.

In *Anti-Oedipus*, Deleuze and Guattari describe the three ways of cutting into a flow as connective, disjunctive, and conjunctive.[85] The first implies encounters and a production of and-and-and series of flows, partial objects, or potentialities; the second implies replacements, recodings, and storage into and-then-and-then series or "building blocks" for future operations; and the third implies becomings or moments of identification with or liberations of aspects of a flow, or so-this-is-it moments. These three forms of the cut are relatively abstract in their philosophy but, to Deleuze and Guattari, are always at play in the production of the real, of subjectivity, and of the social.

Arguably, the Cory Arcangel hack follows a similar tripartite model, an encounter, a recoding, and becomings. There are always encounters with specific coded spaces and audiovisuals that accompany them; they are recoded; and finally, they take on new lines of flight or becomings. This tripartite model can also be used figuratively to separate the development in Arcangel's hacks as they confront different coded spaces, into three types: flow-break hacks, flow-remix hacks, and flow-parody hacks. The first echoes an encounter and its cut; the second, a recoding; and the third, a becoming (however, in a parodic sense). Formally, they rely on three different dominating modes: breaks, remixes, and parody. Each mode or hack type represents a fundamental relation to one or more flows: a break between two flows, a remix of several flows, or a parody of a dominant media flow. However, despite these differences, they all share the fundamental action of the cut into a flow or flows, and, furthermore, even if several hacks are grouped as flow-break hacks or flow-parody hacks, they may contain many different hacking techniques. Even if both *Paganini Caprice No. 5* (2011) and *Working on My Novel* (2009) belong to the flow-remix hacks, they are miles apart with regards to technique and medium; one is a video, the other a novel.

Arcangel's early period used game engines to create a new type of video art. These works typically feature flow-break hacks on the game's narrative flow to explore other potential flow-types in the medium, for instance, related to "invisible" data flows or other nonnarrative or abstract flows. They are primarily associated with ROM hacking, which can be further classified as *program hacks* (modifying the program chip), *graphics hacks* (modifying the graphics chip), or a combination of the two. Most works tend to prioritize one hack type, but there are transitional works that contain elements of all three types, such as the large installation on the history of bowling games, *Various Self Playing Bowling Games* (2011), commissioned as a kind of homage to Arcangel's early works.[86] This installation contained fourteen games and went on display at the Barbican Art Gallery, London. Arcangel modified older and newer generations of game consoles, displayed in chronological order and hooked up to large screens, giving the appearance of a virtual bowling alley, challenging what a museum's space is. They are not ROM hacks but bowling simulations combining flow-breaks and flow-parodies, and their historically correct juxtaposition indicates an encyclopedic flow-catalogue, as well. The games' original controllers (or joysticks) were hacked to record and play back the artist's button input, bowling only gutter balls in an endless loop, foregrounding failure, the failure of flows, the failures of art and technology.

In a narrower but more enlightening sense, Deleuze and Guattari's notion of flow shares some aspects with media historian Raymond Williams's term "televisual flow," also developed during the 1970s.[87] Williams's theory gains some precision by being more limited and media-specific in a way that Deleuze and Guattari's is not. Their perspective was metallurgic, ecological, and evolutionary, but not media-specific. Jussi Parikka developed this into a political "geology of media."[88] Williams's notion of flow doesn't include the ecological and geological layer but shares a focus on powers and forces. Williams is attentive to the forces or powers that are used to submerge a wide variety of contents into one ongoing but intrinsically interrupted media flow. For a television station, it was important that an audience get hooked to a flow, not distinct contents. Williams's televisual flow is constructed by social forces, a molar flow—in other words, televisual institutions and their advertisers mix programmed segments into one continuous flow to draw the attention of the masses to their "product." The strength with Williams's perspective is that he is more sensitive to details with regards to media history than Deleuze and Guattari.

According to Williams, older media or event forms such as books, concerts, movies, or theatre performances were traditionally organized and experienced as distinct, discrete, and programmed events one must physically walk to or reach by the hand, but television introduced a new experience. Early radio and early television tried to recreate the atmosphere of old-style programming of cultural events by introducing long pauses between content types, but gradually, and especially with the introduction of commercials, there was a significant shift in the organization and experience of broadcasting from "the concept of sequence as *programming* to the concept of sequence as flow."[89] The "planned flow" became a "defining characteristic of broadcasting."[90]

However, to understand hacking, the media flow must be explored in its inframachinic complexity, that is, in conjunction with the elemental and computational flows going on behind the screen and under the hood. The media flow must be divided into two interconnected flows, a surface and a substrate flow: one visible, one invisible. The visible flow can be words and images in any media; the invisible flow can be elemental or data and programming language instructing the computer to make a specific audiovisual flow visible. Arcangel famously used metallurgic tools, clippers and soldering iron, to make *Super Mario Clouds* underscoring that flows operate at both a cultural and a computational level.[91] Normally, people relate only to the cultural level, but as a digital phenomenon, they are always connected to a computational level, a coded space. The standard operating procedure of new media is to denigrate the programmable flow of coded space to the benefit of cultural flows. A trait of the Cory Arcangel hack is that it shows the connection between the cultural and the computational flow; the computational flow becomes visible or at least thematized *on* the cultural and aesthetic flow of the work. This is the *schiz-image* in his art. It somehow produces a physical sensation of the coexistence of two flows, *a mattering cut*, a distraction, normally hidden. When appearing together, as strata in conflict, it can lead to an intermittent experiential breakdown. But breakdowns can also be breakthroughs, as for Deleuze and Guattari. Their so-called schizoanalysis, according to philosopher and art historian Stephen Zepke, attempts to accelerate the deterritorializing movements of the strata—for example, destroying specific images or media flows—beyond their reproduction and toward an irrevocable breakdown, a breakdown through which "matter-functions break through the strata."[92] This model of competing strata and forces can be used to describe flow arrangements inside an artwork.

Arcangel makes the inframachinic processes of computation a *matter-function*, the operations of the hack itself break through on the image strata leading to an intermittent breakdown. The breakdown would then be the event where programming itself becomes visible, is felt in the image, or breaks through at the level of the image strata. In works like *Data Diaries* (2003), *T.A.C.—Total Asshole Compression* (2004), *Iron Maiden's "The Number of the Beast" compressed over and over as an mp3 666 times* (2004), *Samsung PS42Q7H Plasma Screen Burn* (2007), or *Permanent Vacation* (2008), the Cory Arcangel hack misuses essential but problematical qualities of digital media such as RAM, compression, static images, and the loop, leading to "catastrophic" breakdowns or alterations of flows. They may lead to crashes, image burn-ins, or "schizzes" as Deleuze and Guattari would call them. To them: "The artist stores up his treasures so as to create an immediate explosion."[93]

Absolute breakdowns of the strata of communication or image flow are typical features in a lot of Net Art. For instance, artists such as Jodi would eradicate the cultural flow completely and show the computational flow only in a freeze, a glitch. Arcangel rarely produces glitch art, but there are schizzes. Usually, the Cory Arcangel hack does not lead to a breakdown but foregrounds a sensation of a coexistence of image and data flows, not blatantly, not necessarily as source code running across a screen, but as indications or indexes included in the installation, somehow. These indications are soft schizzes rather than catastrophic breakdowns.

In the following chapters, we will discuss a variety of breakthroughs or schizzes and explore the forces, territories, perceptions, and imaginaries they create. They will often be described through Deleuzoguattarian terms such as becomings, deterritorializations, and lines of flight.[94] *Becomings* relate to the emergence of new flows after a flow-cut, and Guattari explicitly stated in his later works that "machinic-becoming" after the rise of computation has emerged as a complex topic, both restraining and liberating humans and society.[95] Hacking is, I would argue, a particularly sophisticated mode of machinic-becoming. Its principles will be explored throughout this book. Machinic-becomings as transgressions operate alongside deterritorializations and lines of flight. *Deterritorialization* speaks to what happens when a "territorial" function, like a flow, and I add, an app or an affordance, is defunctionalized and recomposed to erect a new territory, for instance within an artwork or starting from within an artwork.[96] *Lines of flight* are related to sense-making breaches that may go into the evolution of something coming, like new communities or new territories yet to be named.

While Deleuze and Guattari are precise when exploring the social aspects of machines, they are less interested in the actual aspects of technical machines. They are interested in technical lineages but not the minutia of technical details. The term *flow-cut arrangement* is therefore also used to move the attention away from the abstractions and lack of computational detail in much assemblage theory and toward a questioning of the materialities of machination and infrastructuring that reside in concrete technical details. Here, I follow Friedrich Kittler and Wolfgang Ernst's critique of Michel Foucault, a critique that also, to some extent, impacts Deleuze and Guattari.[97] Foucault, Deleuze, and Guattari sought to find the driving forces or *arché* of a culture in the apparatus of knowledge or social machines.[98] *Arché* is a Greek word for origin, command, control, law, and order. Foucault established a theory and a method he called "archaeology of knowledge," a science of the *arché* of knowledge. As Kittler and Ernst have demonstrated, Foucault limited his search for the *arché* of knowledge to discourse analysis, that is, statements found in paper-based archives.[99] With the rise of modern media, this is no longer tenable. Today, any archaeology of knowledge must also be a media archaeology. The *arché* of modern media technologies, and therefore also the circuits of modern knowledge production, are nondiscursive and technical and not to be found in statements or texts alone, according to Kittler and Ernst. Their key imperative—to "go under the hood"—is certainly useful when trying to find the *arché* of the Cory Arcangel hack.

Any hack begs to be reverse engineered. It is therefore valuable that Arcangel has produced films, documents, and interviews about how he did some of his most famous hacks, making it easier to approach them from the perspectives of media archaeology and software studies and to interrogate the step-by-step technical operations involved in hacking. Here, I follow the methods of Ernst's media archaeological research and Robert W. Gehl's software studies research.[100] Gehl writes, "Reverse engineering starts with the final, implemented product and takes it apart, seeking clues as to why it was put together in the way it was, and how it fits into an overall architecture."[101] Technical aspects are absolutely necessary to understand the operational aesthetics of breakthroughs and schizzes in Arcangel's art. Attention to the minutia of technics makes the flow-cuts concrete and tangible, and reveals how codes, tools, and tricks become agents and actors in a larger techno-aesthetic heterogenesis. Furthermore, by highlighting the agency or actor-quality of technical modifications, I implicitly combine media archaeological reverse engineering with Latour's notion of social decomposition.

If it is true as Latour writes that "*any thing* that does modify a state of affairs by making a difference is an actor," then we "have to follow the actors themselves, that is try to catch up with their often wild innovations in order to learn from them what the collective existence has become in their hands."[102] The technical "actors" analyzed in this book reach far beyond the human and include not only social media and search engines but several components of hardware and software, from microchips to EPROM, ROM and RAM, APIs, the Android Debug Bridge, Gould-Pro tools, monkeyrunner tools, code and programming, web crawlers and bots, odd uses of platform mechanisms, and much more. These actors are the raw material of Arcangel's art. They belong to what could be called micropolitical or tactical media or gadgets of the digital infrastructure. The working desk in his studio is often filled with technical objects, cables, video systems, custom-made artist software, and self-playing video controllers (which he calls TIVO), enabling his artwork to run as intended, though often manifesting only as schizzes and interpretative forces (figure 1.3). Reverse engineering the Cory Arcangel hack back to the artist's desktop, with its concatenation of tools, enables one to see the things that will become "actors" reassembling a certain flow, a certain reality.

These "actors" have in part done the job that Latour set out to do with his actor–network theory; they "reassemble the social," to paraphrase the title of his seminal work.[103] "The adjective 'social' designates two entirely different phenomena: it's at once a substance, a kind of stuff, and also a movement between non-social elements," Latour writes.[104] Arcangel's hacks show how connections and alliances are made, and how "*any thing*," human or nonhuman, social or nonsocial, can play a part in this game, and how hacks can reassemble the social in unexpected or skewed ways. I will not only follow the actors but assess what they do and how they differ when they alter, cut, and fragment flows to make new flow-paths or crashes. Furthermore, however tiny these agents are, they become actors in a new collective of agents making up the social. With them, Arcangel teaches us to reassemble and think of the social in new ways.

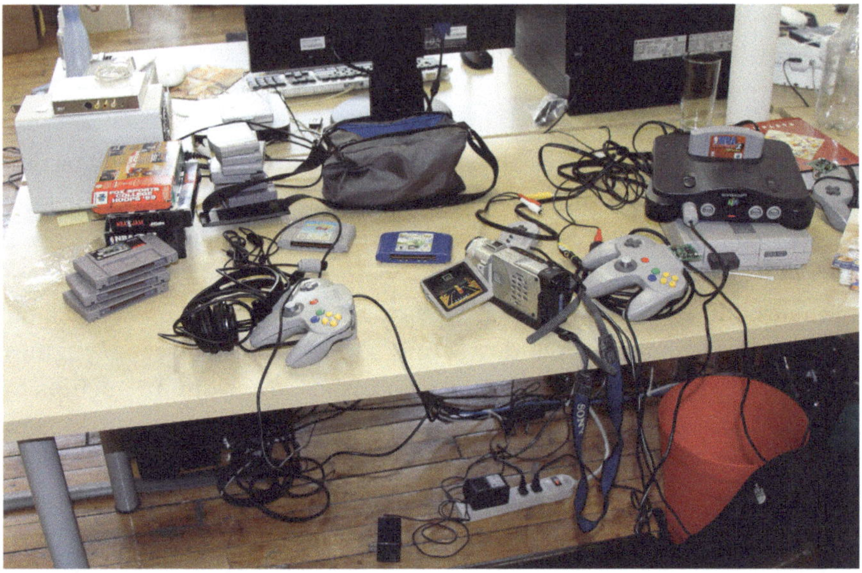

THE COMEDY IMPULSE

Arcangel uses hacking to (mis)treat contemporary art and culture. It is not only an aesthetic provocation, not only an interrogation of how machinic milieus affect the way people express themselves but also, I believe, an exploration of contemporary art's lost opportunity, exemplifying what contemporary art could be if it did not deny the fact that technology is an integral part of the contemporary environment. The techno-philosopher Gilbert Simondon wrote back in the 1950s that "culture has constituted itself as a defense against technics."[105] Even as late as 2012, critic and art historian Claire Bishop concluded that we still need to examine "contemporary art's repressed relationship to the digital."[106] Should not art be where culture is made aware of itself? Perhaps there is an ingrained

1.3

Arcangel's studio, February 8, 2011, Brooklyn, New York. Photo by Cory Arcangel, courtesy of the artist.

skepticism toward technology in the art world despite occasional theme exhibitions on the matter and several strong artists such as Hito Steyerl and Trevor Paglen interrogating these issues. Art and media historians Seán Cubitt and Paul Thomas argue that the art world hesitates to take technology too seriously, fearing it would expose art to the repressive mechanisms embedded in contemporary technological culture.[107]

New media art critic and curator Domenico Quaranta included feedback from readers in his field survey, *Beyond New Media Art*. One reader, Isabel Draves, founder of *Leaders in Software and Art*, refers to a conversation she had with New York Times art critic, Ken Johnson. She writes, "In it, Ken talks about why digital art is not respected in the world of high art. To him, it is because people (curators, gallerists, collectors) don't have any way to tell whether the [new media] art is the result of individual inspiration or creativity or just a 'gimmick.'"[108] This quote reveals much about the paradoxical situation in the art scene, where fear and radical openness coexist in response to postconceptual new media experiments—a situation to which Arcangel is acutely sensitive and is adept at testing.

Accepting Arcangel as a contemporary artist comes with risk. One should think that working with new media technologies inside contemporary art should summon the artist to decency: do not rely on gimmicks! Arcangel gets indecent. The gimmick becomes one of Arcangel's conceptual gambits. There may be a relationship between gimmicks, hacks, pranks, and tricks, and Arcangel seems to push it into the foreground. A gimmick is nourished by the simple, the cheap, the often derogatively labeled special effect, smart trick, or quick fix. Anything genuine may have been manipulated, hacked, or reprogrammed with slyness. This aesthetic experimentation continues a trend the philosopher Stanley Cavell termed the "modernist problematic": the awakening of a suspicion of the artwork as always possibly fraudulent.[109] "*All art becomes intrinsically gimmick-prone after modernism*," cultural theorist Sianne Ngai summarizes in her *Theory of the Gimmick*.[110] Cavell argues that post-atonal music's increasing convergence with technical problem-solving results in an ambiguous feedback loop.[111] The modernist philosopher Theodor Adorno saw this problem but nevertheless believed in the modernist idea of progress in art's technical procedures.[112] Cavell was skeptical. Arcangel is ambiguous. It is as if he uses hacking to implicitly investigate the modernist problematic. Or does he believe in the progress of art's technical procedures only satirically, as when he remixes YouTube cats to play Schönberg?

Many of Arcangel's masterpieces openly acknowledge their trick quality by supplementing the work with a recipe, that is, with source code either as an accompanying catalogue text, online, at GitHub, in his own magazine *The Source*, or in instructional films such as "The Making of *Super Mario Clouds*" (2005). The trick with *Super Mario Clouds* was to simply replace the game's PRG memory chip with a "fake" one. The trick in *Paganini Caprice No. 5* was to remix YouTube videos into incredibly fast guitar players using homemade editing software, and several of the *Century 21* videos are entirely "artificial," made by software agents, bots, and monkeyrunners. These hacks are not necessarily easy, but they are hacker tricks that can be copied by hackers with sufficient skills.

Other works are even more gimmicky; they can be called "hacks by proxy" as they do not rely on hacks proper but instead apply commercial editing tools in unusual, contrived, and deliberately "stupid" ways. In *Personal Film* (2008) and *Structural Film* (2007) Arcangel demonstrates how the flow of abstract modernist film art, known for exploring its own medium specificity, can easily be faked. He calls *Personal Film* "a 'fake' structural film."[113] Once this is known, his work may appear as a contrivance. But we must understand the gimmick at play in these works in the subtlest way possible, as both pedagogy (what can technology do?), a conceptual practice (refashioning modern and postmodern practices), and a theory of the gimmick, as formulated by Ngai.

To Ngai the gimmick is "an aesthetic judgement and capitalist form."[114] It is paradoxical as an aesthetic judgement because it "binds value to labor and time." This speaks again to the art scene's fear of technology: "If the gimmick seems too expensive or too cheap, it is because the technology behind it is too new or too old. And the fact of technology being too new or old often directly accounts for why a gimmick seems to be over- or underperforming."[115] This is fully demonstrated in Arcangel's largest series of prints to date, *The Photoshop Gradient Demonstrations* (2007–ongoing), made as an ironic (?) homage to the Adobe Photoshop tool. The prints demonstrate how something resembling color-field painting or California Finish Fetish minimalism, plastics, or op art, can be made entirely by off-the-shelves software. The prints' titles reveal the exact Photoshop default settings used: *Photoshop CS: 84 by 240 inches, 300 DPI, RGB, square pixels, default gradient "Spectrum", mousedown y = 25130 x = 35700, mouseup y = 0 x = 35700; tool "Wand", select y = 1420 x = 4237, tolerance = 80, contiguous = off; default gradient "Spectrum", mousedown y = 1230 x = 0, mouseup y = 1230 x = 71710* (2018). They are done by opening the software's "paint bucket," clicking and holding it to move the gradient tool, and dragging it according to the settings.[116] There is no emotional magic, only "artificiality," settings following industry standards. One of Arcangel's weirdest-sounding works, also reveals its trick in the title: *Iron Maiden's "The Number of the Beast" compressed over and over as an mp3 666 times* (2004). This work sounds as it does because it is the result of exactly what the title says: 666 compressions.

Indeed, these works openly flag themselves as gimmicks, but they also address the critical intertwinement of strategies available in both conceptualism, minimalism, and certain digital practices—as well as capitalist modes of production in general. Ngai deserves to be quoted at length because her argument goes to the core of Arcangel's ambiguous deployment of gimmicks, why it is disturbing *and* fascinating, its modern prehistory, and why it is a "catalyst for debate":

> The gimmick thus names an experience of dissatisfaction—mixed, for all this, with fascination—linked to our perception of an object making untrustworthy claims about saving of time, the reduction of labor, and expansion of value. No other aesthetic experience so directly invokes, as if explicitly to solicit our misgiving about these promises. At the same time, the hoaxes of Edgar Allan Poe and P. T. Barnum, avid deployers of the gimmick avant la lettre, remind us that the suspicion that the gimmick activates can be counterintuitively enjoyed. In this legacy of deliberately introducing doubt into aesthetic experience, continued in Marcel Duchamp's incorporation of the gimmick's brazenly contemptible form into his readymades (staged collisions of artistic and value-producing labor designed to highlight their equivocal relation, as John Roberts argues), and Alfred Hitchcock's fondness for what D. A. Miller calls "compelling, but meaningless" displays of technical virtuosity, it becomes clear that suspicion does not come only in one unhappy flavor. Poe, Duchamp, and other deployers of gimmicks remind us that it is often rather an occasion for comedy and a catalyst for debate.[117]

This book takes part in such a debate. As we have seen, Arcangel highlights several "staged collisions" between art and technology and between vernacular and modernist aesthetic. He uses the time-saving capabilities of new technology to "mass-produce" modernist and postmodernist styles, questioning innovation and newness, and using the tech-gimmicks as a postconceptual strategy to ask: so, what is art's relation to innovation, what does the art institution celebrate as the new? Furthermore, he points to capitalism's problematical—and funny—usurpation of modernist and postmodernist aesthetics as simple default settings in consumer tools created for profit.

Ngai talks about labor time and value-relations as key to understanding the gimmick. It irritates or disappoints a certain aesthetic attitude because the gimmick seems to be over- or underperforming; it does not fit high art's pattern of expectations. Arcangel complicates this. His *Personal Film* (2008) is a remake of Nam June Paik's *Zen for Film* (1964), using the dust and scratches produced by iMovie's aged film filter, re-editing it on Final Cut Pro, exporting it into a QuickTime movie, and then transferring it to 16mm film. The costly transfer to celluloid underperforms or parodies the filmic and overperforms the digital by turning it into a baffling hybrid film.

Art critic Ed Halter has interviewed Arcangel on the logic of jokes in his work. To Halter, humor has been a prominent but underanalyzed aspect of art in the past century, and he goes on to say:

> the comedy impulse is strongest in the history of media appropriation and conceptual art [. . .]. Even the very way we talk about art overlaps with laff-lingo: we call certain pieces "one-liners," value work for being "wry" or "witty," and discuss whether or not a viewer "gets it." And of course, one of the first things someone will ask who doesn't "get it" is: "Is this supposed to be a joke?"[118]

Tom McCormack calls Arcangel "the king of the new media one-liner."[119] According to Nick Briz, new media one-liners are often driven by a "reference-pleasure" such as a pun or a humorous digitization of other artworks or practices.[120] In Arcangel's work, the one-liners often reflect how digital culture alters expressive conditions, or conversely, how digital quick fixes—such as copy-paste, the loop, or automation—intended to ease flow, also reveal a kind of neurosis or failure. *Sweet 16* (2006) turns a famous guitar lick into a drone and a self-devouring minimalist composition using the phased loop technique; *Self Playing Sony Playstation I Bowling* (2008) is an early bowling game hacked to only throw gutter-balls; and in *Permanent Vacation* (2008), two silver iMacs are stuck in an out-of-office email loop until one of them crashes.

Arcangel's *Continuous Partial Awareness* (2009) is a PDF list of "unused ideas" for artworks, like "Make a record of classic acoustic folk 60's (ish) protest songs and auto-tune all the vocals. Make a series of atonal 'twelve-tone ring tones.' [. . .] Remake 'Black Sabbath' by Black Sabbath but modulate the diminished 5th up to a prefect 5th." And a few ideas that actually became artworks: "Make fake structural films. Make a sculpture where two computers are stuck in infinite Out of Office reply email loops." When read aloud as a lecture-performance, it resonates with various flows and traditions. Accompanied by fancy PowerPoint slides, it echoes the sales pitch of advertising. Framed by personal anecdotes and humorous digressions, it mimics the format of stand-up comedy while also referencing the instructions and scores from Fluxus. As many of the ideas became artmachines, it beautifully realizes Sol LeWitt's famous slogan: "The idea becomes a machine that makes the art."[121]

Arcangel often admits his fondness for stand-up comedy. When he made *Super Mario Clouds*, the idea was to reduce a work to its absolute minimum. It was inspired by Andy Kaufman's famous Mighty Mouse routine, which lives on in Miloš Forman's *Man on the Moon* (1999), starring Jim Carrey as Kaufman. Arcangel explains to Halter:

> Well his [Kaufman's] Mighty Mouse routine was basically playing the song and only singing along to one tiny part of it. So basically stripping away all of the content except for one tiny part of a piece of media. I mean, god, I've made that project thirty times over.[122]

Arcangel's "logic of the joke" is closely related to what Ngai writes about the gimmick—as a form of postconceptual art. He mixes conceptuality with various technical procedures which tend to under- or overperform, like mixing a minimalist or *great* idea with a minimum of labor or at times with a maximum of labor. Both *Untitled Translation Exercise* (2006) and *Personal Film* are based on simple ideas that are committed to a

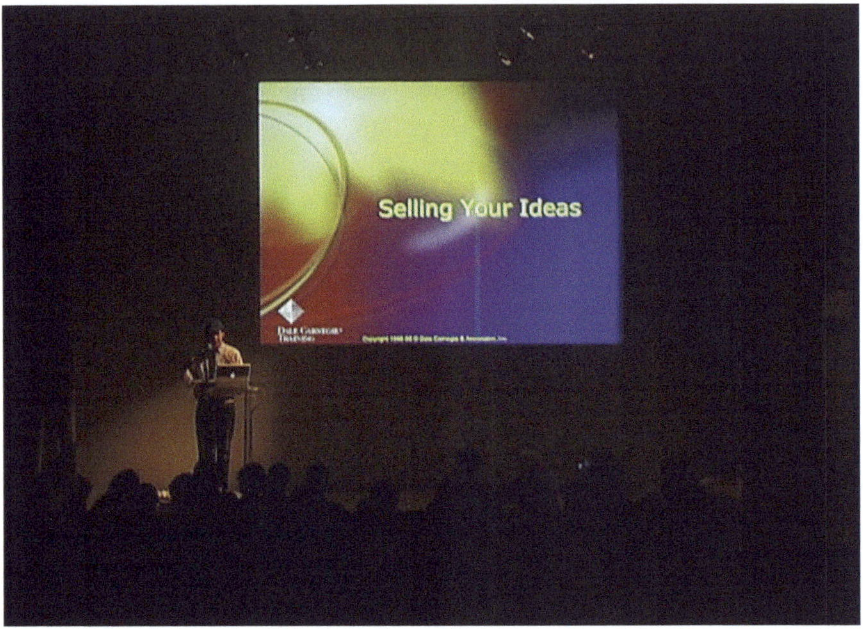

1.4

Cory Arcangel, *Continuous Partial Awareness*, 2008. Lecture. (Performance view: *Continuous Partial Awareness*, New Museum of Contemporary Art via Rhizome, New York, November 14, 2008.) Courtesy of the artist and Rhizome.

deliberate overproduction. The joke in *Personal Film* is "redoing Nam June Paik's *Zen for Film* (1964) but automatized," Halter says and goes on to wonder,

> So that piece also combines an absurd use of defaults (keeping the Final Cut Pro countdown logo), readymade-ness (using video of film footage you found online) and an inordinate amount of work: why transfer a video onto 16mm film, which is a relatively expensive and complicated process?[123]

Arcangel answers: "Yeah, like 'why even bother?'" He chooses not to explain. Flaunting technical skills is not about virtuosity in his art but about taking self-reflection to a point where it begins to question art itself, or more generally, begins to question what we are doing in the world.

Untitled Translation Exercise had an Indian firm dub Richard Linklater's *Dazed and Confused* (1993) into English with Indian accents. The idea seems at first to be utterly silly. Arcangel "automated the procedure by outsourcing it, but then extended it far beyond what was necessary to get the idea," Halter says.[124] The entire 1 hour and 42 minute-long feature was dubbed. As art historian and theorist Jakub Zdebik has shown, it was exactly the conspicuous overdubbing of the entire movie by "voice-over laborers" from India that transformed the experience of the work.[125] "In five minutes you will not be laughing," Arcangel explained in a talk about the movie.[126] After five minutes the laugh is turned into a grin and then into a grim outlook on and critique of how the global entertainment industry utilizes alienated and cheap labor in the Global South. What at first can be shrugged off as a gimmick can in other words be read allegorically as a critique of global capitalism.

ALCHEMY

Arcangel draws attention to how expressions are conditioned by technology, or rather, how the simplicity of the hack is tainted by the force conditioning all expressions in circulation today, by the agency of technology. In this way he makes us see and sense not simply the perceptible, the audiovisuals, but how they are coupled to specific programmable devices or imperceptible mechanisms. His art urges us to see connections and relations between visible and invisible layers of communication and computation. It is a living process constituted equally by human and inorganic agencies, from users to platforms, programs, software, hardware, and screen technology.

Arcangel demonstrates the urgency of hacking as an optics for understanding our times. Hacks intervene in a media system at its subscopic level of operation. They bring forward the machinic as a technical issue. Machines tend to be either functional or dysfunctional. Hacks alter this logic. They install a paralogic: something works, but not the way it was supposed to; or, it may be both functional and dysfunctional; or, simply dysfunctional. This strange undecidability is like a joke which can turn into a morose grin. Arcangel's live command-line hacking for the *Pizza Party* performance (2004), with programmer Michael Frumin, was extremely funny judging from the audience's laughter.

Nevertheless, Arcangel thought the whole performance was "apocalyptic." Hacks can "trash the world," he writes. "That was kind of where my thought always were about it [*Pizza Party*], that it just seemed crazy that we had so much power all of a sudden. Like pressing a button and launching a nuclear missile or something."[127] His hacks, however small, have, in other words, wider ramifications, critically and allegorically speaking. Three dimensions will be queried: how does the hack capture and excise flows, how does it transform them, and how does it make itself visible on the image plane, that is, how is the subscopic operation of the hack visible on the surface layer of the artwork? The first question will be answered through the method of reverse engineering examining a multiplicity of sources both technical and discursive, a method which will be applied in the following three readings; the second question will be addressed shortly as *transcoding*; and the third question pertains to the schiz-image and will be discussed in detail in chapter 2.

Transcoding is a term used in computer science to explain highly formalized and predictable modes of interaction and translation between different layers of abstraction within a computer, like between front end and backend, between high level programming languages and low-level programming languages, between software and hardware, between

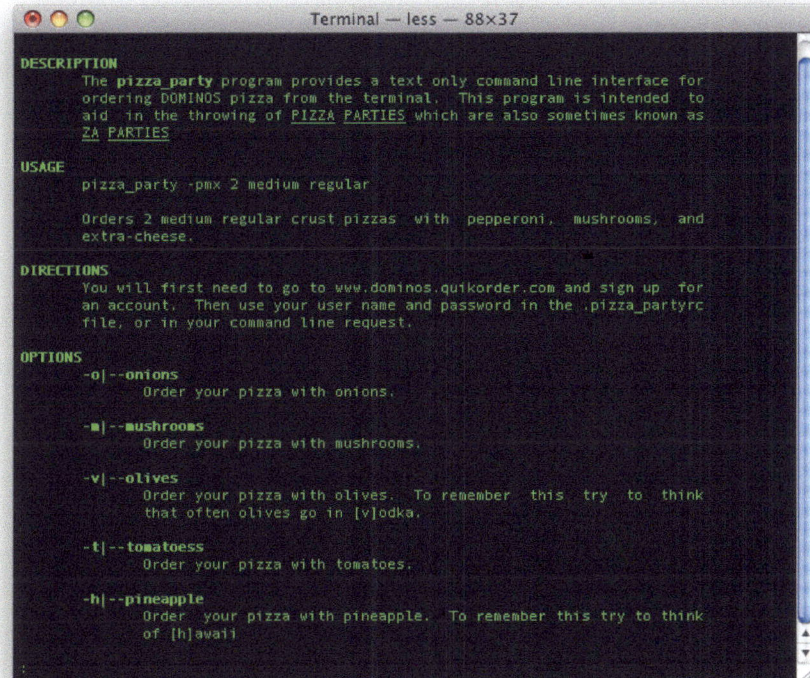

1.5

Cory Arcangel & Michael Frumin, *Pizza Party*, 2004. Software. Photo by Cory Arcangel, courtesy of the artists.

formats, and so on.[128] Transcoding is necessary for the computer to work at all. It is based on a series of automated and standardized procedures. There is a very tight and perfect mapping between one layer and another. Arcangel seems rather to explore transcoding between things that are incommensurable. This is perhaps *misapplied transcoding*. He confronts things that almost but do not quite fit and that show other ways in which data can be organized. Misapplied transcoding can become points of experimentation which conjure forth other notions of collectivity and expression, other notions of sociality and conviviality.

In this way, the hack enables the machine to be coupled to a wide variety of art, media cultures, and strategies, turning each work into an "engine of connotations."[129] It folds the conventions of platform communication and sharing into twisted and uncanny encounters with the conventions of contemporary art in both a humorous and satirical way. It reads the conventions of one media through the conventions of another. *Super Mario Clouds* is iconoclastic; it erases gaming's most recognizable face, the mustachioed Italian plumber, Mario, to leave only a few clouds on repeat as a satire on video art. It is also an iconoclash where consumer culture (action-filled gaming) meets high-art styles (utopian contemplation). The clash is done with comic tenor. It adopts a vaudeville humor resonating with the absurdities of Chaplin's and Keaton's machine art. But while Chaplin's social commentary "has always been almost too legible," Keaton's universe is more complex, according to cinema historian Tom Gunning, and more like the strange withdrawal of Arcangel, I would add.[130] Gunning sees "a truly modern, environmental art form" being developed by Keaton. He reflected "an intricate Taylorized and Fordist environment" where "the absurdist aspect of its vast, recessive spaces and oversized props" are met by "a vaudeville humor of non sequiturs."[131] Perhaps Arcangel creates a contemporary version of this environmental art, not movies dominated by the vast spaces and oversized props of Taylorism but loops based on your "favorite platform" to "broadcast" anything you like.

In other words, his hacks bend the expressions of people who are already formatted by social and technical machines in two directions: first, he reframes the expressions using the styles of art and the techniques of hacking, and second, he highlights a technical infrastructure (software and hardware) by messing it up, disconnecting and reengineering it into something else. These two operations go on continuously in Arcangel's work: reformatting expressions and reloading art.

Arcangel's alchemy, which implies transcoding, destratification, and iconoclashes, adds perspectives, a joke, a worldview, or a perception, on top of the hack. In short, he targets a particular field and hijacks, changes, modulates, or pushes it into new sensuous and critical possibilities. He takes elements of major machines or systems and creates minor machines and becomings that explore new critical articulations. This way of mixing several discourses, tricks, gimmicks, platform aesthetics, vernacular cultures, and postconceptual art produces a vivid sensorium which intermeshes, repels, clashes, and resynthesizes. It conjures "the possibilities for a ludic transdimensionality" opening art to an outside.[132]

Arcangel is not a hacker who only wants to reveal the hidden technical mechanisms of the system. He is not techno-centric. Indeed, there is a media archaeological impulse in his art, which is concerned with how technological shifts determine styles of expression, but the artworks have wider ramifications. They evoke expression as a vibrant interplay between social and technical arrangements. He is both a netnographer asking what people do online, a media archaeologist asking how the machines worked and work, and a media aesthetician and artist asking a series of new questions about the ramifications and possible future uses of media and art. He interrogates how certain subcultures and aspects of the mainstream are shaped by specific conglomerates of media use, styles, and modes of communicating. These human/machine arrangements produce a vast repertoire of flows and expressions that he captures, cuts, and modifies. His career follows not only his personal interests but an ongoing history of socio-technological shifts in recent history, from the subcultural expressions of gamers and hackers (early career), to amateur musicians on social media (midperiod), to users' interactions with celebrity and corporate capital profiles (late to current period). He collects trash and detritus from the freewheeling creativity of hacker collectives to redirect the attention of users sutured to their automated platform feeds. His social bots such as in *elleusa, equinor, equinox, e-trade financial* (2020) record social media scrolling at slow pace, producing eerie moving image monuments to enshittifycation. Every sentence and image of every post that is liked can be read in detail, reflecting slow death and mass physical attenuation under platform capitalism.

When I ask Arcangel about his method, he tells me: "I like to think of it as catching things."[133] Catching also implies an element of rescue and preservation, but again, he is not only an archaeologist or archivist building a cache of techno-cultural means and modes of expression but an artist transforming relics of culture into new, or ever so slightly new, expressions:

> I like to find things and then to do something, but have that something I do be so stupid, so obvious, or dumb, or the things I catch to be so dumb or so overlooked. Somehow the alchemy is: the things that go into the work may seem so insignificant or stupid, but hopefully the transformation becomes profound, in part because what the things are and what I've done to them is so insignificant—there is a relationship there, right—and that the distance between the two are so great that it evolves into something new or amounts to or opens up something infinite.[134]

Arcangel's "alchemy" is about transforming or transcoding a "catch". His flow-mutations imply an awareness of the technical machination at play in the target field, the source of its appropriation. It speaks to the infrastructure of expressions in digital culture. However, his alchemy also plays a trick on this infrastructure by coupling the catch to slightly unfamiliar terrains. Typically, the hack couples the catch to discourses and conventions taken from contemporary art. Two strata meet (app and online culture and high art) and are mixed; an oblique juxtaposition between two seemingly incommensurate practices: video games and video art as in *Super Mario Clouds*. This juxtaposition is also a destratification, because a practice and a series of images are taken from one stratum, a gaming stratum, and bent or mixed to follow the conventions from another stratum, contemporary art. One could also argue, as Matthew Fuller does, that cultural destratification happened most radically with the appearance of the internet.[135] Arcangel's art strategy is perhaps not so much a reworking of pop art, as many commentators say,[136] but a reflection on its dissemination and domestication with the internet's general destratification of everything.

His art is not simply *about* the internet, it borrows strategies *from* the internet. It is not *anybody's* strategy but rather the non-strategy or the confluence of a series of commercial, entrepreneurial, and artistic desires online enabled by the internet machine. Furthermore, Arcangel's art does not appear chaotic, rather the opposite, he tends to purify and simplify his destratification down to a few simple indices. Aesthetic minimalism meets the chaotic maximalism of the internet. The catch, or lab sample, is examined with certainty and calmness. A moment of Zen is epitomized in the slow repetition of clouds in *Super Mario Clouds*. The ease, simplicity, and quiescence in the expression creates a strategic alliance between the conceptual minimalism of art and the minimalism of the hacker code. The ideal for Arcangel is to solve a computational problem in a beautiful way, meaning with as little coding effort as possible. He often achieves this by making small adjustments, such as changing tempo, adding an effect, or erasing the game's protagonist.

The phrase "keep it simple, stupid" appears to be Arcangel's aesthetic motto.[137] There is even a print by him containing a yellow Post-it note saying *SimplySimplify* (2020). While it may seem like a humorous take on minimalism, conceptualism, or the readymade, it also resonates with the KISS principle used by designers and programmers, first noted by the US Navy in 1960. KISS ("Keep It Simple, Stupid") emphasizes the value of simplicity and efficiency in problem-solving. Arcangel first encountered the KISS principle while working as an assistant for Eve Beglarian in the early 2000s when he noticed it as a motto at FedEx while making deliveries. "At the same time in my work, I was trying to find a way to put media art, or code-based art over on a general art audience, and I found that the simpler I made it, the easier it was for people to understand," Arcangel adds.[138]

In the chapters ahead, we will investigate how Cory Arcangel's alchemy transforms the banal into the profound.

2

FLOW-BREAK

Super Mario Clouds and ROM Hacking

"I don't love the games so much, but I really love the system."
—Cory Arcangel[1]

REVERSE ENGINEERING *SUPER MARIO CLOUDS*

Cory Arcangel's most celebrated work from the early period is *Super Mario Clouds* (*SMC*) from 2002. The work lived for a long time as a downloadable ROM, a GIF file with code instructions and comments on his own website.[2] It was accompanied by shout-outs and disses from the hacker pseudonym Anon: "you mess with the best, you die like the rest" and from the controversial rap band Brand Nubian's 1992-hit: "punks jump up to get beat down."[3] The presentation style signaled an alliance to a widespread cracker culture that competed in cracking and removing copyright codes in computer games and to rap culture.[4] In 2004, the work was featured in the Whitney Biennial as a video installation and the young hacker became an artist.

I will in this chapter reverse engineer *SMC* to explain how he modified the original *Super Mario Bros.* (*SMB*) cartridge to turn it into an artwork. According to Arcangel, all he did was "erase everything but the clouds" in the game.[5] The question is, how did he do it? As always, the way Arcangel explains things on his website is an indication of elective affinities. The self-reflexive explanation nods to both Robert Rauschenberg's conceptual

Erased de Kooning Drawing (1953) and Marcel Duchamp's assisted readymades. Arcangel has always had a fondness for simplicity and postconceptual minimalism, but the simplicity of the expression in *SMC* hides complex and cumbersome ROM hacking that will be explained in detail in this chapter. The work's schiz-image exhibits a split personality, engaging with both its sources simultaneously: the cultural layer of standard game graphics, like the clouds, and the computational layer of hacking that breaches these standards. Furthermore, this leads to a discussion of the odd layers of temporality in a digital image and the time of computation. I will argue that Arcangel's infrastructural operation enacts not a becoming with the narrative flow of the game, but a becoming with dataflows or the hacked infrastructure of the game engine.

SMC was based on recycled trash. "I like the idea of making things out of trash (one can easily find an [sic] NES in a dumpster these days) and I like the idea of actually having to break into something even better," Arcangel wrote in the catalog for his first solo show in a museum featuring *SMC*.[6] The trash in question was a found cartridge from the iconic Nintendo game, *Super Mario Bros*. from 1985. He changed it into an ironic and beautiful video art machine.

Modifying and redesigning games was a common practice among video game fans who wanted to fix an old game or change certain features. However, Arcangel took the practice of the so-called ROM hack to another level. Rather than simply altering the game, he used it to destroy the gameplay entirely, making it "the most famous ROM hack" without being a traditional ROM hack at all.[7]

Games machinate the subject to become a player locked to an interactive flow. Arcangel's hack deactivates this machination to replace it with something else. To interrogate the hack and the arrival of "something else," the technical details of the hack and its journey into the postconceptual readymade and the schiz-image must be queried. Following the steps of making *SMC* is a fascinating media archaeological journey. The work is so much more than just an exploration of an obsolescent 8-bit technology and its possible modification; it contains, in this book's perspective, a complex philosophy of flow-cut arrangements. It could be argued that Arcangel performed two opposing technical operations on the old game: restoration and modification. The restoration meant that the game's

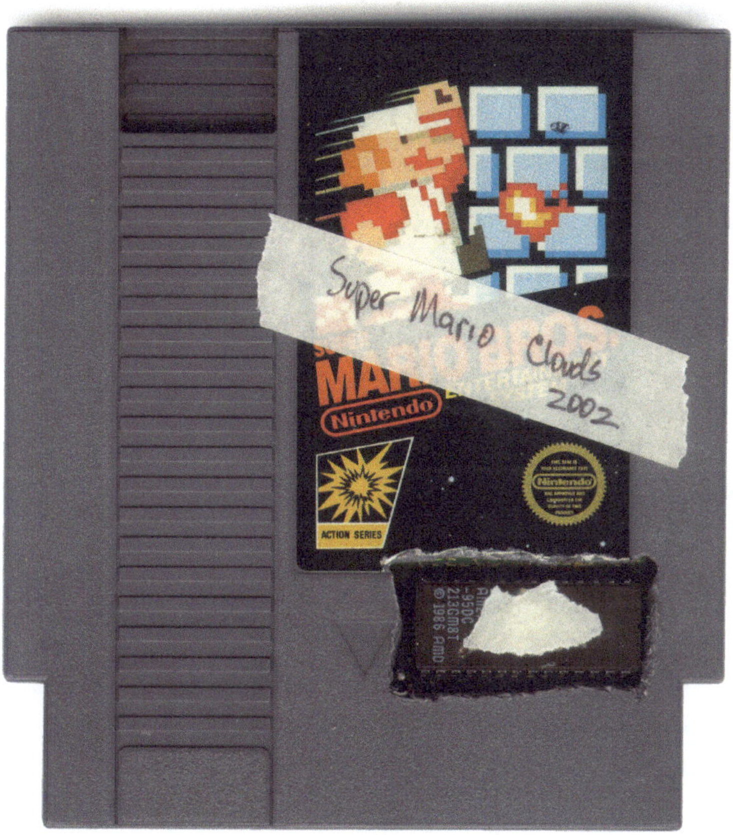

2.1

Cory Arcangel, *Super Mario Clouds*, 2002. Handmade hacked *Super Mario Bros.* cartridge for Nintendo's NES console, artist software. Photo by Cory Arcangel, courtesy of the artist.

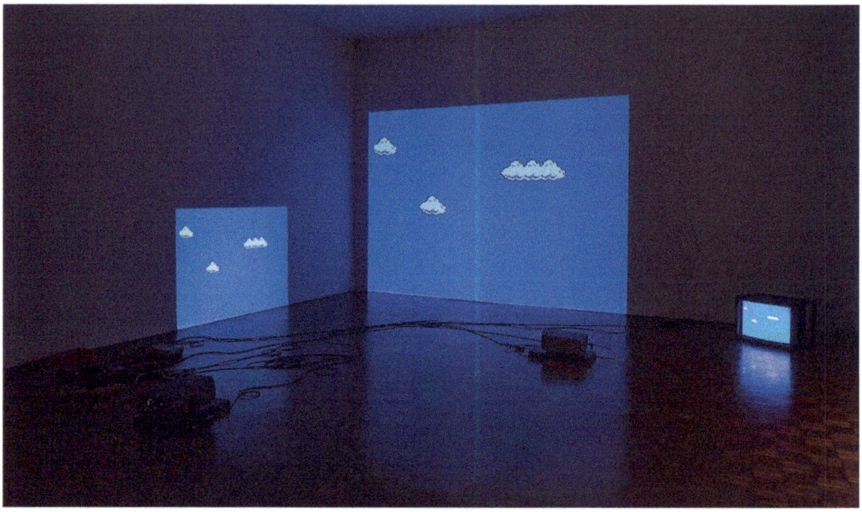

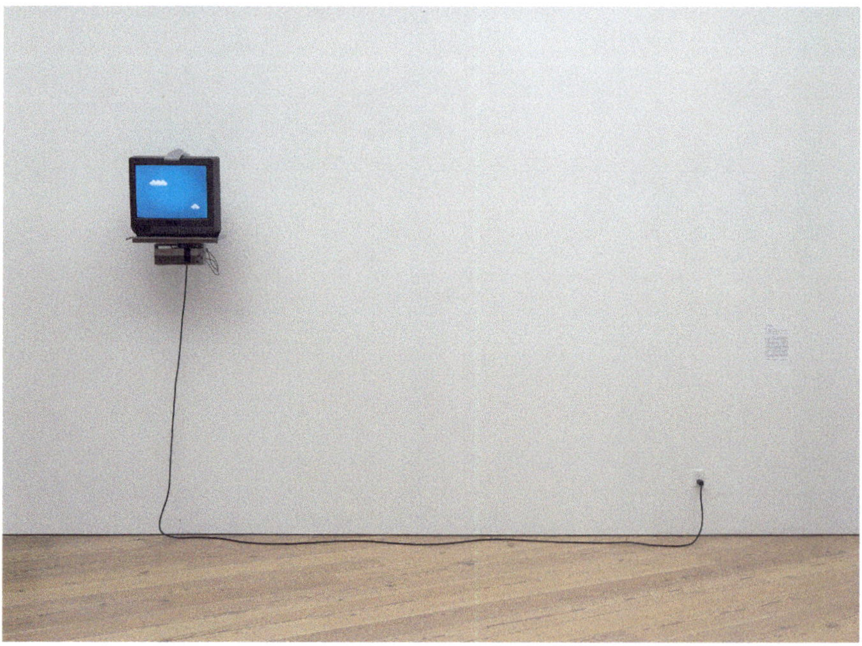

original 8-bit computer-dependent aesthetics from 1985 were kept intact. He originally wanted it to be screened on a 1980s CRT TV, perhaps alluding to a historically informed performance. However, when the work entered art galleries and museums, the CRT TV was, in a compromise between artist and curators, supplemented with large screen projections in a darkened space, making it more immersive, which was the style of showing film and video in art galleries at the time. The gallery versions of *SMC* at Team Gallery (2003), Whitney Museum of American Art (2004 and 2009), and Migros Museum für Gegenwartskunst (2005) were therefore at first labeled as *Super Mario Clouds v2k3*.

However, as every subsequent version of *SMC* varied, many of them only using a small CRT TV with a visible electric cable across the room, as in Whitney's 2018 show, *Programmed*, Arcangel gave up the practice of labelling them as different versions.[8] Personally, I prefer the version using only a small CRT TV as it foregrounds its simplicity and a "historically correct" technical milieu, and therefore more quietly highlights the modifications and the media archaeological aspects of the hack (figure 2.3). The multiscreen installations try too hard to adopt the turn-of-the-millennium trend of immersive video installations (figure 2.2).

The modifications are the most complex aspects of *SMC*. I believe the success of *SMC* in the art world and beyond stems largely from how the hack transcodes the game engine on multiple levels—technically, by combining hardware and software manipulation to alter dimensions and velocity, and visually, by enhancing a seductive pop art palette. Conceptually,

2.2

Cory Arcangel, *Super Mario Clouds*, 2002. (Installation view: *Synthetic*, Whitney Museum of American Art, New York, January 22–April 19, 2009.) Handmade hacked *Super Mario Bros.* cartridge and Nintendo NES video game system. Whitney Museum of American Art, New York; purchased with funds from the Painting and Sculpture Committee 2005. Photo by Sheldan C. Collins.

2.3

Cory Arcangel, *Super Mario Clouds*, 2002. (Installation view: *Programmed: Rules, Codes, and Choreographies in Art, 1965–2018*, Whitney Museum of American Art, New York, September 28, 2018–April 14, 2019.) Handmade hacked *Super Mario Bros.* cartridge and Nintendo NES video game system. Whitney Museum of American Art, New York; purchased with funds from the Painting and Sculpture Committee 2005. Photo by Ron Amstutz.

it not only nods to the already conceptual artists but to hacker culture and, more specifically, to the adventure of the ROM hack. Furthermore, it elegantly exemplifies the procedure of subtraction, or the *erasure*, or undoing of the game. Many things follow, it "reprograms" the player into a reflective viewer, transforming interaction into contemplation. Conceptually and ironically, it forwards art's modernistic essence, to be the "opposite" of entertainment (kitsch) and to be useless, for contemplation only, a becoming-art by undoing play, interactivity, entertainment, the commercial, the functional. All key elements of gaming were removed: There were no longer any protagonists or antagonists, no good guys or bad guys, no controller, no rules, no normal worlds or architecture. It was a process of abstraction. All familiar elements except for a few defining visuals remained. The work is listed on his website as a "modded cartridge." The traces of the hack can be viewed at several levels of the artwork, the configuration of the installation, the screen, and most visibly, through the scars and cracks from the hack on the actual cartridge, which is forwarded in Arcangel's web-presentations as instantiations of the artwork's life as media images (figure 2.1).

Arcangel had experimented a lot with how to use the Nintendo cartridge as a video machine with Paul B. Davis. As mentioned, in their piece *Untitled Landscape Study* (2002, handmade hacked Nintendo NES cartridge), Arcangel had inserted pictures, already used in the *1.44 Megs* exhibition, taken from his grandmother's rooftop and side-scrolled them slowly on a CRT TV. But he felt it "wasn't perfect."[9] He wanted to do something "purer," "simpler." *Super Mario* cartridges were the cheapest to get at the time, and he had many of them lying around. He took them apart and experimented with them, something he had learned from Davis.[10] One night after hours of random tinkering, he got the idea for *Super Mario Clouds*. He had turned the bedroom lights off and stuck an original *SMB* cartridge in and suddenly the entire room was blue. He explains the way *SMC* is based on only two pictures:

Many people think there is a game behind and that things and the colors have been changed, but really there is nothing behind it. Everything's been erased. It's just a little bit of code that takes two screens of clouds and scroll them across and repeats. The way the Nintendo scrolling works is like this. It was perhaps the first video game system that created side-scrolling. It was a great innovation. [. . .] all these backgrounds would be scrolling behind the character, and it would appear as if the character was moving through landscapes. The backgrounds work like this. They are several distinct pictures that come scrolling by behind the character. They constitute lines of images or landscapes arranged as levels (online you can find maps of these, and there are now Mario levels editors [online, not back then]). I was working with only two such images (actually, I could only work with two, because I didn't know more).[11]

Arcangel's technique of erasure was quite groundbreaking in the art world outside cracker culture because it involved modifications, or *mods*, of both software and hardware, and this is what makes *SMC* especially interesting in this book as both a complex flow-cut arrangement and as an experimental attempt at inventing a new lineage in the machinic phylum. Hacking is often based on writing code, but coding is not ordinary writing (*graphy*), it is what can be called *techno-graphy*. When executed and compiled in a system, it *physically* and temporally affects the flow of electricity along conductive pathways in a system.

An introduction to the patterning of those pathways and the architecture of the cartridge highlights the way computation depends on layers of time-bound material processes. Like any electronic device, a game cartridge is designed to control the flow of electricity along conductive pathways. In this case, the pathways are made of thin copper traces "printed" on the surface of a printed circuit board (PCB), which is housed inside the game cartridge. The PCB holds various electronic components, such as the ROM chips, which store the game data. Inside a ROM chip, the conductive pathways are created through a process called photolithography. This process, while similar to the printing of pathways on a PCB, occurs at a much smaller scale on the surface of a silicon wafer. When you insert the cartridge into a console like the Nintendo Entertainment System (NES), the console reads the data from the ROM chips via the PCB, enabling the game to be played. This system relies on semiconductors, where the flow of electricity along conductive pathways is controlled by programming and code. Thousands, even billions, of semiconductor components, such as transistors, form the fundamental building blocks of ROM chips. The switching or closing of gates in a transistor involves applying a voltage to the gate terminal, which controls whether a channel forms between the source and drain terminals (the two ends of the circuit), allowing current to flow. The switching speed of transistors is incredibly fast, often in the range of nanoseconds (billionths of a second). This allows microchips to perform millions to billions of operations per second. This on/off switching mechanism is the foundation of binary logic and digital computation. Machine code or assembly code determines the state of these transistors, effectively turning them on or off to allow or block the flow of electrical current.

In a NES cartridge, the original code or instructions are stored in read-only memory (ROM), which cannot be simply erased or modified. Arcangel needed a special hack to alter its flow arrangement. To speak with Latour, this involved forming an *alliance* with some of the smallest and most untraceable actors of technology, highlighting their agency: the microchip and coding, as well as tools deeply rooted in metallurgy and artisan practices, such as pliers and a soldering iron. These tools were essential for removing the ROM chip from the motherboard. Additionally, hex editors and an EPROM (erasable programmable ROM) device were used to reprogram the chip which replaced the original chip. This is a kind of ROM hack but an unusual one, as it involves replacing chips and rewriting the source code.

A ROM hack gets its name from the fact that it modifies a game by changing the codes in what is called the game memory (or the ROM cartridge) which controls the narrative flow and game functions. The PCB of Nintendo's classic gaming machine consisted of two central memory chips: the program memory chip (PRG or Program ROM) and the graphics memory chip (CHR or Character ROM).[12] The PRG contains the program, the CHR contains the graphics tile data. The first chip is like the warehouse manager who commands and controls all game movements by instructing the second chip, the warehouse, to send certain shapes and colors to the screen. Arcangel's hack was done by removing the warehouse manager, the PRG chip, from the circuit board with a soldering iron and scissors and replacing it with an EPROM chip. The chip's label reads "AM27C256–95DC" (figure 2.4).

The chip is produced by AMD (Advanced Micro Devices); has a storage capacity of 256 kilobits, commonly used in technology from the

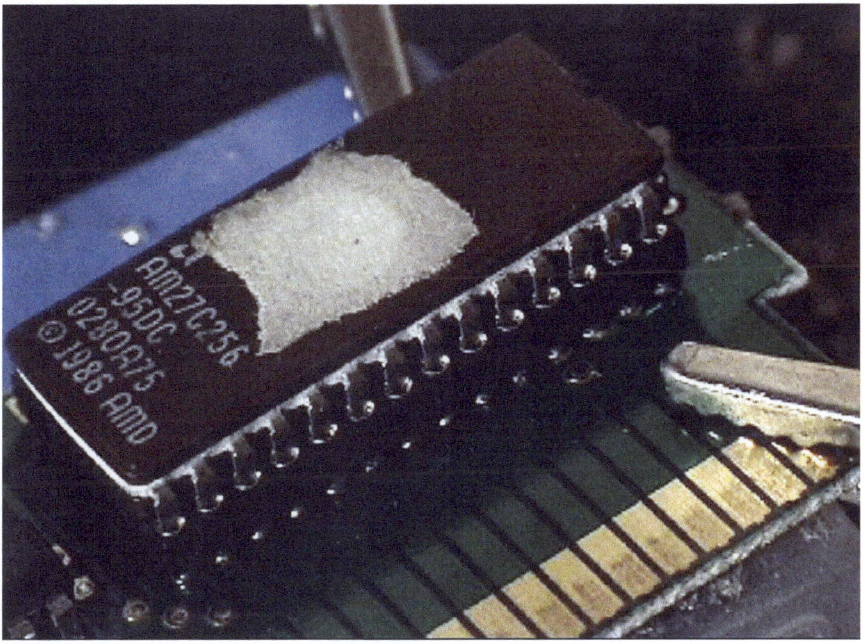

2.4

Cory Arcangel, "The Making of *Super Mario Clouds*," 2005. Text and image tutorial from Migros Museum's exhibition catalog (image B-roll). Photo by Cory Arcangel, courtesy of the artist.

mid-1980s; and "95DC" indicates an access speed of 95 nanoseconds, which is sufficient for maintaining the data flow necessary for *SMC*. Hacking the PRG chip is also called a program hack, while hacking the CHR chip, is called a graphics hack. *SMC* was a program hack, while the game mod, *I Shot Andy Warhol*, also 2002, was, in the main, a graphics hack.[13] Hacking either the PRG or CHR chips with a hex editor or other low-level editor is called ROM hacking. By hacking the PRG chip one can edit pallets, levels, data, and game and music code. By hacking the CHR chip one can edit the character data.

Parallel to this physical process of removing a chip, there was a virtual process of reprogramming the replacement chip. Davis had introduced this technique to Arcangel, and other hackers online, such as the NesDev community site, were important for insights into the way Nintendo programmed its chips. PRG and CHR packaged as a .nes file could be downloaded online. They helped Arcangel to identify the elements needed for *SMC*. He discarded the removed PRG chip, the game's original warehouse manager, and wrote completely new code for a chip to replace it that instructed the CHR chip to send only clouds across a monochrome blue sky to the screen. The code was written in the 6502 assembly language, a programming language from the 1970s commonly used by Nintendo, Commodore 64, the Atari 2600, and many others. As one hacker commented, "Assembly language is a low-level programming language—one where you have almost *total* control over your computer!"[14] Assembly Language operates at the second deepest computer system level, before one reaches the machine codes of 0s and 1s that control the electronic signals in the hardware.[15] Arcangel learned this language online, and he gives credit to his online sources: "a Canadian NEW genius named Chris Covell, who apparently got it from Duck Hunt."[16]

The new code was uploaded via an EPROM burner to an EPROM chip, that was soldered into the empty PRG slot on the circuit board. The procedure is effectively demonstrated in the video "The Making of *Super Mario Clouds*," where the EPROM chip is soldered into the cartridge (figure 2.4).

Because of a socket—which allowed the EPROM chip to be taken in and out many times—the chip was too high to fit into the cartridge. A drill and wire cutters were needed to bore out a hole in the plastic cartridge. That is why the modified cartridge has a hole where a microchip is sticking out. It is visible at the bottom of the cartridge (figure 2.1). It has become the hallmark of the work, but it is usually not visible when installed in a gallery. However, it figures prominently in catalogues, reviews, and on Arcangel's website. Arcangel considers any figuration of the protruding chip in the press or elsewhere as a part of the work:

> You can only see it [the protruding chip] when it's performing as an object in the press. That's also part of the work. . . . The image would communicate the mechanics. The gallery is not any more important area for the work than the press; the work functions all these different places.[17]

The EPROM chip is one of the places to search for the work's *arché*, its origin and control center. It is from this location the work sends its minimal instructions to the graphics chip, and the instruction reads: send two images of white clouds and a blue sky to the screen in a loop! Or in an excerpt from Arcangel's code:

```
load_clouds
lda [addr],y
sta $2007
iny
bne load_clouds
txs
ldx #$01
inc addr,x
tsx
dex
bne load_clouds
```
[18]

The algorithm, which is reproduced here in a small extract, asks the graphics memory chip to upload clouds. It also indicates the clouds' characteristic shape and location in the image. Arcangel also wrote code instructions that would delay the scroll. It created a specific Zen-like aesthetic to the work, but it also highlighted elements of the apparatus. The aesthetics of Nintendo games from 1985 were determined by two basic key hardware constraints: the game processor's 8-bit technology and its interaction with the CRT TV. The 8-bit technology worked so that all data elements appeared as very clumsy and coarse-grained by today's standards since they consisted of only eight binary pieces of information. The cathode ray tube TV image was formed by an electron beam that scanned repeatedly, sixty times per second, across the screen and ignited an image. The scans were too fast to be visible to the human eye. The movement on the screen was determined by the program chip's instruction to send—draw or paint—pieces of graphics on changing coordinates on the TV screen in the short interval between the scanning rhythm of the cathode ray tube technology.[19] Therefore, the movement in the image looked relatively "normal," at least in 1985, but if one slows down the movement, as Arcangel did in his modification, the technical artificiality of the movement is amplified. By adjusting the speed of images, he highlights the way the 8-bit graphics are *infrastructured* by basic constraints. The piece centers on the clunky graphics of the clouds as their jerky slide motion movement is slowed down as if to insert a pause, a reflexivity, in their path. The interval monumentalizes the clouds and brings out the peculiarities of the CRT TV.

The mod at the level of programming alters the program chip without altering the content of the graphics chip. It is the original "factory soldered" clouds from the game's graphics chip that are visible on the screen, as Arcangel asserts in a much-quoted passage on the hack:

> I only modify the program chip, and I leave the graphic chip from the original game intact. Therefore, since I do not touch the graphics from the original cartridge, the clouds you see are the actual factory soldered clouds that come on the Mario cartridge. There is no generation loss, and no "copying," because I did not even have to make a copy. Wasss up.[20]

This in and of itself is correct, but both the colors, the tempo, and even the appearance and location of the clouds are slightly changed in Arcangel's hack, causing much controversy in ROM hacking communities.

THE ROM HACKING CONTROVERSY

Within certain game-oriented segments of the emerging academic subfield of critical code studies, Arcangel was attacked for inconsistencies. This became clear in critical essays by Nintendo expert Nathan Altice and by game artist and media historian Patrick LeMieux.[21] Their views are interesting for their precise and thorough knowledge of game-specific programming like ROM hacking. Within this narrow perspective, their critique makes perfect sense, but when applied to an artwork like *SMC*, their conclusions are highly questionable. They reverse engineer the making of *SMC* and conclude that its hack is inauthentic and that Arcangel struggles to hide it. Arcangel had called *SMC* a simple "erasure of the game." Altice and LeMieux argue *SMC* was much more and much less. According to them it was not an erasure but a rewriting of the entire game. From one perspective, they are right. "Arcangel's ROM hack does not actually contain Nintendo's ROM," LeMieux writes, and therefore it cannot be an erasure.[22] LeMieux refers to the fact that Arcangel did not "erase" codes in a specific ROM chip such as the PRG chip; Arcangel simply removed and replaced it with an entirely rewritten EPROM chip. Therefore, from LeMieux's perspective, *SMC* lacks media-specific criticality. This is largely a debate about diverging notions of media-specific criticality when analyzing a work that has one foot in cracker culture and the other in art.

There seems to be disagreement about what "erasure" is technically and aesthetically speaking. This leads to misunderstandings. First, Altice and LeMieux disregard Arcangel's conceptual and art historical allusions when he uses the term "erasure"; second, the technical aspect of what an erasure is, is also questionable; and third, the fact that Arcangel's erasure also adds alterations to elements like color, speed, and the clouds' contours does not make it less "critical" but rather the opposite, I stress. The alterations, which are highly visible when one studies comparisons between *SMB* and *SMC*, as LeMieux does, are of critical importance to me, because these alterations problematize the conditions of the digital image. They raise more general questions in media-specific terms, and alas, are less about the specifics of *SMB*. LeMieux questions what a digital appropriation is, what a copy is, what a readymade is, and what erasure is after digitization. As Mark B. N. Hansen underscores in *New Philosophy for New Media*, the digital image is unlike what we used to call an image, because it is a numerical image "composed of small 'discrete' fragment or elementary points" that can "be addressed independently of the whole."[23] This is exactly what Arcangel demonstrates and highlights through his transfiguration of discrete pixels. To do this, Arcangel's hack had to follow a different procedure than LeMieux's so-called authentic procedure of erasure. Arcangel rewrote the entire programming code for the chip replacing the PRG chip, altering the velocity and dimension of the clouds and the sky's palette and leaving out (rather than literally erasing) any instructions for other game specific objects such as Mario, the landscape, and the music. LeMieux suggests a more technically precise method of erasure in his "authentic remake," where he modifies the original PRG chip by overwriting specific instructions with 0xFF, effectively nullifying them. This method preserves the media-specific palette and pixel configurations while selectively disabling certain functionalities. If I understand this correctly, LeMieux nullifies specific memory locations in the ROM and considers this a "proper" erasure. In contrast, Arcangel rewrites the entire ROM chip, a procedure deemed "incorrect" by certain standards within the ROM-hacking community for what constitutes a proper erasure. I will not dispute LeMieux's approach from the perspective of the ROM-hacking community's "rules"; his technical expertise in this domain is unrivaled. What interests me is not whether Arcangel is right or wrong according to a particular school or dogma but rather what his hack, erroneous or not, contributes to the larger picture. I will assert that he creates a new media-critical image—the schiz-image—which will be discussed more fully later.

I worry that LeMieux's argument about media specific criticality is reductionistic. To him, media specificity seems to demand that one does not replace chips or add code. The first thing LeMieux did to prove his case was to demonstrate that *SMC* was visually unlike the original *SMB* and, therefore, could not be considered an erasure. He supported his argument by creating a work titled *Coin Heaven* (2013), which he claimed was an authentic example of "erasing nothing but the clouds" in *SMB*.[24] Further proof of authenticity to LeMieux was that this rendition of an erasure kept a technically unerasable feature—the coin or "sprite zero"—intact in the image's upper left corner, something Arcangel purposely erased only in his final gallery version of 2003. LeMieux was not aware that Arcangel's original *SMC* version from 2002, accompanied by a GIF on his website, actually contained "sprite zero." Regardless, LeMieux's next critique of *SMC* was the online video essay, *Everything But the Clouds* (2017). It was composed as a detective story about technical and aesthetical "mistakes" in *SMC*. It seems LeMieux applies criteria from a specific video gaming culture directly on another culture, Arcangel's video art, without any translation or any consideration of artistic modernism's own tradition of media specificity and its ironic dissolution in postconceptual art.

LeMieux starts by respectfully commending *SMC* as "a touchstone in the history and practice of both media art and game; in fact, almost every book invested in game art mentions Arcangel's project," but, according to LeMieux, most commentators got the facts wrong, because they believe that Arcangel had "erased everything but the clouds."[25] To raise the stakes higher, LeMieux indicates that Arcangel's hacker ethos as demonstrated in "The Making of *Super Mario Clouds*" is a posture we should not believe in. He thinks Arcangel's video demonstration is obscured for the purpose of hiding his procedure. Again, LeMieux disregards the artistic references at play. Arcangel's video is stylistically rough and sketchy not to hide his procedure, but to reference in a funny way the shaky handheld camera style typical of the new American experimental documentary film and video genre. LeMieux insinuates:

> despite his transparency, few have investigated what the code reveals about *SMC*, taking it instead as a guarantee of authenticity. However, even a cursory comparison of Arcangel's assembly and Nintendo's ROM reveals that *SMC* doesn't use any programming data from *Super Mario Brothers*.[26]

This is both an interesting and problematical assertion. The term "authenticity" is difficult, almost senseless, when applied to a postconceptual video, despite Arcangel's playful comments. LeMieux's argument seems to establish a front between followers of art and followers of games (the ROM-hacking community), and he uses critical code studies (CCS) as a fact-checking arena to prove that only the latter are honest. Now, the CCS approach is highly needed when dealing with computational art, as few art historians and humanists have sufficient competence, but LeMieux does CCS a disfavor when he disregards the necessary art context. "Authenticity" as optics regarding postconceptual art practices is questionable because these practices implicitly play with authenticity. To reiterate, LeMieux's authenticity check has two registers of comparison. First, if *SMC* does not *look* like *SMB* in terms of color and graphics, it is not authentic. Many have thought *SMC* and *SMB* look the same. LeMieux is correct, however; they do not when placed side by side, as he does in his video essay. Second, comparing the programming code, if the industry standard and the artistic hack use a dissimilar chip or code configuration, the hack is inauthentic.[27] Arcangel's heretic code alters both the shape and tempo of the clouds as well as the palette of the blue background. Arcangel has willingly committed something I will call "an algorithmic iconoclasm." It looks the same, but it is not. Iconoclasm belongs to a long heretic tradition confronting the gospel, which here, is the Nintendo source code. This is where LeMieux's argument gets both interesting and disturbing. It is interesting because LeMieux, like Altice, explains in detail how Arcangel alters the hexadecimal values in the code determining NES's signature palette and graphics, which Arcangel does not address explicitly in his own comments. Arcangel told me that at first, he was not aware of the "value-errors," but as he liked the new color, he kept it. LeMieux thinks that this alteration is an addition and not, strictly speaking, an erasure. He is right, but the argument gets problematical when he asserts that "*SMC* doesn't use any programming data from *Super Mario Brothers*."

The Nintendo ROM has, as we have seen, many layers, both a PRG chip and a CHR chip. One can modify or destroy the PRG chip and leave the other chip intact. Even if the code in the PRG chip is altered or "wrong," the data creating images on the screen are nevertheless generated by the data in the CHR chip. These data are stored in the chip not as readymade clouds but as readymade pixel mosaic tiles that can make clouds in various shapes, but the data, the pixel mosaic tiles, are nevertheless data in the original Nintendo ROM, even if the algorithm in the hacked programming chip selecting pixel mosaic tiles contains programming data that was not in the original programming chip. This is how the system works. In other words, the fact that the palette and shape of the clouds are a bit off, does not mean it is not data *from* Nintendo.

Nevertheless, LeMieux draws several bold conclusions from Arcangel's art practice which he calls "Arcangel's ideology": "Material processes of technology often run counter to the narratives that try to sanitize them, even as those same narratives celebrate their platform specificity and material authenticity," he says, adding, "Before I started this project, I never quite realized how pervasive the dehistoricizing, dematerializing, and disembodying impulse is [in art practices], even in a field of inquiry founded on the exact opposite."[28] Did Arcangel try to sanitize anything? Is Arcangel really dehistoricizing, dematerializing, and disembodying the game? LeMieux makes a big point out of the fact that Arcangel's method even enabled him to erase the game's sprite zero, the lonely blinking coin at the top of the screen. To LeMieux, erasing the coin erases the work's criticality: "It also affects an erasure of the game's medium-specificity, depicting a utopian autonomous zone that renders invisible the game's history of money and materiality."[29] LeMieux's observations on the criticality of the coin are relevant, but leaving it out for artistic reasons, as Arcangel ended up doing, does not mean that the artist disregards the business of gaming. *SMC* activates resonances differently. Arcangel's postconceptual art practice undermines the imaginary of the art world as "a utopian autonomous zone."

I confronted Arcangel with LeMieux's critique. He initially likes it: "It's a cool debate because it is a software–art debate." He elaborates:

We agree, but we disagree on what is a factory-made cloud. [. . .] He would think I would have to leave the program code intact, but not for me. [. . .] Like, what is authentic? My code is public. What more could I have done? I am an artist first, and art is poetics. I first always side with art and poetics, then with code, thirdly with technical authenticity. Art is not about technical authenticity. The clouds on the [CHR] chip are the authentic factory-made clouds. The chip is the factory storage. [. . .] The actual Nintendo doesn't give a fuck whether it's my code or Nintendo's code to scroll the sky. [. . .] And furthermore, no TV or projector ever shows the blue in the same way, so it doesn't matter that much. So, when I exhibit it, I always use the color adjuster and the brightness to make it the best blue for the room. There is actually no "real" color for any video game, it's just a performance that happens through the TV. So, the first version of *SMC* code that went up on my website in 2002 had the wrong blue, the wrong clouds, it even had a bug where there was a big 0 on top left of the screen, like a sprite I couldn't get rid of [. . .] The speed of the game depends on the speed of the walker, and mine is very slow, the speed of the scrolling is very slow. It is laughably clunky, like a joke. It creates a slide-motion. All these "mistakes" really make the piece, I think. So, it's part authentic with the graphics, and part fantasy; [it's] artwork.[30]

Discrepancies between Arcangel's and Nintendo's programming code do not seem to interest Arcangel much; it is all about what works best as an artwork. However, Arcangel is also keen to point out that *SMC* exists in three versions as far as coding is concerned. His original version from 2002 "had a bug" as Arcangel calls the "sprite zero" remaining as a nuisance at the top of the screen. When Arcangel's laptop with his original code got stolen in 2003, he used the opportunity to "fix the bug." The classic version of *SMC* at Team Gallery in 2003 and later at Whitney therefore had a new code. This version of the code was on his website until 2009 when he again updated it. Jack Grahl had told Arcangel about "a bug in the cloud" and gave him a fix for it.[31] Arcangel decided to update his code online, but he did not change the code for the exhibition versions of *SMC*; they still have all the "errors," which Arcangel likes. I asked Arcangel why he changed the code for the web version of the work, but not for the physical version.

Well, I thought this is the way the piece will exist in the world; it is public for people to fix it or improve it, so when somebody did, I changed it to be true to the energy of the intent to make it public. There is no authentic work, both the physical and the online version are both *the* work. Actually, it is [only] one number (one pixel block) that is changed [in the online version].[32]

The hermeneutics of code and versions of the work are in other words even fuzzier and more complex than his critics could imagine, and it does not end there. Arcangel says that for the *SMC* version emulated on cell phones in the work *QuickOffice* (2013 and 2015), he implemented the 2009 code updates.

Also, other artists and critics have objections to LeMieux's critique of Arcangel. Artist and critic Tom Moody calls LeMieux's video a "snide takedown of SMC" setting up a "gotcha" moment. "Patrick [LeMieux], you treat this like a detective story where you discovered a master criminal with clues hiding in plain sight [. . .] (as) evidence of some kind of fraud."[33] Cass Fino-Radin, a tech entrepreneur involved in conservation of digital art practices, wrote a blog post, "Code, Conservation, and Truth," on the issue. He was disappointed that LeMieux "goes beyond material inquiry and questions the artist's honesty, ethics, values, and technical proficiency" and concluded:

> Even though Patrick does underline the affectation present in Cory's practice, his clearly biased theorizing shows a failure of imagination in that he can not entertain the thought that what he views as deception and dishonesty is part of a larger pastiche of Arcangel's put-on. In fact, one could argue that Arcangel's put-on is one that is engaged in a discourse with precisely the kinds of single-minded techno-deterministic perspectives of engineering, hacking, and computer science applied in this criticism of *Super Mario Clouds*. Who else could do this but an artist with education in computer science and the arts?[34]

In other words, LeMieux's critical code studies approach is fair to the game *SMB*, but not to the artwork *SMC*. I leave this debate here but will elaborate on some of my specific disagreements with LeMieux when discussing Marcel Duchamp, the information economy, and the schiz-image described later.

The ROM controversy surrounding *SMC* would later get more serious and demanding. It continued, not as a detective story but as a court case. Arcangel's former Beige colleague Paul B. Davis has asserted that back in 2000, he was "the only person reprogramming video game hardware as art" and that, since he had invented the ROM-hacking technique Arcangel used in *SMC*, copyright to the work should be shared.[35] Davis sued Arcangel in 2021. Some background: While participating in the art group Beige, *SMC* was exhibited publicly at Team Gallery, New York, in 2003 as Arcangel's piece, but in one newspaper article it was credited to "Arcangel and Beige." Davis diligently refers to this article and has even made his own *SMC* industry on the side. When taken to court in 2021, and after several attempts at negotiation, Arcangel's response was to countersue Davis for copyright infringement, unjust enrichment in accounting, and deceptive acts and practices, claiming Davis had held out for sale two products of Arcangel's, without authorization, and had faked historic documents online to erase Arcangel's name and leave Beige as the sole author of the work.[36] Luckily, the costly case was resolved via settlement in 2023. The terms of the agreement are confidential, but crucially, Arcangel continues to be the sole author and rights-holder to the works *SMC* and *Totally Fucked*, another piece Davis had attempted to claim joint authorship of.

Unfortunately, as artists from former loosely collaborative projects go separate ways, some end up in authorship disputes. According to art historian Branden W. Joseph, minimalism has an especially long tradition for it.[37] There are the disputes between La Monte Young and Tony Conrad, echoed by those between Terry Riley and Steve Reich, between Reich and Philip Glass, between Rhys Chatham and Glenn Branca, and now between Davis and Arcangel. As shown earlier, Arcangel never claimed that he did not learn ROM hacking from Davis, rather the opposite, and artists always make works using techniques invented by others. Especially within hacking, the techniques are always multi-authored, but an artistic idea and its execution can be unique in essential ways.

THE DIGITAL READYMADE

SMC should not be judged solely with regards to how Arcangel (mis)treats *Super Mario Bros.* but equally with how he situates his hack in alliance with video and conceptual art traditions, and as a critical practice with wider societal ramifications.

Take the term *erasure*. Obviously, it relates to both Robert Rauschenberg's use of the term and Duchamp's assisted readymade. Furthermore, the term should not simply be taken literally, as LeMieux does, but as conceptual and pedagogical rhetoric. Arcangel seems more interested in challenging possible similarities and differences between the worlds of hacking and conceptual art than in doing forensic work on *Super Mario Bros.* When Arcangel says that he used the hacked program chip to find "the actual factory soldered clouds that come on the Mario cartridge," it is of course a play on, or an attempt at, trying to make us think about what a digital readymade would be. Some have therefore claimed that with *SMC* media art received a "playful rearticulation of Duchamp's *Fountain*."[38] Duchamp was and is undoubtedly a source of inspiration for Arcangel. However, according to LeMieux, *SMC* is closer to Andy Warhol's *Campbell's Soup Cans*, which were redesigned by the artist rather than found. *SMC* is therefore, to LeMieux, not medium-specific or a found digital readymade, but a rerepresentation of the *Super Mario Bros.* clouds as a pop icon within a mass-entertainment, commodity aesthetic. But perhaps the piece is about both Duchamp and Warhol, and both medium specificity and commodity aesthetics? Eddie Lohmeyer addresses this possibility in his PhD dissertation on digital art practices. He writes:

> Arcangel's clouds, through their continual scrolling, become analogous to Warhol's grids of Campbell soup cans in that repetition and seriality transform the familiar commodity icon into abstract forms. If the erasure of a work in essence always possesses some trace of the original, then Arcangel's scrolling clouds playfully question erasure and appropriation as conceptual practices by having us question if, in fact, a palimpsestual residue of the CHR-ROM remains on screen.[39]

Indeed, Arcangel's clouds "playfully question erasure and appropriation as conceptual practices." The alliances, forces, and affects the work's erasure provokes bring on spectrality and the ghostly and establish a relationship to what is barely there or not there at all, but nevertheless has an impact. Ghostly presences proliferate—from what is erased from the game, like the hero, Mario, to other artistic strategies, Duchamp, Warhol, and Rauschenberg, to what is going on in the hardware and software, ghosts in the machine, and finally, to digital labor.

Art historian John Roberts discusses in *Intangibilities of Form: Skill and Deskilling in Art After the Readymade*, how a postconceptual work tends to function as "a temporal nodal point in a larger flow or network of art's productive relations."[40] As Nicolas Bourriaud wrote, artists become "tenants of culture" and "specialized workers of appropriation."[41] Roberts expands the argument to explore how the art of appropriation and the readymade after the digital implies a curatorial and mnemotechnical engagement in past practices and situations that are at once aesthetic, conceptual, and economic. "Renarrativization, reinscription, and disinscription" become integral parts of the art process.[42] Roberts elaborates:

> Consequently, these shifts have had a profound effect on the circuits of artistic authorship as the dissolution of the category of art has come to be identified with a form of archival writing: *the interpretative re-narrativization of extant works of art converges with the re-narrativization of the readymade in the electronic flow of production.*[43]

Furthermore, Roberts points to an analogy between the digital postconceptual artists of the information economy and the early avant-garde. The latter experienced "a convergence between the deskilling of artistic labour (cf. the readymade) and the deskilling of productive labour (cf. Fordism) that both might constitute the basis for the reskilled technical domain (of mass production and distribution)."[44] Roberts's analysis keenly observes how art as flow-arrangements also include circuits of skilling, deskilling, and reskilling, processes that transgress aesthetic and socioeconomic boundaries.

Duchamp was interested in processes of deskilling and reskilling, and they have only intensified after digitization. Through Roberts's perspective, the logic of the Cory Arcangel hack can be illuminated as a specific industry intervention. The layers of appropriation and design in *SMC* explore the technical architecture of the digital entertainment industry's merchandise. The Nintendo Entertainment System as an industrial and digital object bears singular traits belonging to the new information economy. The NES industry was based on a delicate balance between the open and the closed, interactivity and proprietary software. One must go under the surface, symbolically and technically, to see how the merchandise as information operates and is black-boxed. The cartridge and its split ROM architecture could be called a factory and distribution facility consisting of, as shown previously, a warehouse and a warehouse manager. Arcangel's hack instructed the warehouse manager with its prosthetic hands, the algorithms, to bring out and put together certain readymade industry-determined CHR 8x8 pixel mosaic tiles from the warehouse. Therefore, the video in *SMC* is built not from "found footage" but from "found pixels."

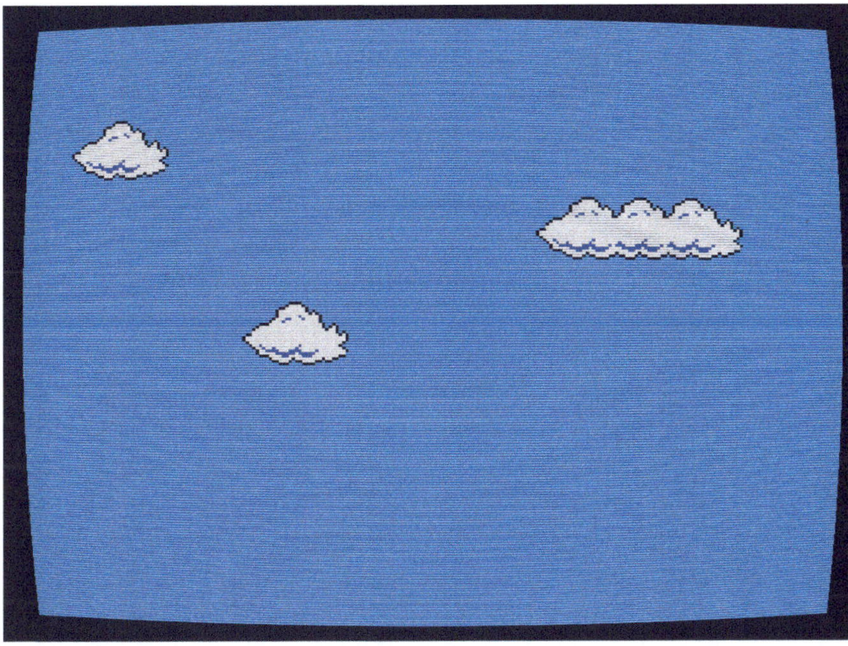

2.5

Cory Arcangel, *Super Mario Clouds*, 2002. Handmade hacked *Super Mario Bros.* cartridge, Nintendo NES video game system, artist software. Photo by Cory Arcangel, courtesy of the artist. Historically accurate screenshot created using OpenEmu.

In other words, the pixel mosaic tiles that shape the clouds are taken from the game's digital inventory. They are digital readymades, stolen and "assisted," as Duchamp would have said. They are not made by a matter supplied by Arcangel but by somebody else. What is the status and condition of this "somebody else"?

Digital game artifacts are unlike Duchamp's predigital industrial readymades, engineered by programmers as a new workforce, as digital labor. They are the ghost workers of the information economy. The digital readymade highlights a process of deskilling which affects both labor in a factory and the contemporary artist. Furthermore, it represents a deskilling with regards to earlier media like graphics, sculpture, and painting, and a reskilling with regards to intellectual and conceptual capacities related to programming and digital marketing, again, affecting both the industry and the artist. Arcangel's work mirrors this process both in terms of the complexity of its "marketing" and his special enactment of the split ROM architecture. The vast literature of comments, images, and instructional videos like "The Making of *Super Mario Clouds*" made by Arcangel himself, highlights the way the artist intervenes, not in a factory, but in its proxy, the ROM architecture. He could not just walk into a factory or shop to pick up what he needed like one would assume Duchamp did; Arcangel had to enter the information society's postindustrial distributed factory premises, the ROM, a hidden and restricted abode, to extract reminiscences of a readymade dispersed as pixel mosaic tiles, only reachable, not by hands, but by algorithms.

Arcangel emphasizes the hybrid nature of the digital commodity by entering into it. The modded circuit board in the cartridge alerts attention to a new image-producing "machine" residing in the interaction between two chips on the circuit board. This interaction is governed by software as an invisible flow of code that opens and closes logic gates of electrons that are then converted into visible images on a screen. To intervene in this interaction, one must disguise as factory-made instructions in a PRG chip, as Arcangel did.

This exchange of codes takes place in an essentially restricted area. Information capitalism copyrights the codes, algorithms, and software, but it was not always like this. At first, it was impossible for tech companies to patent software because lawyers saw them as mathematical innovations that should be treated as scientific truths and unpatentable laws of nature. Not until 1981 did the Supreme Court of the United States recognize the patenting of software, which was by then seen as the gateway to turning general computers into specific machines that could perform special tasks.[45] Only then did software become a commodity companies could build an economy around, and it is this new software economy that Arcangel intervenes in.

Roberts claims that Duchamp's interest in the industrially produced commodity as an art object thematizes the transformation of the status of skill and knowledge after capitalist Fordist mass production.[46] Arcangel's interest reflects an additional transformation as the information economy redesigns the division of labor and the customer. Customers in high-cost countries need no programming skills in their leisure time. The digital entertainment industry is outsourced to low-cost countries in the Global South where anonymous and low-paid programmers, representing the game industry's so-called ghost work, do all the programming.[47] Arcangel's break-in illuminates the black-boxing of commercial design after digitization and animates ghost work somehow, but in a way that is reskilled as a form of creative and conceptual craft used to redirect the flow of industrial codes and pixels, nodding to both Duchamp and Warhol. The hacker's countercultural programming in Arcangel's art rewrites three sources: ghost work, hacker tricks, and avant-garde strategies.

If one accepts the premise of McKenzie Wark's *A Hacker Manifesto*, that hacking is a work of liberation, hackers can function as a countercultural community that liberates and takes the industrially produced software away from the capital owners.[48] Hacker networks do not attack or exploit the underpaid workers in the Global South that punch in the copyright-protected codes under strict surveillance; they crack the protections held by the owners and bring the merchandise out into the open through processes of sharing. The anonymous efforts of hackers and ghost workers are given agency within a longer history of art and creativity in Arcangel's exhibition. The way he defunctionalizes the game's interactivity and refunctionalizes it as an artistic dialogue with Duchamp's readymade after the paradigm of the information economy is not dehistoricizing and dematerializing the game, as LeMieux indicates, but rather demonstrative of the potential and complexity of hacking on the bigger picture.

THE SCHIZ-IMAGE

The Cory Arcangel hack forces substrates and surfaces to confront each other; what is going on under the hood is traceable at the surface level, somehow, somewhere. This strange event, which can easily be neglected, despite its irritating or fun breakthroughs, is what I call the *schiz-image*. It appears almost everywhere in Arcangel's art and is especially significant in *SMC*. It is specific to the uncanniness and ambiguity in his art and reflects a broader issue with, in particular, digital images, as they nearly undo themselves when tracing their means of production. It is difficult to pinpoint the exact cause of the schizzing tension between layers or strata in the hack. This tension seems to arise when one layer breaks through to another. *SMC* may help illustrate this phenomenon more clearly. It relates to an infrastructure issue. In critical infrastructure studies, it is often noted that infrastructures remain invisible until they break—only then does everyone become aware of them. The schiz-image operates according to a similar logic. It remains invisible until a certain awareness breaks through, seizing the viewer's perception. At that moment, it becomes undeniable. I will therefore conclude this chapter with an in-depth exploration of the schiz-image in *SMC*, examining various aspects of it through a confrontation between the time-image philosophy of Deleuze and media archaeology.

In appropriation art, a modified image may displace, enrich, or impoverish its meaning with regards to its original function and qualities and increase or decrease the circuit of actors at play in its making, aesthetically and technically. In *SMC*, the modification decreases the number of elements from gaming but increases the number of resonances as it makes tangible several ghosts from art and entertainment such as Duchamp and Mario. Not only that, but media-specific ensembles such as ROM, microchips, and programming language become tangible in new ways. Every modification signifies an action at one or multiple layers. For instance, consider the almost invisible yet deeply felt delay programmed into the piece, making the images in *SMC* move much slower than in *SMB*. The slowness is motivated both aesthetically and techno-logically. The jerky movement of the clouds deprives them of their diegetic background function and forwards them as 8-bit objects to be explored. The clouds' intensified artificiality forwards both the strangeness of a digital commodity and the hack itself as a prank. The hack's many oddities constitute what could be called, after Deleuze's *Cinema* books, "false movements" and forms; they are "breakthroughs" on the image plane and make *SMC* an "open work" with unexpected sensations.[49]

The slowness foregrounds technical constraints by making the technology work contrary to how it was intended. Pushing technology toward a breaking point turns the attention away from a functional flow and toward the minutia of a potential performativity hidden in the game's infrastructure, hardware, code, hack, and screen. The game's original speed was set up to weave an image best fitted to the scanning rhythm of the CRT TV. *SMC*'s delay, as one of several elements in the schiz-image, renders the gaps between the electron beams igniting the image sense-able. Consequently, the digital-to-analog conversion performance characteristic of early video games is tampered with. The slow-motion instructions as code look like this:

```
nmi:
dec DELAYSCROLL
bne .end_no_scroll
lda #$20
sta DELAYSCROLL
```

The DELAYSCROLL displaces the game world's functional pace and brings on a different spatiotemporal rhythm. The absurdity of this otherworldly slow rhythm is intensified as another key element of the game—interactivity—is removed. Interactivity was crucial to the development of the computer, as discussed in connection with cybernetics in chapter 1. Interactivity in games determines the function of both the use and the images. The user is determined as a game player where the intuitive and semiautomatic sensorimotor link between the image and a player's action is prioritized in games such as *SMB*. Equally, the images are determined according to a figure/background schematism where objects are obstacles, conquest tokens, resources, and so on. As interactivity vanishes, the schematism ascribing specific roles to images and users also vanishes. The game arrangement is deterritorialized and the elements are taken on a line of flight. The new image-flow loosens its sensorimotor link and begins to crack. In the cracks, other qualities begin to shine through. This creates a flow-cut arrangement where other matters become expressive. The game engine is techno-aesthetically denuded and its qualities as a programmable artifact become expressive in a variety of ways. What was seen as a technical constraint, the 8-bit technology, comes forward as an anachronistic *jouissance*. The "delayscroll" brings on a magical stutter, as if the machine itself begins to speak. The computation as a theater of possibilities corrupts the "message" of the image, and it begins to emit strangely "a-signifying particles" bringing on a physical intimacy with the workings of the hardware, the software, and the screen technology.[50] This starts a process of knowledge and curiosity, or, as Deleuze and Guattari would say, the subject is produced through these sensible and infra-sensible powers of organization; the subject is taken on a line of flight into other becomings.[51]

SMC and *SMB* produce two very different viewer/user-subjects. In *SMC*, the user is no longer a player in an environment of action images. The game controller is completely removed in Arcangel's installation. There is literally no longer anything to hold on to. Most significantly, the user becomes a viewer or a voyeur in a strange environment. There is an openness and an expectation of something else arriving in the moving image. As one realizes that it is looped, another type of reflection sets in. This transformation of the user into a voyeur is also key to understanding Deleuze's distinctions between two image-regimes: the *movement-image* and the *time-image*. The movement-image keeps the viewer/user's attention within a sensorimotor linkage or locked to a more or less predictable chain of perceptions, actions, and reactions, while the time-image opens the viewer/user up to new insights. This happens when a narrative scheme somehow dissolves in cinema and is replaced by a character-situation where the world appears open and no linkage to a sensorimotor reaction is imminent. To Deleuze, this leads to an attitude where the world is read critically rather than simply followed; it is an attitude of curiosity and criticality. The image–viewer arrangement "becomes questioning, responding, objecting, provoking, theorematizing, hypothesizing, experimenting," writes Deleuze.[52] Similarly, this is what happens in *SMC*. To understand the terms of this new criticality, a detour into Deleuze's philosophy is needed.

Deleuze's thinking about images in philosophy, cinema, and the arts is useful for understanding breaks and ruptures. He saw thinking and the unfolding of being as a process of individuation and becoming with flows (also image-flows) and capacities of matter in the world. This is explored succinctly in two volumes, *Cinema 1–2* (1983–1985), inspired by Henri Bergson's *Matière et Mémoire* (1896), where the world is viewed as image-flows vibrating as and in between the temporal forces of matter and memory. Deleuze made a taxonomy of images to "think with."[53] It illustrates how philosophers can learn from directors and artists. He saw the emergence of a new kind of image in Italian and French cinema after WWII, characteristic of a new creative openness. This image was characterized by a special relationship to time as open, as a different flow-formation not locked to narrative or binary chains of suspense and release. He called this the time-image.[54]

In the last chapter of *Cinema 2*, Deleuze asked what kind of images we might expect with the advent of digital technology. He did not have a clear answer in 1985. In his late essay, "Postscript on Control Societies" (1990), he saw the digital less as a technique and more as the result of a new regime governed by computers and cybernetics, a regime of control *and* new creative and critical possibilities, foreseeing platform capitalism by decades. We have to imagine the digital time-image as different from the time-image of analogue cinema, not necessarily because it *looks* different but because it is part of a different set of relations, regimes, and powers, affecting every aspect of interacting with it.

It is necessary to start with three fundamental aspects of the time-image from *Cinema 2* and project them into the digital regime and the Cory Arcangel hack. They are: 1) time is no longer the measure of movement but an exploration of other time/space-arrangements; 2) the image does not primarily tell a story which can be detached from the image but directs attention to "an analytics of the image"; and 3) the image attains "the function of thought," becomes "theorematizing," as mentioned previously.[55] Deleuze explores in particular Jean-Luc Godard's critical play with and use of clichés. We live in "a civilization of the cliché," Deleuze writes.[56] Clichés are particularly salient markers of culture and its technologies of inscription, storage, and dissemination. Deleuze discusses clichés and the way Godard could treat them cinematically in the 1960s and 1970s. With digitization the culture and technology of clichés is radically altered. Unlike Godard, Arcangel *hacks* the clichés of digital culture amid their flow-trajectory. He grabs them at an inframachinic layer of the stack where images linger in a fragmented state as pixel mosaic tiles and analytically redevelops and destroys the image from its inside. Image-flows are cut by the powers and capacities of a new technology and the Cory Arcangel hack taints the resulting image with scars of the hack. This creates an image with a split personality, a schiz-image.

Schiz comes from the Greek word *skhizein*, meaning to split, break, separate, or divide. The schiz-image is ambiguous. Its "split" may not be immediately perceptible, but it lurks in the image as an indication. It is and is not what you see or is perhaps more about seeing what you cannot really see—the rustle of an inframachinic stack from before the image is born. The technical strategies of the unborn image, the capture and containment of pixel mosaic tiles, somehow speak through the image. This opens the image to a difference, to the technical imaging itself. The schiz-image denaturalizes the givenness of images in circulation and forwards them as technical objects belonging to a specific control regime.

The term "schiz-image" is loosely inspired by Deleuze and Guattari's so-called schizoanalysis. In *Anti-Oedipus*, they analyze capitalism as basically a schizo-project, which at the same time liberates and contains or restricts flows of desire. They do not talk about a schiz-image but about the "schiz" as an event, a flow-cut taking place when two opposing flows meet.[57] It creates a breakdown followed by a breakthrough. It is used to describe both societal and aesthetic phenomena, as when they explore schizzes or breakthroughs in early modern paintings. Here, the term designates moments where elements of abstraction break down figurations and lead to a dissolution of sensorimotor coordinates. These breakdowns are followed by breakthroughs that instigate new openings and possibilities. "It is a space of virtual conjunction, grasped as a pure locus of the possible," writes Deleuze.[58] The schiz-image is related but different.[59]

Micropolitically, the schizzes, the breakdowns, and the breakthroughs in Arcangel's art articulate inframachinic mutations at the levels of both code and the digital regime. Inframachinic flows—coded instructions and pixel mosaic tiles—clash with the remains of images (for example, the clouds and blue sky) on the image plane. The schiz-image vibrates with an uneasy sense of both closure and opening. Furthermore, the schiz-image as a techno-aesthetic construct also points toward flow-cut arrangements or territories where other memory techniques are available that can imagine and reassemble the social differently and instigate lines of flight away from the straitjacket of sensorimotor causality (i.e., clichés that operate directly on the body and nervous system). This latter aspect resonates with what Deleuze saw in the time-image, namely a new "belief" in the world through its creative possibilities, an opening to new connections and alliances, a new multiplicity. When the time-image appears in new cinema, Deleuze writes, paraphrasing Godard, "It is not the cinema that turns away from politics, it becomes completely political, but in another way."[60] This is valid also for the schiz-image. It may seem like a withdrawal from its surroundings, but it is the opposite; it articulates, physically and symptomatologically, the forces that surround it as a techno-aesthetic machine. There is also the resistive quality of the schiz-image. It evinces a strong attachment to the madness of the digital regime—that is, an image can easily be both realized and destroyed—but this madness is also a reflection on its technical condition. It flickers with the wild imagination of where it comes from and its future. Many of Arcangel's hacks have this mad and eerie dimension.

Here I must note the importance of curator and critic Ed Halter's conversation with Arcangel about the moving image in his work, as he was the first to demonstrate how Arcangel's oeuvre can be viewed through a focus on various moving image variations.[61] However, my perspective is different from Halter's cinema-centric understanding of Arcangel's work. Halter said in the conversation that *SMC* was a game-changer because it transformed the video game image into cinema. It may be correct if "cinema" refers to all kinds of moving image art styles including video art, but now, what interests me is rather the way *SMC* critically examines not cinema or video art but the digital regime and its associated subcultural elements: gaming, programming, hacking, and the glitch. The disavowal of gaming and interactivity in *SMC* defers the sensorimotor system of the typical action and reaction *SMB* imposes on the user and instead throws the viewer into a *jouissance* which is analytic and theorematic. The image points equally to the Zen-like bliss of the clouds and to the medial condition of the image itself. It is like a diagrammatic image which maps a relation of forces between an image plane and the inframachinic. At the same time, unexpected resonances appear. All the clouds and blue skies in art history become connective resources—for example, Venetian Renaissance paintings, John Constable's cloud studies, the blue colors of pop art, Californian Finish Fetish minimalism, plastics and op art, or Vik Muniz's *Clouds* (2001), where a skywriting airplane drew cartoony nimbuses in the sky above Manhattan.[62]

The strange combination of a blue sky with clouds and machinic stutter strengthens *SMC*'s quality of being not simply a work that undoes the image through glitch and breakdown but one that alerts attention to hacking as something dreamy. Forwarding substrates and infrastructures is not done in a harsh way, but with a stutter, as if a stranger temporality is at play—not the temporality of a game flow, but a temporality which speaks to or from the machinic itself, as if there is a different nonhuman time at play here; the time of computational processes hiding in or behind a stutter.

SMC is haunted by the materiality of its hack. My focus, however, differs from the way *SMC* is haunted by absences, as explored in Jaimey Hamilton Faris's insightful study *Uncommon Goods: Global Dimensions of the Readymade*. Faris emphasizes how the *SMC* hack transforms the user from a consumer of stories into a voyeur, haunted by the erased commodity—Mario himself. Faris formulates the hauntology thus:

> Divorced from the motivating force of the game, and typical consumption of contemporary media streams, there is instead a strong sonic and optic hypnosis as each repetition of the cloud moves across the screen. [. . .] The viewer is forced to reckon with the ghost of Mario and experience their confusion and unmet expectation in this new materiality of time. [. . .] Without being able to see Mario as guide, and now controlled by the logic of his ghostly movement, the video game atmosphere become a bit eerie.[63]

It's as if we are witnessing what is no longer there—Mario—invoking a cascade of memories of what should have been present. Drawing on Deleuze, she refers to *SMC* as an "affectual readymade."[64] Indeed, *SMC* engages a network of affects, but the haunting could also direct the viewer's attention to the materiality of time, understood through the lens of hacking and engineering.

The hauntology here could be metatechnical. Playability is gone; Mario is gone, but the interactive operations in the ROM remain. One is haunted by the traces of a hack—electronics, code, executability. Arcangel's image points to a new materiality of time that is highly specific to computation. The hauntology is not nostalgic about memories of game playing as some commentators think; as this chapter's epigraph states, he "loves the system" and its specific connections to computational processes. The hack operates on the possibilities of the system. Therefore, the hack is foregrounded with all its allies—clippers, solder, chips, and code. *SMC* is about a different kind of interactivity, participation, and performance, asking: how can the flow of data be addressed—as clouds? The jerky clouds are an entryway into the materiality of time as conditioned by computation. The hack makes the imperceptible—computation—the perceptible; the "inauthentic" rendition of *SMB* questions the work of rendition, of misappropriation, as a technical feat. The agency of the player is replaced by the agency of a hacked microchip. The clouds' jerkiness isolates them as clues to a game mod.

Arcangel's anachronistic fondness for a dirt-style 8-bit aesthetic flaunts mediation. Its artifactuality dramatizes media archaeology and questions its *arché*, its operational origin—where do the clouds come from, how are they made? Arcangel's way of reprogramming the PRG chip dramatizes the 8-bit aesthetics of *SMB* by slightly changing the clouds' dimension and velocity, making them a bit alien, and slowing their speed down to a stutter, an eerie slide motion, where each frame is about to halt or crash. This hack is "radical media archaeology."[65] A slight deviation, a few altered hexadecimal values and an odd duplication of the graphic mosaic tiles creates a flow-break and a stuttering flow-cut arrangement. *SMC* does not install the human as a game player but as a hacker in Wark's sense, as someone setting up new arrangements of humans and technology.

The schiz-image is a clash between the image plane and its substrate; it frustrates both an image-centric and a technology-centric perspective. Both image flows and elemental or computational flows are given a specific agency. Technology is of course always present as a *sine qua non* safeguarding the image plane, but the Cory Arcangel hack makes this presence problematic and theorematic. A "theorematic" image makes "thought immanent to the image," according to Deleuze.[66] But the Cory Arcangel hack makes the unthought of thinking or the unthought of the image—its technical undoing—tangible as thought, as image. At the same time, the minimalistic simplicity of the new image hides the complexity of this problem. One needs to reengineer the experience of the image slowly to grasp its theorematic problem. Three media philosophical approaches can be sketched here: the post-phenomenological positions of Faris or Hansen, underscoring the human embodiments present in the image; the hacktivist position of Wark, underscoring the image's techno-politics; and the media archaeological position of Wolfgang Ernst, underscoring the image's possible openings to what he calls "the microtempor(e)alities of computing."[67] Faris and Hansen stress human and nonhuman affects; Wark, the potential of hackers; and Ernst, the nonhuman time of computation. All positions would view *SMC* as a deviant space/time entity determined by and created through the manipulation of computational time-flows, but each would interpret it differently.

Hansen and Wark, and we could add Donna Haraway here, would perhaps explore how the digital enables and liberates new forms of embodiment and new "worldings," as Haraway calls them.[68] Hansen could explore how computer-processed forms prepare for a new access to human and nonhuman infrastructures of affects beyond natural perception; Wark sees the potentiality for new hacks. Hansen explores the computational production of the real, differently from Ernst. Where Hansen finds a richer variant of human embodiment in *machine time*, Ernst finds a nonhuman real, not directly experienceable to humans.[69] Hansen uses an artwork at the opposite end of the art video spectrum from Arcangel, namely Bill Viola's *The Passions* series (2000–2001), to illustrate his case. Viola's ultraslow-motion rendition of humans in the series is, to Hansen, about substrates—not technological substrates, but bodily substrates. Viola offers a new entrance into the "non-lived [. . .] the material infrastructure of the enlarged now itself, or in other words, the affective texture of the neuro-dynamics that [. . .] conditions time-consciousness."[70] Arcangel's work, whether it uses compression or slow-motion as a gimmicky and humorous stutter as in *SMC*, or the superfast flicker in his supercuts, is less about affects, as I see it, and more about technical machination and machine time. I appreciate Ernst's post-anthropocentric exploration of machine time, but my position is somewhere between Hansen's and

Ernst's, as I also explore the hack as a manifestation of human entanglement with the agency of microchips and machine time, creating a flow-cut arrangement where human capacities are harnessed through a becoming-machinic in Deleuze and Guattari's sense. However, much can be gained by a media archaeological approach.

In *Technológos in Being*, Ernst interrogates the relationship between computers and technical instructions such as code as a relationship between *techno* and *lógos*. To become *technológos*, code must be executed. Once Assembly code is compiled to become machine code, it is embedded in physical matter, in silicon. Code becomes operational through a "nonhuman technical embodiment."[71] Hacking is *lógos* coming into being as *technológos*.[72] *Lógos*, or written code, "becomes temporal beings," embedded in physical matter as electric pulses and flows of electrons determining processes where logical gates open and close.[73] These processes and pulses take place at superspeed; they contain microtempor(e)alities. Computer time constitutes a multiplicity of times where innumerable instructions are carried out at different speeds and layers. Quoting the father of cybernetics, Norbert Wiener, Ernst calls this the "time of nonreality," because it is inaccessible to human sense perception; it is a trillion times faster.[74] Computational nanospeeds are subscopic, below or beyond human perception. Nevertheless, the time of nonreality, is the *real* time of computating capitalism; it is the microtempor(e)ality *infrastructuring* medialife.

Paradoxically, the time of computational high-speed processing is forwarded by Arcangel's experiments with slowness. When the laughably clunky clouds are brought to a standstill for a fraction of a second, the screen vibrates with the converted workings of the time of nonreality. The iteration of the clouds' momentary standstill conjures forth the perception of something imperceptible, the *technológos* of "erroneously" coded clouds. The standstill induces a theorematic *movement*, a "noosign," which enables thought to sense the inexperienceable, the time of nonreality.[75] *SMC*'s line of flight is not an escapism from the real but a becoming with the microtempor(e)al conditions of the digital regime.

By drawing on Deleuze's cinema-thinking as becomings, as a way of constructing more comprehensive and transgressive bodies with machines, we can explore the multiple dimensions of Arcangel's schiz-image.

The uncanniness of the "stupid" clouds in *SMC* draws attention away from the clouds being just clouds and to the network of technical actors transforming a world. The schiz-image instigates a machinic becoming, but inspired by Wark's *A Hacker Manifesto*, it is more like a becoming-hacker, and a becoming with the a-signifying particles in the image-stutter that impacts or constructs a search-impulse seeking out the reprogrammable in any system. The impulse implies an ethos, saying the given is never fixed, but it is programmable. Therefore, the schiz-image restores a belief in the world, but in a slightly different sense than Deleuze's.[76] In the time-image, the camera functions as an "intermediary of the liberated sense organs" in a specific constellation with characters, their movements and gazes, and "the inventory of a setting."[77] When used in a particular way, cinema as a technical ensemble produces a time-image that can "restore our belief in the world."[78] Deleuze's notion of "belief" is far from straightforward and has inspired much debate.[79] The seemingly radical absence of actual bodies in the direct time-image is not an occasion for melancholy or disbelief but rather where the forces of becoming reside—instigating new bodies, linkages, flow-cut arrangements, and new thoughts, which can produce new "cultural strategies for imagining and imaging the world."[80]

If Deleuze found in the direct time-image a way to restore our belief in the world after fascism—that is, a belief in humanity's ability to envision new modes of living together, new communities—perhaps certain forms of new media art can do the same after digitization. If the time-image relies on a particular use of the camera as an "intermediary of the liberated sense organs," the schiz-image relies on hacking as an intermediary of the liberated sense organs. To Deleuze, the time-image emerges when an image is a-centered and deanthropomorphized, deferring action and sensorimotor time/space coordinates, and when a nonhuman camera conjures forth the "any-space-whatever," changing the inventory of the image.[81] The schiz-image, which is noncamera-based, both reduces and expands the autonomy of "the inventory of a setting."[82] The eye of a camera is replaced by a hack reassembling agents and subagents operating in the intervals of matter to readjust the flow-paths of bits and bytes. If configured in the right way, they bring forth a sense of the time of nonreality as an action upon and an undoing of the image. It is a becoming, that is, an unworlding and a reworlding, toward the open, the outside.

The schiz-image lets the viewer experience the image's infrastructure in its deviances from the industrial mold. In a sense, the schiz-image is instructional as it visualizes the situation of a hack, but it is done without deploying what Harun Farocki calls "the operational image," which is an image that does not depict, represent, entertain, or inform but rather tracks, navigates, activates, oversees, controls, visualizes, detects, and identifies a human or nonhuman process or operation. Operational images are instruments that perform tasks and carry out functions as part of a larger operation.[83] They are conductive within a larger flow arrangement. The Cory Arcangel hack is eco-operational in the sense that it relates to a larger system, but it breaks connections and cuts flows and, in this way, displaces eco-operational relations to a larger system. If the hack deploys operational images, it is only ironically.[84]

The stuttering image is key to understanding *SMC*. It reminds the viewer of the artificiality of the system. The viewer enters the intervallic gaps between the stillness and the motion of the clunky clouds to (re)imagine the computational processes. It brings on the experience of a complex flow-cut arrangement that speaks to the infrastructure governing the system. However, the arrangement is not displayed as a trap or a trick, instead reflecting an opening onto a malleable outside. The schiz-image reveals rather than conceals its own mediation. The use of 8-bit aesthetics, drawn from the childhood of visual computing, serves as an anachronism that underscores the artifactuality of computing. This approach highlights that any technical milieu is constrained by limited data processing, formats, and specific display technologies, despite the assurances of today's optimists. The modifications forward the technical constraints of "nondiegetic machine acts."[85] Rather than immersion in gameplay, the modifications direct attention to the machinic as both infrastructure and a stepping stone to other hacks, other artworks. The viewer becomes aware of generic features and thereby a "machinic-becoming," a potential becoming with the *arché* of media. The schiz-image directs the viewer's attention to his or her ability to perform the world, imagine the world, and connect the matters of the world in new ways. Arcangel evokes the act of hacking as a becoming in the interval of matter after digitization.

3

FLOW-REMIX

From Supercuts to *Working on My Novel*

"[A] post-body [. . .] set in motion by various laws, decades, minds, inventions, bodies, fingers, conventions, coincidences, emergencies, fashions, borrowings, machines, media, rebellions, thefts, and resurrections."
—Paul Morley[1]

REMIXING THE WEB

The social media platforms that emerged at the turn of the century—from Blogger (1999) to Wikipedia (2001), Myspace (2003), Facebook (2004), Flickr (2004), YouTube (2005), and Twitter (2006)—transformed the means of expression, creativity, and sharing, while also shaping and controlling influence. Being a connected individual became a simple technical enterprise. The mid- to late '00s was "a period in which the web was still transitioning from quasi-lawless creative outpost to monetized, polarized aggravation machine," *Wired* magazine wrote in a summary.[2] This chapter will analyze a handful of works from what I call Cory Arcangel's remix period. "We live in an age of quotation, appropriation, recycling, and repetition," Arcangel would claim in an article he wrote in *ArtForum*, wanting to make something "sicker than the remix."[3] After 2006 Arcangel explored the amazing amount of user-generated content on social media. He made an experimental novel based on tweets, as well as several video works experimenting with the YouTube genre that would later be called the *supercut*.[4]

YouTube (acquired by Google in 2006) launched itself as a platform for sharing self-made amateur videos, an "alternative" to watching television. It "promised to revolutionize the experience of lean-back TV into lean-forward interactive engagement and pitted user-generated content (UGC) against professionally generated content."[5] In 2006 "YOU" became the person of the year in *TIME* magazine. By 2012, Google, Facebook, and YouTube were the three most popular internet sites in the world.[6] Many believed Tim O'Reilly's idea that Web 2.0 being "an architecture of participation" would turn the user into a media producer.[7] "Culture has always been about remixability—but now this remixability is available to all participants of Web culture," Lev Manovich asserted.[8] "The new speed and scale of the circulation of media objects between people, devices, and the Web" gave "remix culture" a new meaning.[9]

The term "remixing" originated with the emergence of the multitrack mixer in the music recording studio in the 1950s. Postproduction techniques were already used by the early avant-gardes and filmmakers, but during the 1950s postproduction became a widespread standard practice in commercial television, film, and video production processes, referring to all stages of production occurring after principal photography or recording. In-studio composition began to flourish. Several artists changed their style. We got the Beatles of sound engineer George Martin, the Miles Davis of sound engineer Teo Macero, and composers like Stockhausen and Schaeffer. The virtuoso concert pianist Glenn Gould retired permanently from public performance in 1964 and become an outspoken champion of electronic media, studio recording, broadcasting, and filmmaking. Gould's inclination to perfect his recording through postproduction editing, that "splendid splice" as Gould called it, fascinated Arcangel forty years later and inspired him to do several remix homages to Gould.[10] Gould saw what would come: "It will not, it seems to me, be very much longer before a more self-assertive streak is detached in the listener's participation, before, to give but one example, 'do-it-yourself' tape editing is the prerogative of every reasonably conscientious consumer of recorded music."[11] Indeed, remix culture would explode. After Web 2.0 and increased bandwidth, it soon became a practice affecting all kinds of digitized content. "This is the age of the remix," *Wired* magazine declared in its 2005 *Remix Planet* issue.

"Here comes everybody" became a slogan nervously embraced by Post-Internet artists. It went back to the early Web 2.0 era, epitomized with a flare of optimism in Clay Shirky's book *Here Comes Everybody: The Power of Organizing Without Organizations* (2008). He explored models for understanding online social interactions, group dynamics, and collaborative production, ranging from the supposed blogger/journalist dichotomy to open-source code creation and fan interactions. Shirky wrote, "No one person can take credit for what gets created, and the project could not come into being without the participation of many."[12] Notions of collective creative processes had already long been addressed by a range of postmodern philosophers in terms such as "intertextuality" and the "open work." It was perhaps prefigured by the most experimental novel of the century, James Joyce's *Finnegans Wake* (1939), which twisted and recirculated the phrase "Here comes everybody" again and again. This multilingual text, a "bringer of plurability," carried a dream of a truly global citizenship, and as many commentators have speculated, prefigured cyberspace, "in which *Everybody* meets *Everybuddy*, staving off *Everybully* (as Joyce cautions)."[13]

Arcangel believed in the opportunities of the new remix age of "everybody" in his early career years, and he thought artists had not sufficiently grabbed the moment.[14] He wrote the preface, "Everybody Else," to Olia Lialina and Dragan Espenschied's collection *Digital Folklore* (2009). Many believed "that net.art had finally freed the artist from the tyranny of the museums and galleries," Arcangel writes, but did it?[15] Web 2.0 platforms had made online publishing easier for "everybody," but they hadn't changed contemporary art; everybody *else* but the artists were online. The biggest show in town is not contemporary art but "everybody else," Arcangel concluded. He was sympathetic to Lialina and Espenschied's effort at preserving user-generated content (UGC) online. The question for him seemed to be: how can artists become like the big "everybody else", or, how can the artist, ironically or not, merge with "everybody else"? Gould's prediction had manifested—"The audience would be the artist and their life would be the art"[16]—and it frustrated some new media artists. Art groups like Paper Rad, active from roughly 2000–2008, lost interest or did not find a way to continue as artists after the social media explosion.

The interactive platforms of social media promised to make culture more participatory, user-centered, and collaborative. Users were not *lusers* but possessed crowd-wisdom, were noble amateurs, and practiced folksonomy.[17] "Web 2.0 applications exponentially enhanced the natural human need to connect and create," the media platform historian José van Dijck asserted.[18] "Media is no longer a one-way street," was Arcangel's view.[19] The old one-to-many media, for example, newspapers and television, had been replaced by many-to-many media. "When we change the way we communicate, we change society," is one of Shirky's famous quotes. With social media, the social and the nonsocial (machines and technology) converge in ways never seen before.[20] To be part of the new game in town, Big Tech, entrepreneurs, and artists had to extend "the range of entities at work in the world" to capture the processes of a new collectivity.[21]

Arcangel's work in this period traces this collectivity through new flow-arrangements. He went from gaming platforms to social media platforms and developed new techniques to explore different flows. His solo show *Here Comes Everybody* in Berlin in 2010 collected and centered around such works. He had engineered a way of mining or playing the web like a musical instrument using his own software and hacker techniques.[22] The videos reflected the web's emerging sociality. The vloggers he remixed were hobby musicians. They did not perform in concert halls, on big stages, or in fancy studios, but in their own living rooms. The living room with a webcam had become a new production site for an alternative sociality, a site where various vernacular practices shared desires and modes of attunement through technology. Initially, this was a decentralized and nonmarket form of production, not yet merchandized by Big Tech.

Arcangel allied himself with what he would later call some of the "unstable forces" of New York's art and media landscape, some of them among the most productive blog and social media developers in New York at the time.[23] One of them, entrepreneur and researcher Jonah Peretti, became a big influence on Arcangel.[24] Peretti came from MIT, taught at NYU's Interactive Telecommunications Program (ITP), had set up eyebeam OpenLab (2003–2007) as a research lab exploring tools of engagement with the web, and would go on to cofound *The Huffington Post* (now *HuffPost*) (2005) and BuzzFeed Laboratories (now BuzzFeed) (2006).[25] Many of the new tools and exploits of the "sharing culture" of Web 2.0 were developed in these collectives.[26] Facebook had introduced "likes," Twitter introduced "followers," Google introduced commercial datamining, and Peretti made words like "viral," "internet meme," "reblog," and "clickbait," viable for both commercial and artistic interventions.[27] The tools of copy and paste, cuts and connections, mimetic desires and beliefs, began to proliferate. "Media ecology is a cascade of parasitism," Matthew Fuller wrote at the time.[28] New affordances, platforms, teams of developers, entrepreneurs, start-ups, hackers, and artists constituted a strange media ecology that would both liberate and exploit the common. Fake websites, prank sites, and the mass hoax were part of leftist activism at the time.

Big Tech would sweep the landscape for any inventive affordance it could buy; media outlets had to change their business and information models; and entrepreneurs and artists had to invent new ways of tapping into the watershed of content and techniques. At eyebeam OpenLab, Peretti ran research projects like Contagious Media and reBlog.[29] Arcangel was artist-in-residence at the lab alongside inventive hacker-programmers like Alexander R. Galloway and Michael Frumin (the latter as technical director). Frumin stated in an interview that the purpose was to explore "how the world of artists and hackers could mingle."[30]

Peretti had already made headlines with his ironic intervention into Nike's ad campaign which allowed customers to order shoes personalized with any word they might like. Peretti asked Nike to brand his shoes "sweatshop" to draw attention to their alleged use of child labor. Nike refused, and Peretti emailed his correspondence with Nike to ten friends, and it went viral. "Nike has the advantage when it comes to mass media, but activists may have the advantage with micromedia," Peretti wrote in a comment.[31] His manifesto, "Notes on Contagious Media," blended digital entrepreneurship with conceptual art alluding to Sol LeWitt. Peretti declared, "contagious media is a form of pop conceptual art" in which "the idea is the machine that makes the art, and the idea is interesting to ordinary people."[32] For that reason, "a contagious media project should represent the simplest form of an idea. Fancy design or extraneous content made media less contagious."[33]

BuzzFeed, originally known for its "internet popularity contest," online quizzes, listicles, and pop culture articles, started as Peretti's research project on internet culture with a particular focus on memes.[34] He experimented with bot technologies and automated forms of copying, redistributing, and reblogging specific thematic elements from the web's new wealth of information and developed a type of journalism without journalists and editors—algorithms did the job. Algorithms and bots would "cull stories from around the web that were showing stirrings of virality."[35] They were redistributed using an instant messaging client called BuzzBot. Peretti hired several inventive minds to work at BuzzFeed, such as Arcangel, the YouTuber and online performance artist Ze Frank, and entrepreneur Christopher "moot" Poole, who had made the anonymous imageboard 4chan and launched the first "lolcat." Back then 4chan was a radical hacker channel, only later to be hijacked by the incels of the alt-right.

In the middle of this craze, Arcangel explored how Google, YouTube, and Twitter could be treated artistically, and would soon be "at the forefront of a new kind of culture," one journalist claimed, "call it democratic art, or focus on its wholesale limb-splicing and call it FrankenArt, in a nod to Mary Shelley's science-fiction horror story."[36] Arcangel developed hacker techniques that could intervene directly in the information processes of search engines and social media. Many of these works were humorous and light—and some darker. They would often highlight the stupidity of information services. Early experiments such as *Dooogle* (2004, with code helper Frumin) was a prank site, a fake search engine mimicking Google, but *Dooogle* would, regardless of the search word, only return results for the sitcom character Dr. Doogie Howser.

Punk Rock 101 (2006) was a conceptual Google ad hack. Arcangel posted the legendary rock star Kurt Cobain's tragic suicide letter as a webpage that a stream of Google ads would flow into. Google's ads are produced and monitored by an automated, purportedly impartial, computer algorithm. "AdSense can deliver relevant ads because Google understand the meaning of a webpage," Google claimed at the time.[37] Google ads are supposedly generated from the text of the webpage they appear on. The Google ads that quickly began to accumulate and surrounded Cobain's tragic suicide letter on Arcangel's *Punk Rock 101* website, however, were ads for social anxiety support, natural lighting solutions, love support, therapy, and public speaking training (figure 3.1).

The website was up for a while, Arcangel writes on his portfolio website, "but after getting digged google decided to remove the ads from the page."[38] Arcangel took some screenshots of the webpage while Google

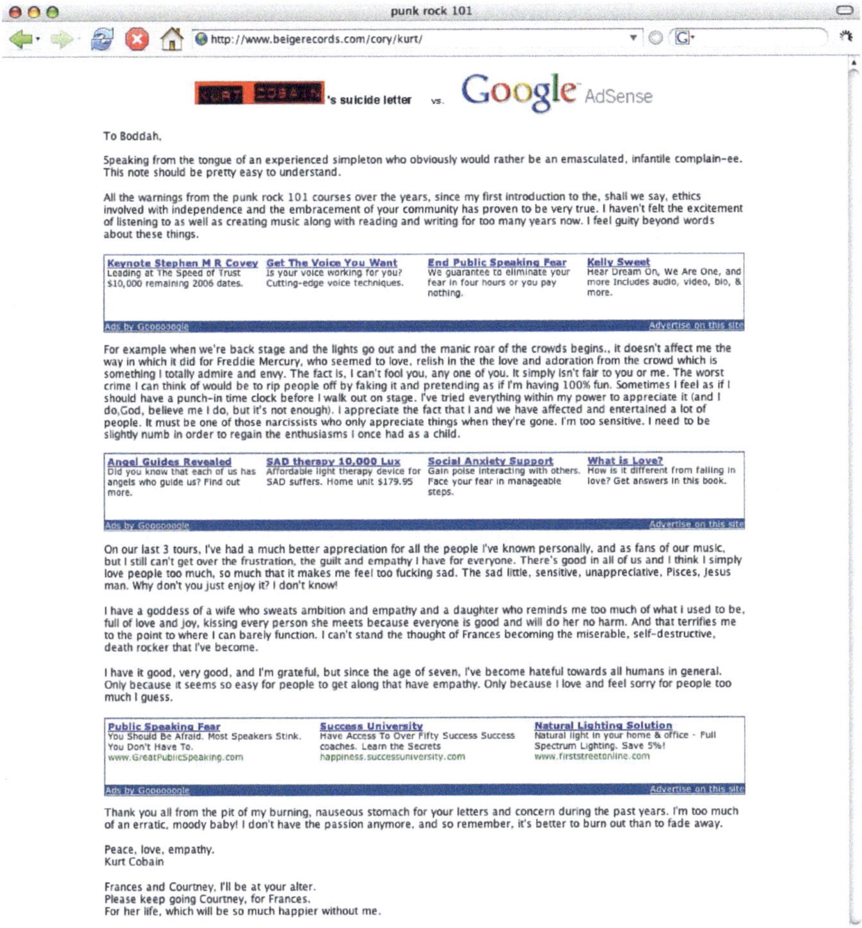

3.1

Cory Arcangel, *Punk Rock 101*, 2006. Website. Screenshot by Cory Arcangel, courtesy of the artist.

AdSense was running. The work has been much discussed as an example of artificial stupid intelligence. Art and design teacher Aubrey W. Baker called the work "a darker statement on the emotionless utilitarism [sic] of commercialism, juxtaposing this against a high-profile tragedy still raw in the heart of many."[39] Rhizome declared it "the best internet art of the year [2006]."[40] Art critic Paddy Johnson wrote, "This is quite possibly the most brilliant subversion of the medium [Google] I have seen."[41]

THE SUPERCUT AND THE GIMMICK

While *Punk Rock 101* activated and disarticulated the automated interpretational and connective logic of Google's main sources of income, Google AdSense, Arcangel's odd supercuts called attention to other aspects of information processing and self-publishing. I will analyze three of Arcangel's supercuts and a closely related work, *Working on My Novel*. The three music-driven supercuts are based on YouTube material and re-edited on Arcangel's own editing software, Gould Pro. Arcangel calls them supercuts, but they are not typical to the genre.[42] The term supercut was coined in 2008 by writer and net-culture observer Andy Baio. It describes a metatextual genre of popular vernacular video montages that started appearing with YouTube in 2005.

> ["Supercut" was] a catch-all term for a new wave of fast-moving, detail-obsessed videos that isolated a recurring pop-culture trope. Some supercuts were specific to a movie or series, like a compilation of every ridiculous one-liner uttered by David Caruso on *CSI: Miami*. Others cataloged decades-old Hollywood cliches, like dramatically yelling "It's showtime!"[43]

Supercuts were often humorous and demonstrated a fan-style fetish observation of a cultural trend, or they could simply be an efficient summary of a series or a movie. Over time, they developed into an array of vernacular forms of editing cultural content. One of the earliest supercuts, a so-called YouTube Poop, was "The Adventures of Super Mario 3 Remixed," a video remix of an episode of the 1989 cartoon series *The Super Mario Bros. Super Show!* It was uploaded by a user with the online handle SuperYoshi (a 15-year-old kid) on the website SheezyArt in December 2004, before it spread on YouTube.[44] "YouTube Poops, as they are known, became an artform perfectly attuned to the internet age: provocative, absurdist, surreal, and with a good dose of *trollololol* devilishness," tech writer Luke Dormehl summarizes.[45] No doubt, this was already familiar terrain for Arcangel. The remix genre's quality of being secondary, not the real thing, a supplement, a parasite, a joke, resonated with Arcangel's game mods.

Arcangel writes on his website that he had a go at the supercut initially to make a meme.[46] If so, his supercuts are brilliant failures, and especially his seemingly most stupid of them all, *Drei Klavierstücke op. 11* (2009), containing cute cats cut to play a masterpiece of atonal music. Sure, it had a meme ingredient, cute cats, but would that be enough to turn Schönberg, the perhaps most unpopular of all composers, into a meme? As I see it, Arcangel's early embrace of the supercut was more than a mere attempt at meme-making; it opened up a new arena for debate on aesthetic questioning, for a very short while, before it all got swallowed up by excesses. I hope to engage with some of these debates, their strange ways of being conceptual and experimental wagers and funny failures. They lingered uneasy in between being dumb and ingenious, transcoding a popular genre into weird postconceptual art. Arcangel's only true supercut, by which I mean his most genre-faithful supercut, is *There's Always One At Every Party* (2010), on YouTube titled "Cofee [sic] Table Book About Coffee Tables Supercut." It's a quick summary of everything about the character Kramer's coffee table book in the TV series *Seinfeld*. Kramer's idea about a coffee table book about coffee tables that can itself be turned into a coffee table with foldable legs is useless to the point of being totally ridiculous, and it fails tremendously, of course.

As always, Arcangel tends to appropriate and recontextualize aspects of popular culture that also become metacommentaries on his own art. Kramer accelerates a farcical idea into an absurd machine resonating with late capitalism's gimmick-driven start-up scene. All of Arcangel's supercuts are prankish and slightly bawdy in a technically exaggerated way. He explores the potential of synchronizing image-cuts and music faster than ever before, creating what I call it an "algorithmic humor," which flaunts the skills and wit of hacker culture. As digital arts lecturer and curator Olga Goriunova writes in the introduction to *Fun and Software*, "in particular hacker performances and objects, fun may come in the guise of wit [. . .] and technical or mathematical proficiency."[47] Fun is the hacker culture's "curious method of connecting"; "fun is their medium," Goriunova writes.[48] Arcangel's fondness for a compelling, but seemingly meaningless "display of technical virtuosity," is also typical of the gimmick.[49] Hence, his algorithmic humor connects to hacker culture and to the gimmick as a societal and artistic phenomena in contemporary business and art. He seems to excel in and mock the proclivities for quick fixes in digital culture and design.

Sianne Ngai's *Theory of the Gimmick*, as mentioned earlier, treats aesthetic confusions after modernism in a historical perspective and offers a fresh analysis of conceptual and postconceptual art practices. These art practices, from Duchamp to Arcangel, do not deny the problems of capitalism but highlight them by ironically aligning themselves with the capitalist economy's fondness for the gimmick—as a joke—and use the art institution as a place where the joke can instantiate laughter and serious reflection. According to Ngai, the gimmick is "capitalism's most successful aesthetic category but also its biggest embarrassment and structural problem."[50] When addressed in art, that is, "aesthetic risk-taking experimentation with the gimmick's compromised form," it challenges the critical core of the art institution, aesthetic judgement.[51] It provokes an encounter which challenges both Kant (traditional aesthetics critique) and Marx (traditional critique of capitalist economy). This gives rise to a confusion and an irritation. Ngai writes: "In the gimmick, specifically, our spontaneously affective, explicitly aesthetic appraisal of an object's form as unsatisfyingly compromised triggers and comes to overlap with economic and ethical evaluations of it as cheap and fraudulent."[52]

The gimmick as a form of judgement is intimately connected to the logic of late capitalism, for Ngai. The value of merchandise is no longer tied to use-value or labor value; value and the "necessary" accumulation of things are rather linked to seductions, quick fixes, an update, a reload, a new trend, or a "smart" solution. Quality, use-value, and fraudulence get blurred during modernity. This aesthetic confusion in capitalism's own logic, infects judgment in art, as well. Aesthetic judgement is sabotaged by nonaesthetic prejudices concerning economic parameters, labor, time, and value. The gimmick as judgment brings economy and aesthetics together in a way not envisioned by either Kant or Marx. Gimmicks are "overrated devices that strike us as working too little (labor-saving tricks) but also as working too hard (strained efforts to get our attention)."[53] In other words, the gimmick is both "an aesthetic judgement and capitalist form."[54]

"With and after modernism, specifically, the invocation of doubts about artistic value and labor for which 'gimmick' becomes shorthand seems inevitable," Ngai asserts.[55] As already stated, Marcel Duchamp was among the first artists to reveal and deploy this socioeconomic development and logic to art through his "incorporation of the gimmick's brazenly contemptible form into his readymades."[56] His strategy of doubting both the art institution and its environment, capitalism, served in the same gesture as "an occasion for comedy and a catalyst for debate."[57] Arcangel continues this tradition.

Arcangel's use of the gimmick is both a homage to avant-garde artists like Duchamp and also a way of intensifying the gimmick with reference to the digital vernacular and subcultures online. He (mis)uses commercial toys and platforms to conjure an unexpected alliance with the avant-garde. Among his purest gimmicks using a commercial toy to celebrate highbrow art, is *Composition #7* (2010), where a *Guitar Hero*–style game with a plastic toy guitar is hacked to play La Monte Young's static "Composition #7" from 1960. Young's score instructs the performer to hold a "perfect fifth" (B and F#) "for a long time."[58] Recall, Young was inspired by John Cage, was a member of the Theatre of Eternal Music (a.k.a. the Dream Syndicate) with Tony Conrad, and had meetings with Yoko Ono that led to the Fluxus movement. Arcangel's *Composition #7* demonstrates an alliance with both avant-garde artists and rock. His use of an electric guitar to perform Young's interval nods to the ultimate power chord of rock, the perfect fifth, usually E and B or A and E as is the opening of Eddie Van Halen's game-changing guitar solo from 1978, "Eruption," used in Arcangel's *Historically Informed Performance in Relationship to Eddie Van Halen's 1978 Recording of* Eruption *on the Self-Titled Album Van Halen* (2003), where Arcangel explains all the licks in the guitar solo and demonstrates them on his electric guitar. The choice of Van Halen as example is no coincidence from a hacker's point of view, because Van Halen is known for having modded both his amplifier (altering the voltage flow) and guitar pick-ups to create his special "brown sound." The historically informed performance opens with Arcangel striking a heavily distorted—hacked—power chord on his guitar as he smiles with a childlike joy to the high-art audience at New Museum in New York.[59] Arcangel's supercut, *Paganini Caprice No. 5* (2011), also starts with the same power chord on an electric guitar. While Young's minimalism is taken on a flight to resonate with rock guitar, Arcangel's *Sweet 16* (2006), takes the pentatonic rock guitar intro of Guns N' Roses's "Sweet Child o' Mine," on a flight to resonate with the experimental minimalist compositional phased loop technique of Steve Reich, using a dual channel video. Reich would later assert that minimalism's experiments with looping audio samples "laid the groundwork for hip-hop, dub and electronic music."[60] Arcangel's blues-rock addendum to this story is a dead serious gimmick.

In his supercut gimmicks, Arcangel uses a homemade software, Gould Pro, to rewrite rock, classical, and avant-garde music deploying found-user generated content. It is a crazy postconceptual *tour de force* remixing UGC, Niccolò Paganini, Glenn Gould, and John Cage. A vernacular flow is taken onto other paths of discovery, meaning, and collectivity merging universes and resonances. Perhaps, Arcangel does not explore participation in a sociological sense but, like Latour, asks how technology can reassemble the social, creating an odd transhistoric participatory collective. He becomes a *bricoleur*, a handyman, engineering UGC and classics as each other's plug-ins, creating a monster art with "world-making abilities."[61] Four examples demonstrate this differently.

THE WEB AS A MUSICAL INSTRUMENT

While *Super Mario Clouds* transcodes game engines into video art machines through an exploration of the agency of a microchip, Arcangel's supercuts transcode the web into a musical instrument with the help of Gould Pro. Arcangel's rock-guitar background made him see certain liberating aspects of the technical sharing culture. YouTube, with its imperative to "Broadcast Yourself," transformed digital folklore and enabled talented musicians to practice and distribute their living room performances directly to peers and a wider audience. Within the field of rock,

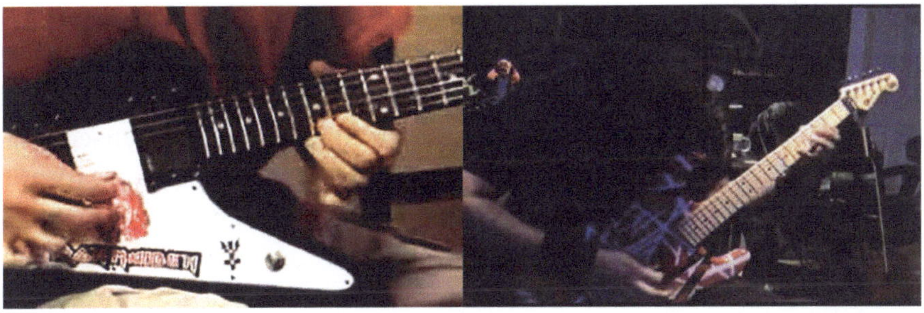

one experienced the emergence of a new culture of virtuosity. Some of the best "unknown" guitar players could quickly have a huge following online without ever having had a concert or recorded an album. The popular music educator Rick Beato said in a 2018 vlog on his YouTube channel "Everything Music" that "we live in the era of virtuosos because of YouTube."[62] He refers to two things: YouTube has become a vast educational archive of past virtuoso performances going back to the 1940s, and second, the new sharing culture has created a new type of musician, who sits at home copying all kinds of virtuoso tricks and sharing them in tutorials online. What if all the lonely individuals could play something together?

The video work *A Couple Thousand Short Films About Glenn Gould* (2007) consists of about 1200 video fragments from YouTube of electric guitarists and keyboardists playing various solos at home in their living rooms (figure 3.2).

Arcangel reorganizes the music videos into an audiovisual data stream playing Johann Sebastian Bach's *Goldberg Variations: Variation 1*. The experiment could also be a nod to the first sound experiments performed by MIT hackers in the 1950s which transformed an abstract data stream into music by Bach.[63] This is tricking the computer to misapply

3.2

Cory Arcangel, *A Couple Thousand Short Films About Glenn Gould*, 2007. Dual channel projection from a digital source. Photo by Cory Arcangel, courtesy of the artist.

transcoding. In computing, compilers make sure transcoding between layers of computing translate smoothly. However, when hackers turn code into music, a technical latency in computing is made manifest. It is a kind of algorithmic humor. Arcangel's supercuts take misapplied transcoding to another level. Code and music scores are program notifications, idealizations, and abstractions to be executed. Arcangel challenges this analogy by allegorizing transcoding. By cutting and reconnecting the flows of UGC using Gould Pro, he transcodes 1200 video clips or notes into expressing one single melody. Gould Pro does between strata what transcoding does between layers or stacks of computing. But how does Gould Pro work?

Gould Pro is uploaded to GitHub. It contains four scripts that "allow one to re-construct in video a musical score from sinipts [sic, "snippets"] of notes from other videos. They require an input of youtube videos at 340 * 240 resolution, and can reedit them together using sample based precision at 44100 samples / second."[64] It isolates individual tones from thousands of downloaded music videos and makes them play things like Bach. However, Gould Pro involves an extensive process: 1) downloading YouTube videos; 2) converting them into mp4s; 3) separating video and audio by extracting individual notes as aif (an uncompressed audio file format); 4) uploading them to Arcangel's feature, "the gould-maketranscriptions .mxb64," which separates video and audio; 5) the plug-in of a free runtime tool enabling the user to "write" a "score file"; 6) the score mimicking any musical score fed into it, like a Bach-variation; 7) a video score file is generated. The directory showing the latter parts of the process should look like this:

```
gould-maketranscriptions.mxb64
gould-makevideo.pl
gould-makeaudio.pl
gould-makescore.c
MovieSeq/
aif/
303.aif
g1.aif
    mp4/
303.mp4
```

```
g1.mp4
   transcriptions/
303.txt
g1.txt
   allfiles.txt
   music-score.txt
   video-score.txt
```
[65]

And finally, 8) the video score file is used to generate a jpeg sequence and aif, which are then glued together and can be opened for testing by clicking "add to movie" in QuickTime. That is how *A Couple Thousand Short Films About Glenn Gould* was made. Technically, the process is itself a piece of innovative virtuoso hacking. At the time, most video editing tools like Adobe Premiere, Echo Nest, Max, Jitter, and Open Frameworks were only accurate down to the frame rate of the video, but Gould Pro is accurate to the sample rate of the music (in the aforementioned case, 44,100 samples per second).

A 255-page book entitled *A Couple Thousand Short Films About Glenn Gould: A Book in Relation to a Project by the Same Name* (2008), edited by the director of Film and Video Umbrella, Steven Bode, and designed by Dexter Sinister, contains an interview with Arcangel by Michael Connor from Rhizome, essays by Bode and Paul Morley from The Art of Noise, an essay by Arcangel on decompression, and appendices with musical scores and source code. The contributions explain and interpret the project's history, context, and Gould's studio technique and visions for the "electronic age."[66] Both the video and the book seem to be a tribute to Glenn Gould as a postproduction artist. It had surprised Arcangel to learn to that Gould used "studio techniques like splicing tapes together" to delete and replace poorly executed piano strokes with better ones.[67] Gould would do dozens of recordings of the same piece and then compare and mix the best sequences, not because he could not play the piece correctly but because he wanted it to be "perfect."[68] It was considered as "a dishonest and dehumanizing technique" to many critics and admirers of his concert hall performances at the time.[69] François Girard's film *Thirty-Two Short Films About Glenn Gould* (1993), a heavily montaged movie based on Gould's life and texts, tended to mystify Gould's own technique of splicing and editing. Where Girard's film cultivates the eccentric and inspired Gould, Arcangel's video pays tribute to Gould as a hardworking postproduction artist. With Gould Pro as a DIY machine, Gould's legacy lives on as a postproduction software for "every reasonably conscientious consumer of recorded music."[70]

The Canadian composer and sound artist Tim Hecker has argued that Gould developed "utopian theories of interactivity and network-mediated creativity."[71] He had not given up the concert hall for the recording studio out of anxiety. He wanted to eliminate distractions from music. The concert hall and the commercial market's false idea of the artist as a single visionary prevented music from reaching its potential. "Let's ban applause!" he wrote in 1962.[72] Gould believed—and hoped—the concert hall would cease to exist as a cultural institution in the twenty-first century.[73] Rather than obeying "the demands of the market" and a "public responsibility," the artist has an "archival responsibility" on behalf of music, and it can best be served by a commitment to the recording studio, its machines and electronic media.[74] The studio was a "technology of self-erasure," fostering a posthuman "technological self."[75] His friend and neighbor, Marshall McLuhan, had in 1964 called media "extensions of man."[76] The same year, Gould thought that "electronic culture" would lead to a "multilevel participation in the creative process," changing "forever the value we attach to art."[77] Art is no longer a single human's vision but part of a collective and technological becoming. Gould promoted an idea of cultural communication as an "invisible" media network, where artists disseminate works to "creative listeners." The creative agency of the listener was to cycle back into the development of works as a feedback loop, generating a "benign boomerang" of ideas that would oscillate from the studio to society and back again.[78] Gould called it a listener-to-zero network. The zero designates the feedback loop and the erasure of the artist.

In many ways Gould's "invisible network" resembles Arcangel's studioscape, but with obvious differences. Arcangel works from an information perspective, both liberated and restrained by the far-reaching fluidities of cybernetic control casting a shadow on any artists using bits and bytes as material, and he seems to be without an "archival responsibility" to classical works. Rather, he bends bits of information out of proportion and into monsters as if to allegorize a fluidity out of control. I make "sick supercuts," he once told an interviewer.[79] Nevertheless, Bach is resurrected, ironically or not, as a software plug-in to gather and organize the dispersed for the purpose of a work. It is as if the scars, glitches, blurs, and poverty of images in the remix question the status of a work or the possibility of making one at all—that is, the possibility of subtracting, domesticating, and framing bits and pieces from an overwhelming cybernetic flow of dividuals (the already divided and dispersed, the already desubjectified).

Morley states that Arcangel's programming technique changed the idea of music performance and recording.[80] Gould Pro or Glenn-Gould-as-software could play music with near mathematical precision. Also, it did something to the music tradition, to Bach, to content and form, to performance and technology, to bodies. This chapter's epigraph is from Morley. He thinks the piece

> suggests a post-Nintendo Wii, post-body, post-history, post-everything-happening-at-once, post-everything-influencing-everything-else future for music that takes with it the spirit, and spirits, as suggested/chosen/touted/observed by Johann Sebastian Bach—and ultimately, as set in motion by various laws, decades, minds, inventions, bodies, fingers, conventions, coincidences, emergencies, fashions, borrowings, machines, media, rebellions, thefts, and resurrections.[81]

Morley's notion of a "post-body," indicates that he believes Arcangel is not interested in an anthropocentric or a physical and ethnographic body, but an informational body. He reassembles bodies as pieces of information that can be hacked into almost anything. The meaning of this posthuman approach becomes clearer when compared to Natalie Bookchin's *Mass Ornament*, a video art installation from 2009 that uses YouTube material and music in a different way.

Bookchin's installation projected fragments of YouTube shorts as multiple simultaneous and shifting windows in a single channel video not easily assimilable to the "normal" YouTube flow. Arcangel's was a dual channel video. He would later do only single channel supercuts which could be more easily assimilated with the formats of YouTube memes. "2 b honest I was hoping for a meme hit! So why I made the first one dual channel I have no idea (aka, not really the utube format). The second, and third one ended up better in this respect," Arcangel wrote on his portfolio website.[82] The key similarity between Bookchin's and Arcangel's works lies in their use of YouTube as an archive of potentials, of "found collectivity," meaning that both artists re-edit videos with a view toward a new collectivity.[83]

Bookchin shows multiple clips of people dancing alone in their rooms. The soundtrack is both diegetic ambient sounds from the clips and added samples of music from Leni Riefenstahl's *Triumph of the Will* and Busby Berkeley's *Gold Diggers of 1935*. The latter highlights a reference to the Tiller Girls dance, a topic in critic and film theorist Siegfried Kracauer's infamous essay "Mass Ornament" (1927). Kracauer analyzed the connection between capitalism's modes of production and entertainment. The synchronized acts of chorus line dancers were viewed as reflections of society's Fordist industrial factory work. Bookchin's montage also demonstrates how the individual YouTube dancers "seem to perform the same movements over and over as if scripted."[84] These dancers were most comfortable as themselves when doing the same as everyone else—without anyone asking them to. Paradoxically, the imperative to self-mediate shone through, not a multiplicity but another homogeneity, perhaps another version of being "alone together." Bookchin juxtaposes two flow-arrangements: "the machinery of the Fordist era was mechanical, post-Fordism is digital."[85] Nevertheless, in a comment, Wendy Chun remarks, "[Bookchin's] *Mass Ornament* is not simply a negative critique—hey, we're all the same—but also a helpful revelation of an unconscious community or what Jamie Baron has called 'found collectivity,' traced throughout the mass archive."[86]

Both Bookchin and Arcangel share this ability to find "unconscious," or rather, latent communities, but where Bookchin locates her critical ethnography explicitly in a line from Kracauer and into contemporary popular culture, Arcangel's critical distance is suspended by a search for virtuosity, a quality further enhanced by his editing tool. His use of tech mimics both high-tech and rock culture's strange alliance with baroque virtuosity. The high speed is essential. The editing tool conjures forth excellence rather than alienation; he does not so much analyze a situation ethnographically as take its flow on a trip where the remix connects the dots into a concert, a new algorithm, a people of post-bodies, a body–sound–tech arrangement. Again, the high-speed data processing technology is a *pharmakon*—both a remedy and a poison. It turns the potential to play together into reality, while simultaneously threatening the integrity of every player by bifurcating them into mere information. Gould Pro reflects the contemporary corporate media system's own use of similar high-speed data-processing technology—and presents a skewed caricature of it. This parody element is perhaps more evident today than when the work was made, because attention to big data issues is more widespread now, as reflected in a recent exhibition (*Cybernetics of the Poor*) to be discussed in this chapter.

Arcangel highlights a clash between the latency in both computational operations and cultural expressions. The players are released from their confinements to perform together but are manipulated as big data. Like a parasite, he simulates cybernetic control mechanisms, comparison, segmentation, and clustering, to remix a material. However, they are not segmented according to taste values and likes, as they are in the tech giants' software, but rather according to tone values.

THE DEMONIC

The physically intense supercut *Paganini Caprice No. 5* (2011) integrates the topic of virtuosity or mastery with a self-indulgent and ironic view on heavy metal guitar playing and hacking.

It is based on the early Romantic virtuoso freelance violinist and composer Niccolò Paganini, who composed twenty-four caprices around 1810. The "caprice" or "capriccio" genre had been closely tied to the idea of humor since it first appeared during the Renaissance. The term usually identifies a piece that is whimsical, tricky, and short. To the Romantics, a caprice was also a cadenza in a concerto, often improvised and excessive. Some composers like Paganini would write them out. Paganini's virtuoso playing style was also considered "demonic." According to the most popular legend, Paganini, like Faust, made a pact with the devil to acquire magical powers, enabling him to create effects on the violin beyond the reach of anyone else. Others, encouraged by the spectacle of him lashing the violin with his bow, considered him "demonic" in the Gothic sense

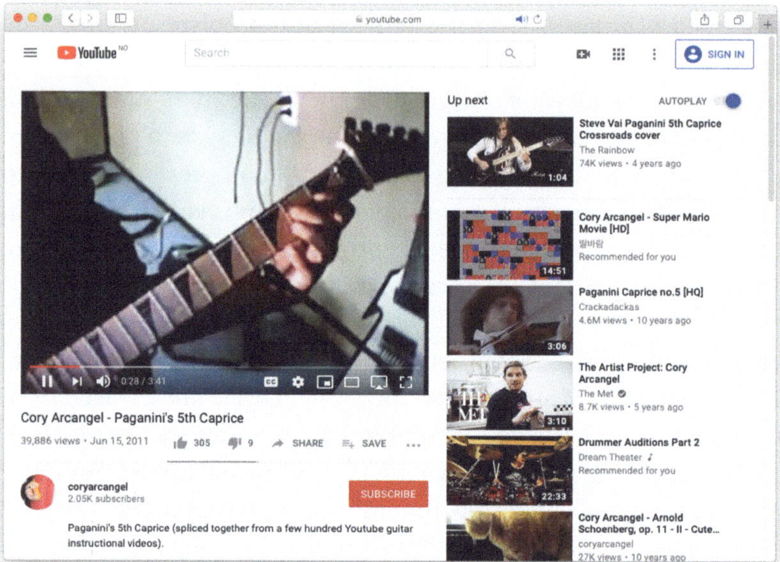

of being corrupt and perverted, a licentious criminal in the tradition of Marquis de Sade and Lord Byron's hero-villains.[87]

Arcangel's *Paganini Caprice No. 5* forces or liberates hundreds of YouTube amateurs to play one note each of Paganini's Caprice No. 5, a piece considered impossible to play for amateurs and quite difficult for professionals. Arcangel's Gould Pro lifts this barrier and lets the amateurs participate in a culture of virtuosity. The move from the amateur to virtuoso is illustrated by the opening clip, where a young amateur guitar instructor shows a simple power chord, A, at the second fret, as an initiation ritual, preparing "everybody" for the journey of becoming a virtuoso. Interestingly, the last clip of the piece is a handheld camera panning over a guitar

3.3

Cory Arcangel, *Paganini Caprice No. 5*, 2011. Single-channel video, YouTube, (optional) contemporary art venue. Photo by Adam Reich, courtesy of the artist.

effects pedalboard, reminding us that modern heavy metal guitar-playing demands artificial compression and distortion.

The Paganini version presented in this video reflects a particular electric guitar history. Paganini was rediscovered in the 1980s by neoclassically oriented heavy metal guitarists like Yngwie Malmsteen.[88] This led the "best" among them to create their own versions of the Paganini piece to show off their skills. Arcangel's heavy metal–inspired version adds explicit references to the virtuoso guitarist Steve Vai's famous version of the piece. He is known as one of the most influential rock guitarists of all time, having tirelessly toured the world, done "Alien Guitar Secrets" Masterclasses, been a guitarist and note transcriber for Frank Zappa, and been a member of David Lee Roth's rock band. He is among the unique guitar players along with Eddie van Halen, Jason Becker, and Malmsteen who introduced the virtuoso technique of tapping and shred guitar, an awe-inspiring superfast heavy metal guitar style popular when Arcangel was growing up as a heavy rock guitar player in Buffalo. "Everybody" tried to copy this playing style, he says.[89] Before YouTube it seemed impossible, but after YouTube one could see, hear, and learn the finger-techniques from YouTube tutorials—for free.[90]

Vai's lightning-fast version of Paganini's Caprice No. 5, called *Eugene's Trick Bag*, was written for the movie *Crossroads* (1986), directed by former blues musician John Fusco. The movie is a musical drama inspired by the legend of blues musician Robert Johnson, who in his song *Cross Road Blues* (1936), hints at how he sold his soul to the devil in exchange for musical talent. It became one of the songs "that shaped rock and roll."[91] Vai's Paganini piece was used in the movie's guitar battle scene, where Vai had his film debut playing the devil's guitarist, Jack Butler. His part was so technically challenging to play that Vai admitted that he could not do it live at the time; it had to be done in postproduction. The movie also did well at demonstrating what postproduction could do at the time. In the aforementioned scene, Vai's character, Butler, fails to play the piece, while his competitor, played by Ralph Macchio (who cannot in real life play guitar at this level at all), plays like a virtuoso. It was Vai who performed all the guitar parts for the scene, nicely sutured to Macchio's fingers in postproduction.[92]

Both *Crossroads*, Arcangel's video, and Paganini's caprices seem to be made as homages to the virtuosi; *Crossroads* to the history of guitar-playing, Arcangel to the vernacular energy and creativity represented by the found collectivity of amateurs shredding tirelessly on their guitars and sharing it on the web, and some of Paganini's 24 Caprices for Solo Violin to virtuoso musicians who had visited him in Italy 200 years ago. However, Arcangel's and Paganini's modes of inscription, storage, and performance are dissimilar. Paganini's mode of inscription and storage was the handwritten musical notation, and the performance was a live concert. Arcangel uses executable code as mode of inscription, storage, and performance. He fed Paganini's piece and a bunch of YouTube files into his Gould Pro software, and had this machine select the appropriate cuts. It is stored as a digital file, exhibited in galleries, and performed as an executable file with the click of a button on YouTube.[93]

Arcangel's video is, of course, far removed from the classical Hollywood style of representation dominating *Crossroads*, even though they share the same music. A key characteristic of Arcangel's *Paganini Caprice No. 5* is the DIY dirt-style. He appropriates both the sound and image quality of the homebrew style of amateurs and intensifies it by adding a virtuoso melody and editing speed. In this way the high speed of the music is strengthened by the hallucinatory effect of the image cuts. The cuts of individual guitar players sitting in different places, different postures, different colored clothes, and at different camera angles, passing by at the speed of Vai's guitar playing, create a strong physical sensation of almost pure flicker.

Gould Pro's editing speed made a new type of flicker film possible. Arcangel's informatization of the image depersonalizes and compresses the musicians' personal expressions into super-rapid frequencies of microcuts. The cuts pass by at speeds provoking a hypertrophy of the eye, reminiscent of the flicker-films of the 1960s like Tony Conrad's *The Flicker* (1966) or the 16 mm films by Paul Sharits where the flickering abstract light created visceral perceptual effects. But where the classic flicker films would often highlight the sound of the sprocket holes going through the projector, Arcangel organizes the rapid flow of images by letting the sound of the rapid and compressed plectrum attacks accompany the flicker.

The stroboscopic effect was a flicker phenomenon explored by 1960s avant-garde light, film, and video artists from Brion Gysin to Peter Kubelka and Tony Conrad. Psychophysical experiments as far back as the 1920s had shown that stroboscopic effects could affect the brain directly and produce vivid hallucinations altering the sense of time and self. Avant-garde artists would later use the flicker effect to explore "self-transformation and alternative modes of collective being."[94] Arcangel works with a technically already *given* collective; he connects and transforms the dispersed individuals of neoliberal tech into a massive rock being, capacitated by the psychophysical forces of heavy metal, the flicker, and the elemental media of computing. The guitar—encompassing strings, pick-ups, and electronics—and computing, in its production, are prime examples of what natural forces and metallurgy can do together in terms of the production, emission, and amplification of signals and data flows. The machines of rock meet the metallurgy of computing and the psychographics of the flicker.

The editing possibilities arising when everything is reduced to 0s and 1s seem unlimited and sublime. Arcangel's supercuts may simulate film frames, but they are not; they are datapoints, bits, and bytes. If a clip lasts one second, it equals a sample rate of 44,100 samples per second. The computational speed of calculation far surpasses the speeds of any earlier media, and its abilities to transform and control collectivities are developing rapidly. This ambiguous and perhaps darker side of Arcangel's *Caprice* was thematized when the piece toured Europe as part of the curators Diedrich Diederichsen and Oier Etxeberria's show *Cybernetics of the Poor* in 2020–2021. To them the piece exemplifies an odd version of cybernetics:

> Cory Arcangel teaches us the notoriously difficult virtuosity of Paganini [or Bach, Gould, or Vai] the same way that computers process and control the world: by sampling an unimaginable number of individual guitar players, whose swarm intelligence or ant-like ambition makes them seem, in a sense, themselves a kind of random access memory.[95]

Diederichsen and Etxeberria use Deleuze's analysis of "societies of control" as a guiding thesis. According to Deleuze, social formations always correspond to specific technical machines, and the current society is dominated by what he called computers and cybernetic machines which govern by assessment and control of large amounts of data which also turn individuals into "dividuals," data nodes.[96] As Diederichsen and Etxeberria see it, Arcangel simulates the analytical techniques of cybernetic capitalism, that is, the recursive and processual technique of collecting, finding, matching, and returning samples of individual expressions to compose and control a larger structure. Their reading illustrates how the Cory Arcangel hack can be interpreted differently as technological regimes change.

The phrase "cybernetics of the *poor*" designates the styles, capacities, and infrastructures available to amateurs after neoliberal capitalism. Firstly, it is about the styles of "the poor image," in Steyerl's sense, "a lumpen proletariat of the class society of appearances," a lure and a decoy "often degraded to the point of being just a hurried blur," and "the trash that washes up on the digital economies' shores."[97] These amateur images cannot match the perfection available at Big Tech budgets—and they are not interested in it. Arcangel adopts the low-fi DIY style of the YouTube videos; when projected on a big screen, their low resolution becomes so pronounced that the guitarists at times become ghostly abstractions playing the guitar. Secondly, these amateurs do not work with big data processed by supercomputers to extract behavioral products; they work small scale and extract rather alternative projections, glimmers of difference and hope. And thirdly, they use tactical media to intervene in Big Tech operations and infrastructures. Arcangel's game hacks and supercuts are not merely interventions in gaming and guitar-playing techniques but in a broader media ecology of technical standards and platforms, which are ultimately leveraged by large corporations for data processing and user population management. Behind a joyful surface, the hacks highlight the exploits of the masses, the manipulative computerization of vernacular culture. However, rather than emphasizing technology's alienating impact, Arcangel allows the multitude to play virtuosic music in a carnivalesque manner. The sublime and sacred (Bach or Paganini) meet the popular (the rock guitarist) and the everyday (the home video). He transforms the "found collectivity" of guitarists online into a virtuoso block of sensations, a "machinic-becoming" contesting or showing an alternative to the exploits of Big Tech.[98]

The machinic-becoming points to a complex field of forces: a collectivity of guitar players brought together by YouTube and Gould Pro, a rough and rapid edit that brings out the physicality and power unleashed by the sound of vibrating strings compressed through a distortion pedal, echoed in the compression of YouTube's MP4 files, its preferred compression format. Even if the image flow in this piece is very different from the slow-moving *Super Mario Clouds*, it produces a schizzing clash of incommensurable forces. The virtuoso flow of guitar licks is both completely artificial, a virtuoso machine-edit, and at the same time an extremely physical experience of real players flaunting chops in medium to ultra close-ups. Again, the schiz-image brings out a discombobulating sensation of physical bodies and post-bodies, and an almost pure flicker transporting the viewer into the vibrating cracks of the time of non-reality of computation, approaching a nonrepresentational layer of the image where its surface blends with its technological infrastructure.

BECOMING-ANIMAL

All supercuts are transformations where flows are remixed by software. Arcangel highlights the editing software as a flow-agent creating a clash of not only styles and conventions but also physical bodies, sounds, and machinations. This is also what creates his typical schiz-image. Schizzing the image enhances ambiguity and, in the following piece, an uncanny connection to machinery and to animals. The alliances and the borders between entities and flow-agents (sounds, images, performers, and technology) in the remix, seem unstable. The becomings in between the machinic and the animal produce a different schiz-image.

Arcangel's *Drei Klavierstücke op. 11* (*Three Piano Pieces op. 11*) was subtitled *Cute Kittens* (2009). It demonstrates how machinic-becomings converge with animal-becomings. Human piano players are replaced by cats that walk randomly on various pianos. The edit rearranges the real gestures of cats into a performance of Arnold Schönberg's Drei Klavierstücke, op. 11 (figure 3.4).

Arcangel's version is close to the sensitivity of Gould's version of the piece. Did Arcangel know that Gould once said: "By the time I was six, I made an important discovery that I get along much better with animals than humans"?[99]

As always, Arcangel's appropriation gains strength and coherence by being viewed in light of the history and context it intervenes in, and in this case, it comprises the heart of the development of modernist aesthetic in music and the arts. The choice of Schönberg's Drei Klavierstücke as a subject is significant. At the time, it was 100 years after Schönberg's celebrated piece was written. It was music history's first free atonal composition. Gould has often talked about its importance. In the liner notes to his own recording of Drei Klavierstücke, Gould wrote:

> It was about 1908 that Schoenberg began to use the piano as a solo instrument. Perhaps no other composition was as crucial to Schoenberg's future, and [. . .] then also to 20th-century music, as the *Three Piano Pieces, Op. 11*. [. . .] *Opus 11* was the first major test of the possibilities of survival in a musical universe no longer dominated by a triadically centered harmonic orbit. And the survival potential was, on the basis of *Opus 11*, eminently satisfactory.[100]

Gould addresses Schönberg's free atonality as a way of liberating music from "a triadically centered harmonic orbit." Schönberg nullified the rules of traditional techniques of composition where all notes were organized in relation to a tonic key.

Arcangel's reinterpretation forwards an aspect of Schönberg's musical revolution that John Cage, as well as Arcangel's teacher Pauline Oliveros and others, had seen, namely that Schönberg's exploration of matters of expression and his free compositional technique, implies an openness and an indeterminacy with regards to musical material, pointing to the new future of music. Drei Klavierstücke, op. 11 contributed to making Schönberg "the most progressive person in modern music," writes Martin Jay.[101] The three piano pieces vary in tempo and technique. The third one is considered the most innovative. It isolates its musical parameters—mode of attack, rhythm, texture, register, and agogics—and employs them in a structural though unsystematic manner that perhaps foreshadows the integral serialism of the 1950s, which later was extended into electronic music by Pauline Oliveros, among others. Musicologists have discussed exactly how radical Schönberg's break with tradition was in this piece. Schönberg himself is clear; he insisted in a letter to the pianist Ferruccio Busoni in 1909 that this piece implied a "complete liberation from all forms, from all symbols of cohesion and logic. Thus: away with 'motivic working out.' Away with harmony as cement or bricks of a building."[102] However, some musicologists have been able to describe

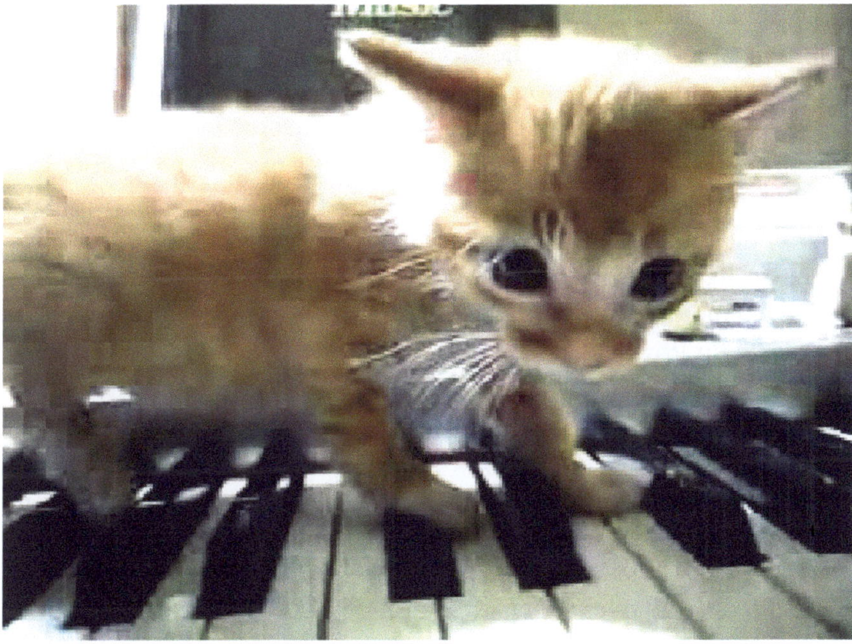

3.4

Cory Arcangel, *Drei Klavierstücke op. 11*, 2009. Single-channel video, YouTube (optional) contemporary art venue. Courtesy of the artist.

remnants of tradition in complex motivic processes, melodies, harmonies, and rhythms that give the piece coherence as a whole. Others have stressed its complete "amotivicism" and call it a totally free product of expression and improvisation.[103] What is clear is that the piece stands out as a turning point in musical modernism. Schönberg's free atonality had a dramatic and lasting effect on Western music, but its tendency toward dissonance over the typical consonance and resolution procedure were abhorred by the general public of the day.[104] As this was research, Schönberg prohibited membership to music critics and the gratitude of applause at his Society for Private Performances in Vienna. He seems to have agreed with philosopher of music Theodor Adorno's premise that "from the middle of the nineteenth century on, good music had renounced commercialism altogether."[105]

Schönberg was in alliance with other artists at the time, such as Wassily Kandinsky, in the insistence on art's development toward abstraction. This did not necessarily lead to an absolute destruction of tradition, but rather to a process of abstraction where any cliché, any worn-out gesture from "classical" patterns, was critiqued in an effort to drive art toward a relative autonomy, as Adorno would say.[106] Adorno went to Vienna to study composition under Alban Berg, a disciple of Schönberg. Adorno viewed Schönberg as essential for understanding the crises in Western art and music and saw his triumph over tonality as a triumph over a "decaying form of bourgeois music."[107] In Adorno's *Philosophy of New Music*, written in exile in 1940–1941 and released decades later, Drei Klavierstücke, op. 11 is viewed as a moment of truth in the historical development of musical material.[108] Schönberg takes control of the expressive material of bourgeois individualism and makes it a vehicle for the "undisguised and uninhibited expression of the psyche and of the unconscious *per se*."[109] The critical modernist notion of the unconscious as not simply personal but collective, or as a way of working through (*Durcharbeitung*) the logic of a milieu, called the tradition or musical material, resonates with the way Arcangel works through the logic of the contemporary networked milieu.[110] Adorno writes:

Schoenberg's formal innovations were closely related to the change in the emotional content. They serve the breakthrough of its reality. The first atonal works are depositions, in the sense of psychoanalytic dream depositions (*Traum*

Protokollen). In the earliest book published on Schoenberg, Wassily Kandinsky called the composer's paintings "studies in the mind laid bare." The scars of the revolution in expression, however, are the disfiguring stains that have become as deeply fixed in the paintings as in the music—in opposition to the compositional will—as emissaries of the id, distressing the surface and as little to be wiped away by correction as are the traces of blood in fairy tale.[111]

Adorno teases out a societal truth by a historical examination of the development of the musical material in Drei Klavierstücke. A key takeaway is how Schönberg was able to forward the repression of bourgeois culture. His music brings out the deepest conflicts in the human psyche. Free atonality was able to go into modes of expression denied to composers who relied too much on the rules of tradition. Schönberg, along with others, taught Adorno to view musical material as a historical category and not as a natural category. Schönberg had insisted in *Harmonielehre* from 1911 that dissonance was not a natural category but historical and determined by taste and culture. Music would evolve through a gradual process of change whereby certain dissonances came to be integrated as "normal." The harsh diminished seventh chord was shocking at the time of Beethoven but was already considered a cliché or a "harmless consonance" at the turn of the last century, according to Schönberg. His experimentation in music and Adorno's influential music philosophy was founded on the concept of musical material as a historical category.[112]

Many experiments in new music after Schönberg, and especially since the 1950s, have challenged Adorno's concept of musical material as a historical category. Musicologist Max Paddison discusses Cage in particular. Cage said about his five operas *Europeras* (1987–1991): "For two hundred years the Europeans have been sending us their operas. Now I'm sending them back."[113] *Europeras* was a collage of musical quotes and found or readymade music from "great operas," organized by computer-assisted chance operations. In Europe, reviewers were quick to see that Cage's material had become "matter as *Stoff*—that is, naturalized and removed from history."[114] These are "relics of tradition" organized as "chance-derived fragments."[115] Paddison concludes by quoting musicologist Carl Dahlhaus: "Adorno's concept of material is a historical category, whereas Cage's idea of matter is a natural one."[116] They are two different ways of understanding and using sounds as matter. Musical matter viewed as historical material can be developed according to notions of necessity and logic, as Schönberg did. If viewed as natural material, it can be quoted randomly, as Cage did. Cage's operation establishes music as matter, like anything-whatsoever in nature/culture, to be picked up or left alone.

Arcangel's *Drei Klavierstücke* can be disassembled as a compressed version of modern music history and aesthetics, as shown previously. However, unlike Cage, Arcangel adds a theatrical and carnivalesque layer by using the medium and styles of vernacular new media practices. Arcangel's use of the power or flow of conventions is also a metacommentary on popular affects and aesthetic judgements of modernist music, Schönberg's atonality, and modernist aesthetics. Furthermore, Arcangel seems to play a joke on both popular prejudice against modernism *and* Adorno's notion of modernism and musicologist Malcolm MacDonald's insistence that Drei Klavierstücke reveals the depths of tradition or the human psyche. MacDonald writes in his Schönberg study that free atonality enabled the composer to follow no other law but man's deepest emotions, "an extremely subjective emotional expressionism."[117] In Arcangel's reconstruction, man's deepest emotions are executed by cute kittens. A turning point in modern music undergoes a "becoming-animal." As always, Arcangel's add-ons are never arbitrary; the cat signifies not just any species but one of man's favorite "companion species."[118] According to several "paw-some" rankings, the cat was an instant favorite in both mainstream and subcultures. Early 4chan was swarming with cat pranks and lolcats. Arcangel's Schönberg cats connect both the internet and classical culture. They simulate a shock to both cultures; the animals' potentials are transformed by an unfamiliar framework. The work is, of course, mostly a jab at the seriousness of traditional high modernism, but also, as I read it, it is a critique of the anthropocentric understanding of this tradition.

High culture has been swallowed by the chaotic environment of memes. It is perhaps the well-known clash between the respect for mainstream modernism and the rupture and play of the avant-garde, or as literary historian Ástráður Eysteinsson summarizes the avant-garde vision:

Is this not also a moment where "art" runs seamlessly into "real life" and vice versa (according to some the very dream, the *jouissance*, of the avant-garde)?

And do we not witness here the experimental and playful aspects of the avant-garde desire to unveil the contingency, the made-up-ness of grand meanings?[119]

Arcangel's prank on modernism and prejudice reassembles a world of views, styles, players (lolcats) from the living room, and imaginaries. His comical "recreation" of Drei Klavierstücke establishes a collective of multiple actors, in Latour's terminology, staged as a funny drama of opposites.[120] It is a destratification in every sense of the word. It involves both animal-becomings and machinic-becomings and a play with cultural codes and clichés. Indeed, it is a meeting between the high (modernism) and the low (kitch), and between human *expressivism* and nonhuman *(in) expressivism*. The marvelous dance of agencies can be traced in detail. A key influence is the flow of memes and especially cat memes online. Arcangel writes that *Drei Klavierstücke* emerged from what "I have been interested in lately [. . .] mainly 'cats,' copy & paste net junk, and youtube's tendency in the past few years to host videos that are as good and many times similar to my favorite video artworks."[121] He was, as mentioned, working in the BuzzFeed environment at the time—with memes—so it was not surprising that he was into "mainly" cats. However, when the artist watches art movies and cats at the same time, YouTube's recommendation algorithms start to generate a menu of cat videos with an unpredictable blend of art and the popular. Arcangel wrote about experiencing a transition in recommendations from the so-called *Infinite Cat Project* to *Pussy versus Printer* to *Panta improvising on the piano featuring my cat* to cats listening to music to *Watching the Paint Dry* to *Andy Eating a Hamburger* to the Warhol-pastiche *Infinite Warhol*.[122] Digesting this, one can imagine, led to Arcangel wanting to make his own cat video, and since he listened to Glenn Gould and it was soon 100 years since Schönberg wrote his seminal piano piece, why not fuse the two: cats and Schönberg?

Arcangel's procedure nicely illustrates Deleuze and Guattari's three-step procedure for transgressive machines, as described earlier.[123] First a flow is cut, then it is connected to something else, and thirdly, it conjures forth a new becoming. The flows that interested Arcangel are intimately connected to the capacities of various images and techniques. Arcangel delegated the selection of cat videos in part to YouTube's recommendation algorithms. This is how one cat video automatically led to another, establishing a corpora of cat videos. The dataset was cleaned by separating the sound bites from the images, and then downloaded onto two distinct pieces of editing software, Comparisonics and Gould Pro, where it was matched with Gould playing Schönberg. Arcangel describes his approach, thus:

> First I downloaded every video of a cat playing piano I could find on Youtube. I ended up with about 170 videos. Then I extracted the audio from each, pasted these files end to end, and then pasted this huge file onto the end of an audio file of Glenn Gould playing op11. I loaded this file into Comparisonics. Comparisonics, a strange free program I found while surfing one night, allows users to highlight a section of audio, and responds by finding "similar" sounding areas in rest [sic] of the audio file. Using Comparisioncs [sic] I went through every "note" (sometimes I also did clusters of notes) in the Gould [Pro], then selected my favorite "similar" section Comparisonics suggested and wrote it in the score. After going though [sic] the 1000's of "notes", the completed scores were turned into a video by some perl scripts I wrote.[124]

Arcangel carefully mentions all the actors at play: computers, YouTube, cats, and various software. The files were cleaned and uploaded to the software-agent he describes, Comparisonics.[125] Comparisonics then selected (in a more refined way, mathematically and according to frequencies and tone values) the cat videos that matched Schönberg's *op. 11* in Gould's version best. The total number of "raw material" for Arcangel's piece is 170 YouTube videos. These can be reedited as single notes or a cluster of notes and used in different orders across the three piano pieces: 191 cat clusters for piano piece I, 344 for II, and 117 for III. Arcangel enumerates each note or cluster of notes by pencil in the original Schönberg score. Each number refers to a fragment of a cat playing from one of the 170 YouTube videos (figure 3.5).

At times, it can be wonderful to work with machines rather than humans, because a software like Comparisonics makes *no difference, no distinctions* in terms of the cultural value of the material fed into it. Values are based on sound frequency and mathematics. There is no human editor and no educational or editorial principles separating the found material into aesthetical or educational hierarchies. All of it is assimilated or domesticated as files to be automatically and algorithmically analyzed regardless of content (cats or Schönberg). This posthuman approach to music liberates the material from cultural hierarchies and opens it to a strange conceptuality where anything can play anything-whatsoever. The cuts and connections made at a technical level (the flows of cat videos on the web modded to fit the flow of a Schönberg piece) affront the cuts and connections made at a cultural level (the flows of cultural codes and clichés ordering culture into taste patterns—highs and lows, elites and the vulgar), thus effectively staging an ambiguous aesthetic experience.

Again, Arcangel uses "the gimmick's brazenly contemptible form" (fast editing of cute kittens playing the piano) on a found piece of classical music.[126] Like Duchamp, he conceptually stages a collision between what is estimated in terms of time (long vs. short duration), value (economic vs. aesthetic value), and labor (manual vs. automated). The high artistic value and labor duration of Schönberg's composition, developed over several years, cannot match cat videos which are beyond value; they are cute, priceless.

The confrontation between high modernism and kitsch is here multiplied in terms of clashing aesthetic sensations at both the level of sounds and images. Hearing Schönberg but seeing only cats creates a clash between hearing and seeing, and a clash between what is usually considered as human *expressivism* (intentional acts) and nonhuman *(in) expressivism* (unintentional acts). Arcangel foregrounds these clashes as a shock to thought before they became the stylistic hallmark of thousands of YouTube videos. Even if the work's idea or concept—cats play Schönberg—seems simpler than its technical execution, its aesthetic impact still preempts certain objections. The work *shows* the cliché prejudice against modernist forms of abstraction: even a cat can do that! It enacts the ambiguous play between the imaginary and the real—*for real*; it transforms the (un)thinkable ground of the prejudice—Schönberg is like cats playing the piano—conceptually and physically into the register of the real, the visible and audible. It makes the verdict blush. With the help of technology, cats *can* play Schönberg.

The video enacts a certain game between the impossible and the visible on the borders between the sayable, seeable, and audible. It makes visible and audible the sayable, that Schönberg *is* cats playing the piano. However,

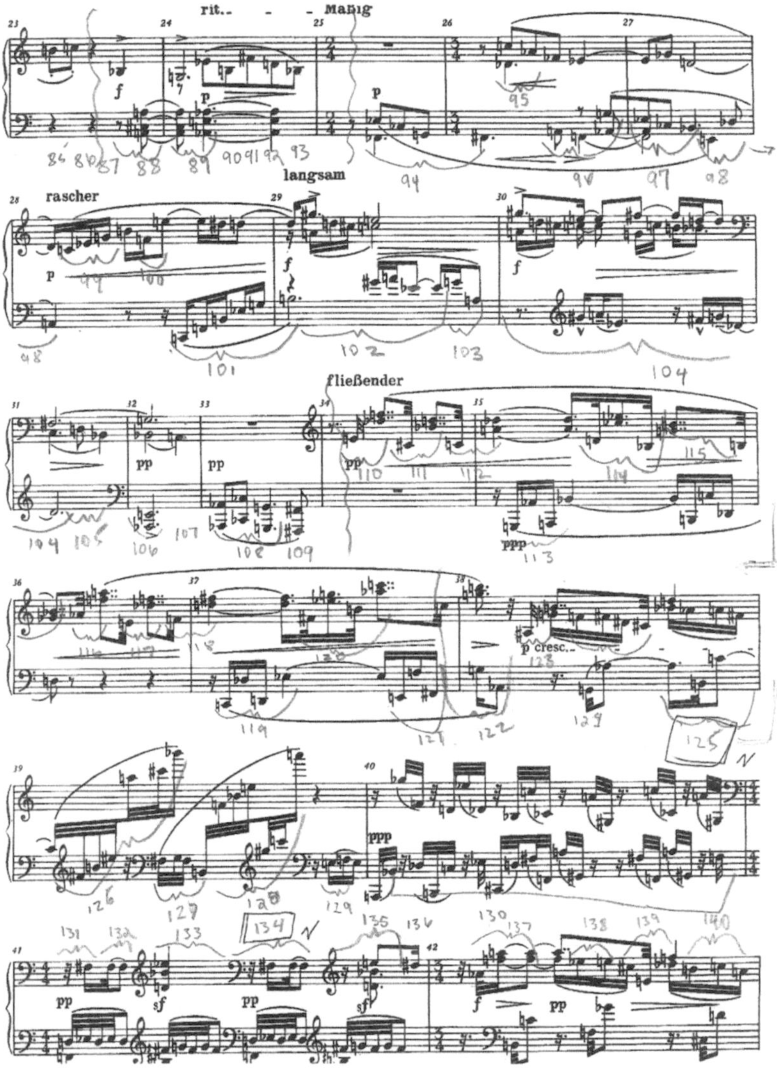

3.5

Cory Arcangel, *Drei Klavierstücke op. 11* (video mapping score), 2009. Pencil on paper. Photo by Cory Arcangel, courtesy of the artist.

what you see is not what you get—as always with digital media.[127] These cats do not really play Schönberg; it is a trick, a gimmick made possible by montage and software manipulations. A gimmick can be both a lie and a creative gesture at the same time. The task of the interpreter is to find the most interesting tensions or machinations in the work. It is at these junctures that the work reassembles the sayable, seeable, and audible in new ways. The cuts and connections of Arcangel's *Drei Klavierstücke* question the *body* of art. Which body owns this artwork: Schönberg, Gould, cats, YouTube, Arcangel, or technology? Who is occupying whose territory?

Such questionings resonate with what Deleuze and Guattari called a process of deterritorialization. They explained it by a reference to how animals like birds sing to mark a territory.[128] When they fly to a new territory, somebody else's territory, they sing and thereby, deterritorialize the new territory, as if taking it from someone, and secondly, they reterritorialize the territory, as if saying, "this is now mine." Appropriations and reappropriations like these are common in art. Arcangel's video is an elegant example of Deleuzoguattarian deterritorialization, because high modernism is turned into a lowly charm where animals mimic human creativity. This is of course already a cliché in Walt Disney animations. The slapstick arises when Arcangel "documents," note by note, that real cats can *play*. It asks, what is possible? It simulates a shock to the senses, to common sense, and ridicules the cliché that Schönberg sounds like cats on a piano. It removes the debate from a popular prejudice to its opposite, an avant-garde stance.

What at first seemed like a delightful joke, is perhaps an attempt at exploring a certain avant-garde tradition by other means. The video performs a *sympoiesis*, to use Donna Haraway's term, which is a becoming-with or a *making with*. Haraway writes:

> Becoming-with, not becoming, is the name of the game; becoming-with is how partners are [. . .] terms, rendered capable. Ontologically heterogeneous partners become who and what they are in relational material-semiotic worlding. Natures, cultures, subjects, and objects do not preexist their intertwined worldings.[129]

In Arcangel's *Drei Klavierstücke*, music, video, the machinic, and human's oldest companion, animals, become together. This *intertwined worlding* make technical machines and animals express the environment differently. The environment in this case is both free tonality and culture as a set of aesthetic norms and practices. The Cory Arcangel hack transforms the expressive logic of Schönberg (how can music liberate human expressiveness?) toward an expressive logic of environments (how can a musical machine be used to include contingencies or sounds produced by animals?), as a becoming-*with* both animals and technology. "How can music become-with the nonhuman?," the artist may have asked. Can this video be a flight-line, proposing and showing a multiplicity of becomings with the environment, which can include popular expressions, new media, and various art and music traditions—and animals? Arcangel's *Drei Klavierstücke* has this ability to conjure forth a transgressive sympoietic collectivity.

The moment music is viewed as natural matter, as Cage and Oliveros did, there is no limit to what music is, where it is, or how it is made. The environment itself is music if it is sensed or framed in the "right" way. Oliveros's electronic Expanded Interactive music System (EIS) was created for the purpose of enabling musicians to improvise together with any environmental sound during live performances. There is no longer any limit to whom or what in the environment (whether it is animals or technical machines) one can collaborate. Even the humming of a computer can be a companion species. A musician can improvise or become with-everything-whatsoever-everywhere.

Arcangel's *Drei Klavierstücke* were shown at the solo exhibition *Here Comes Everybody* and at many other shows. They were also posted on YouTube, where they generated a large audience outside the art world. 230,000 people have seen them on YouTube, and many have left comments.[130] They are generally divided into three groups: those who view them as a "postmodern joke," those who view them as an interesting supplement to the Schönberg tradition, and those who seem to agree with both views. The profile "Pit-trout" writes, "I don't know about coryarcangel, but I for one love (much of) Schoenberg's music and also love this video! You can appreciate a piece of music and still enjoy making a joke of it."[131] The profile "trickhips" answers:

> i [sic] think this is wonderful and i agree with PitTrout. i know more about Arcangel's work than Schoenberg. i do not find this the least bit disrespectful of

the composer. i can't stop thinking about the work it took to find, arrange and piece all of those clips together in the right order. i think it's more in the spirit of Schoenberg than some music snobs might be willing to admit.[132]

There are also more typical prank comments like this one from "Planet-Thoughts": "Maybe the original music was also composed this way? I believe Schoenberg was cat-holic in his preferences."[133] Others seem to have visited the video because they have taken a class in remix studies, where Arcangel's *Drei Klavierstücke* has become a standard reference.[134] Arcangel's supercuts supplement remix studies with examples which not only explore popular culture but equally modernist aesthetics and the avant-garde. His next exploration of the genre goes one step further, erasing the conditioning medium, social media, and replacing it with a book, a novel.

TWITTER AS A BOOK

Arcangel's supercuts culminate with a remix book based on tweets. Speed relations change drastically. While the supercuts discussed previously accelerate flows, the remix book decelerates flows by montaging them into the slower yet more stable medium of organic paper. While the supercuts were image- and sound-oriented, the Twitter-based work *Working on My Novel* (2014) explores the web's text-based folklore. In its initial phase, Twitter was a cumbersome and inaccessible medium in archival terms; one could not search its full archive and there was no metadata tag like the #hashtag. Only Twitter itself had the full overview of its contemporary archive.

In *Working on My Novel*, Arcangel examines Twitter by conducting a series of search and organization experiments that would highlight collective currents in the material. They are organized around certain expressions, clichés, topoi, and sayings, found by using the search function on Twitter as a compositional technique. Initially, he did a few works leading up to the "novel." First, he organized a search for messages that included the phrase "working on my novel" (figure 3.6).

These were retweeted as a listicle on BuzzFeed called Great Twitter Searches Volume # 1 'Working on my novel' (2009) (see figure 3.6). The

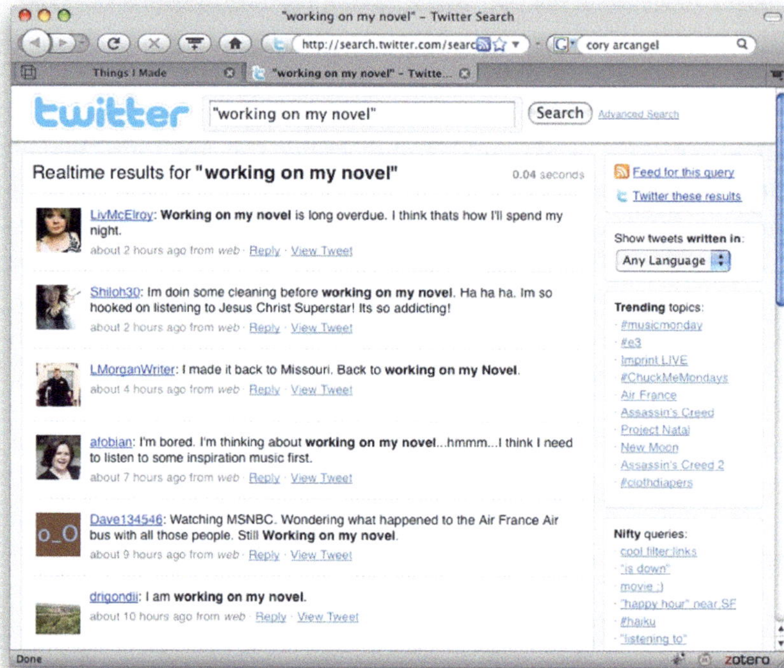

3.6

Cory Arcangel, *Working on My Novel*, 2009. Twitter search results for "working on my novel." Screenshot by Cory Arcangel, courtesy of the artist.

work *Sorry, I Haven't Posted* (2010) was generated via software that harvested posts from the popular Google Blog Search based on the phrase "Sorry, I have not posted." Curated posts were published automatically on a blog page using Peretti's reBlog tool. It became a text- and image-based work or a "Blog which re-posts the best blog posts of people apologizing for not posting to their blogs."[135] Today, this work is a relic from a techno-aesthetic chapter in the history of web publishing regimes, the early blogosphere. The focus on apologetic phrases like "Sorry, I have not posted" articulates the pressure exerted on bodies and brains affecting those connected. The blogosphere does not only make people express themselves but also formats the users' affects, drives, and desires. Once you have started a blog, you are plagued by automated reminders that it must be completed.

A publisher at Penguin noticed Arcangel's work and asked if he could write a novel for them. The cross between literature and social media was in vogue at the time, as if publishers also felt a pressure. Penguin had already published *Twitterature: The World's Greatest Books Retold Through Twitter* (2009), edited by Alexander Aciman and Emmett Rensin, which received many sequels in other countries, and Craig Dworkin and Kenneth Goldsmith edited the concept literature anthology *Against Expression* (2011), which explored new copying and appropriation techniques in literature after the computer. Twitter also got involved in the #TwitterFiction Festival in 2012. And in 2014, writer David Mitchell published his short story "The Right Sort" on Twitter and Frode Grytten published a collection of novellas, *Waiting for Birds*, based on a Twitter-based experiment in micro-short stories. While Mitchell and Grytten joined ranks with the Twitterature that tried to use Twitter's mini format (the 140-character maximum) to create a feeling of micro-narratives or micro-plots, Arcangel's tweet collection does not tell a story but is instead a panorama of the affective condition of the connected crowd, its neurosis, paranoia, fear, and desire to write a novel, as well as its craving for intensity, fun, and distraction; the tweeters' preparations for writing a novel become an archive of procrastinations. It is "paraliterature," designated by Roland Barthes as a "counter-writing," "non-writing," or "para-graphy," but in Arcangel's universe, it sounds more like the murmur at a clinic, a symptomatology.[136]

Arcangel made an archiving tool (a web crawler or an internet bot) that could capture and store tweets.[137] He picked out about 300 of them and made a semiautomatic database driven CMS (content management system) that would set up a permission request to reuse tweets. It was important for Arcangel that this process would not look like a spam or a robot attack, so he would additionally write a personal letter to each tweeter. A little less than half of them accepted the request. The remaining 120 tweets were montaged into a 128-page book, one tweet on each page, including a tweet midway in the book, signed by Arcangel, saying: "Working on my novel."

Arcangel emphasizes that the book has the structure of the joke:

> When you search that phrase ["working on my novel"] on Twitter you get all these people talking about how they're working on their novel. The joke is of course that if you're twittering about how you're working on your novel, you're probably not working on your novel! I love these situations.[138]

The joke also hides seriousness. *Working on my Novel* is not *written* by Arcangel but rather *curated* by him. It remixes tweets written by tweeters who are putatively at work on their novel but are infatuated by the influence of entertainment industries. They have domesticated distraction as a way of life. Uncannily, they are pulled into a machine dominated by an unreasonable rhythm, nodes in a foreign network of the all-too-familiar. Like the ball in a game of ping-pong, they are being tossed between different media platforms. The search phrase "working on my novel" discloses contemporary living conditioned by an unforeseen media addiction. The book brings out the aberrant and the anomalous through a new type of montage, where each fragment somehow constitutes an allegory of the schiz, a clash between flesh and metal; the desire to write a novel, to become with a novel, is short-circuited by a craving for more media entertainment and the inclination to post, to become with platform media. The bloggers are caught in an impossible spider-web of diverging flow-paths. The tweets, as segments of time, evoke a process where the subjects seem to be in control. Indeed, I will work on my novel, but first I must do this or that, on and on. Eventually, the story, which is of course not a story, reveals, through a series of fragments, a systematic pattern of interruptions.

Normal and everyday experiences of distractions begin to evoke a pattern of compulsive repetitions, a pathology, as if these people have become slaves of a new normal, the sickening flow-cuts of contemporary media life, which is a hyped vesion of media historian Raymond Williams's notion of a televisual flow.[139] Some examples:

> . . . working on my novel but Garth Brooks Live from Vegas is coming back on TV . . . nothing will be done the next two hours
> [. . .]
> Having way too much fun on Pinterest . . . should be working on my novel
> [. . .]
> That's it, that's it, I'm getting off Twitter and working on my novel. Right after I finish this episode of Are You Afraid of the Dark.
> [. . .]
> Should be working on my novel but I'm stuck in the quicksand of a blog entry I'll probably never post anyway.[140]

The efficiency of new media at capturing the attention of consumers through its programmed flow evokes being "stuck in the quicksand of a blog entry." It has become a habit zone, so absorbing that its flow cannot be cut. Media that came after the book consistently lures the tweeters away from what they were staunchly supposed to do: work on the novel. There is an implicit media hierarchy at play in the imagination of the tweeters here. Around 2010, for the digital nonnatives the novel was still privileged as a *serious* medium, with a different and more complex flow. Tenacious notions about the value of the novel are established through humanities traditions, school and education, but also through more intangible currents and forces in society related to affects and emotions which are maintained by mass media and popular culture.[141] Arcangel's collection of tweets forms an affective cartography of the networked self that struggles in an oversaturated media landscape between the dream of self-realization in the traditional sense, writing a novel, and the demand for constant self-mediation, the Twitter addiction.

Working on My Novel maps the new Web 2.0 human who (in)elegantly tours many sharing and participation platforms: the monstrously dispersed human being. The tweeters have all sorts of new media in the living room but dream of realizing themselves in a predigital medium, as if only the novel, the Book with a capital B, can give the world meaning and the individual an identity. But Arcangel's book is also a gift to the desperately dreaming tweeters; finally, they end up in a novel, albeit in a somewhat unusual novel. By fulfilling the tweeters' dream, the book can short-circuit the postindustrial machine's capture of the user. The tweeters are lifted out of a tech giant's platform, and incorporated into Arcangel's book—an offline medium, ideally outside and beyond the postindustrial machine's profiling and feedback mechanisms of platform capitalism. This makes *Working on My Novel* a complex flow-cut arrangement. It portrays the contemporary media flow as comically disjointed yet reassembles the fragments into the flow of a paperback. By employing the new technique of the web crawler, as a mega-camera capturing expressive flows to write an old-fashion "novel", Arcangel transforms a vast quantity of frustration ("I cannot write") into a concentrated intensity ("I can write").

The result is a machinic novel rich in heartbreaking affects, powerful enough to move even the most cynical reader. Once again, Arcangel masterfully combines the material—affects and phrases—of popular culture with the ethos and aesthetics of experimental modernism, an art tradition where fragmented forms, unlike new media fragments, are considered to hold a unique truth value.

Arcangel's *Working on My Novel* is his most reviewed single work in the press, most likely because it is his only work in the medium of the novel. Literary criticism is far more widespread and esteemed in international press than art criticism, and literary criticism follows the rhythms of literary productions, one book at the time, rather than, say, a group of works or exhibitions, which is usually the rhythm and focus of the art world. A striking thing with the in-depth reviews of *Working on My Novel*, which are all done by literary reviewers, not art critics, is that they primarily explore it as a novel in the experimental tradition and not as an artwork of appropriation or new media art using an old format.

Critic Jonathan Jones of *The Guardian* places the novel in a tradition of antinovels from Cervantes to Sterne, Calvino, and Warhol's *a: A Novel* (1968):

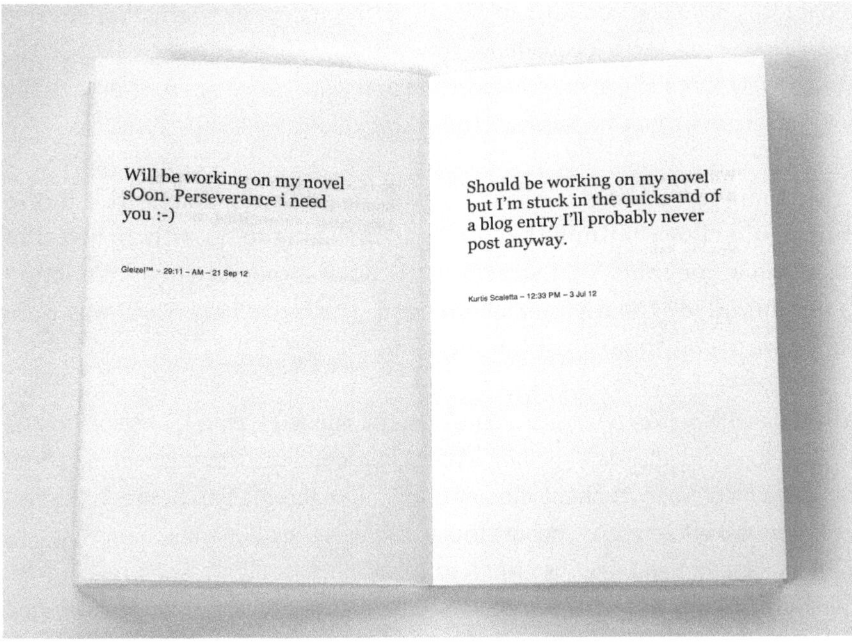

3.7

Cory Arcangel, *Working On My Novel*, 2014. Paperback. 144 pages. Photo by Gil Gentile, courtesy of the artist.

In this struggle to find new ways to joke about the impossibility of fiction, *Working on My Novel* feels like a joyous move forward. Cory Arcangel has created something deeply liberating, at once cynical and optimistic. Once again, as always, the novel is reborn in the contemplation of its own death.[142]

Critic Dan Piepenbring's review in *The Parisian Review* start with a motto from Saul Bellow: "I think that art has something to do with an arrest of attention in the midst of distraction."[143] What happens when distraction is not annulled? Creativity is challenged. *Working on My Novel* was published with a blurb raising that question:

What does it feel like to try and create something new? How is it possible to find a space for the demands of writing a novel in a world of instant communication? *Working on My Novel* is about the act of creation and the gap between the different ways we express ourselves today. Exploring the extremes of making art, from satisfaction and even euphoria to those days or nights when nothing will come, it's the story of what it means to be a creative person, and why we keep on trying.[144]

Piepenbring thinks differently. *Working on My Novel* is "the story of what it means to live in a cultural climate that stifles almost every creative impulse and why it so often seems we should stop trying."[145] He wonders why the novel has such a high status among the tweeters. They seem to view the novel as a kind of therapy, he suggests, not as "an artistic mode but as a kind of elevated diary" that will cure but also be a feat "proving that we have reservoirs of mindfulness and discipline deeper than our peers." Paradoxically, *Working on My Novel* is a testament to how the novel as a radical critique of the therapeutic society "has instead been co-opted by that society," Piepenbring concludes.

Louise Benson writes her review from what she calls "the age of distraction." The novel speaks to contemporary modes of subjectivity: "What distinction can we draw between our online and offline lives, when (particularly for the creative industries) career advancement can hinge on how 'online' we are. And who is to say which version of ourselves holds greater value?"[146] Posting updates becomes just another way of preparing the self as a commodity. Benson quotes from a series of recent essay collections where writers complain about "digital distractions." Most literary reviewers discuss new media as a source of distraction. The strength of Arcangel's book lies in its ambiguity; he shares both his reviewers' view *and* sees beauty in distraction.

Arcangel freeloads these distractions as a creative source. As a hacker trained in the nerdzones of Beige, Paper Rad, and Radical Software Group, and later in the research collectives of Jonah Peretti, he learned that platforms or elements in their ensemble can be tapped into, decomposed, reconstructed, and redistributed. The Cory Arcangel hack multiplies the number of possible actors making up a social and aesthetic collective. UGC is turned into cuts, fragments, flickers, and notes, and the tools Gould Pro and Comparisonics reassemble them into new collectives.

The Cory Arcangel hack traces the possible actions of these actors onto the verge of wild innovations. It decomposes a world into a thousand fragments taken on a line of flight, deterritorializing their original associations and connections, and building new ones. But the flight brings on connections and associations to both creativity and radical cybernetic control. Especially *Working on My Novel* may represent a shift in Arcangel's career toward the darker sides of new media, producing not so much multiplicity and heterogeneity as uniformity and homogeneity. Arcangel's "joyous move forward" was perhaps also a move toward a different approach to art-making that will only become more evident in his forthcoming works and exhibitions. While many postdigital artists might overtly reject or abandon the online world, the Cory Arcangel hack appears to embody a schizophrenic stance, simultaneously participating in and critiquing it, simultaneously using digital and analog media of display. It is not easy to place his work on a map of critical attitudes. In a discussion of the term "postdigital," Florian Cramer aligns it with a critical tendency observed in early Post-Internet art criticism such as Gene McHugh's analysis, which argues that the new internet "became not a thing in the world to escape into, but rather the world one sought to escape from."[147] Arcangel's schizophrenic attitude embodies both tendencies, and perhaps becomes especially challenging in his subsequent exhibition, *Century 21*.

4

FLOW-PARODY

Bots and Monkeyrunners

"With increasing aggressiveness, one of the artist's functions, I believe, is to specify how technology uses us."
—Jack Burnham[1]

CENTURY 21

Century 21, Cory Arcangel's first big solo show in the US after he moved to Norway in 2015 took place at Greene Naftali in New York in 2021. While Arcangel's earlier shows such as *Here Comes Everybody* would joyfully play along with the unfettered creativity of the multitudes of social media, *Century 21* is dominated by something different.[2] The feel of the works is different, and the humor is less tangible. Rather than relying on subcultures, he uses the devices and affordances of the platform economy as artistic material. The online exhibition catalog states: "Cory Arcangel uses the systems and social mores of the Internet as artistic material, lending solidity to what he calls the virtual realm that 'both consumes us and fits so neatly in the palm of our hands.'"[3] To sneak up on this material, it is as if the artist has withdrawn or is hiding behind bots. He hacks into the API of Android cell phones to simulate the flows of human–computer interaction, using social bots to click and game across platforms. Five such works will be analyzed. They are all by Arcangel and involve a series of different types of bots that are programmed with help from his studio, in particular from his production manager at the time, Henry Van Dusen. *elleusa, equinor, equinox, etrade_financial* (2020) involves four bots programmed to automatically "like" every post on the Twitter profiles of major multinational corporations. *we deliver / the king checked by the queen* (2020) sets up two bots instructed to play chess across a variety of profiles on Instagram, ranging from celebrities to big corporations, brands and heads of state. Two other works are live action transmissions of bots doing more complex tasks. */roʊ ˈdeɪoʊ/ Let's Play: HOLLYWOOD* (2017–2021) is a custom-built RPG software bot instructed to play the cell phone game, *Kim Kardashian: Hollywood*, on an LED wall in the gallery's main room. *Related to your interests* (2020–2021) is an autogenerated audiovisual gossip news archive on a YouTube profile; a bot scrapes text- and image-based news stories from low-end clickbait websites, repurposing the content using a text-to-speech software tool and posting them as YouTube videos on the profile. This artmachine set-up had made more than 800 videos by the time it was taken offline. Finally, *Inspos* (2021), a series of prints, contain quotes from aggressive incipits from Twitter and similar platforms. These artworks testify to a new cultural condition dominated not so much by the creativity of the multitudes, journalists, and artists, as by the cynicism of nonsensical bot farms, AI hype, super corporations, and celebrities. In sum, the tone is apocalyptic.

PLATFORM CAPITALISM

This chapter will discuss how these works interact with and display some of the devices and discourses that regulate the flows of platform capitalism, such as the widespread use of smartphones, the like button, commentary, scrolling, games, clickbait, fake news, divisive language, the dominance of super corporations and celebrities, as well as the influence of the AI industry and its rhetoric. I use the term *platform capitalism* to designate the affordances of a selection of platforms and their redefinition of labor as cognitive and immaterial, meaning the corporate takeover of platforms as well as their inventive techniques for extracting surplus value from the flow of human labor or users for targeted purposes. Platform capitalism is different from traditional capitalism because the "factory" has been extended to include any activity, private or public, online or offline. The platformization of the web enables anybody to cannibalize everybody. All that is needed is a smartphone.

Three interconnected aspects of the Cory Arcangel hack that relate to platform capitalism will be explored: subjectivation, technology, and documentation. The hack connects to these three aspects in fun, critical, and even gimmicky ways. First, subjectivation is perhaps the most complex issue. It deals with the production of subjects in coded space, like, how is addiction created? More generally, it is about how specific platform affordances capture, shape, and entice the platform-user subject to stick with a platform for as long as possible. Arcangel foregrounds specific techniques such as the use of the like button, commentary, or other aspects of "gamification," that platform capitalism relies on to instill a certain obedience into its users.[4] Naturally, Arcangel tends to use these affordances in a disobedient way. Second, the topic of technology speaks to how Arcangel hacks into a platform and how this reflects the architecture of the platform itself; the artwork's use of bots speaks to the increasing saturation of bots and bot farms on the internet. Third, documentation relates to Arcangel's peculiar form of archival writing; the way he rewrites and renarrativizes what is happening online. Implicitly and explicitly, the artworks document the technicity of digital culture though highlighting aspects of computation and the web. Arcangel is always attentive to the minutia of certain media-specific details, and that is one of the reasons his artworks can quickly attain an archival aura. As digital technologies change rapidly and are often based on large science budgets *and* the economy of artificial obsolescence, Arcangel's artwork can even resemble dumb fossils. There is something odd with the rapid development of digital technologies. "Imagine trying to play Bach on the piano if they switched keys around every few years . . . and charged you for it!" he said once.[5] Archival art in the digital domain is often a homage to creativity—or a monument to cultural stupidity. Arcangel seems to opt for the latter.

Elleusa, equinor, equinox, etrade_financial (2020) consists of four single-channel screen recordings erected on top of each other on the wall like a totem, containing four live bot performances on Twitter from November 20, 2020. The bot is programmed to like every post on the named companies' feeds "till the feed would not reload anymore," as it is written on Arcangel's YouTube account, which contains samples of these recordings.[6] The work features a hack for Twitter via bot-generated user input using a monkeyrunner API for Android devices. "The monkey tool runs in an adb shell directly on the device or emulator and generates pseudo-random streams of user and system events."[7] The ADB (Android Debug Bridge) is a versatile command-line tool that allows you to communicate with an Android device from your computer. It enables various actions, such as installing debugging apps, transferring files, and accessing the command-line interface provided by the Android operating system on a device. It is particularly useful for performing advanced tasks on Android devices—or it can be "misused," as in the Cory Arcangel hack, where it fakes finger presses and swipes on a phone.

Arcangel's bot simulates a regular cell phone user, doing nothing fancy or interesting, just clicking "like" on every post on one of the four super-company profiles mentioned in the work's title. He has referenced big brands in his art earlier, but tuning in on the companies' branding practices through social media is something new. Their branding practices incorporate other big players in the field, such as the cell phone companies Samsung and Apple, and social media platforms Meta (Facebook and Instagram) and Twitter (now X); they are the "super corporations that control the fate of the world."[8] *Elle* is a worldwide women's magazine offering a mix of fashion, beauty, and lifestyle content, "receiving 100 million unique monthly visitors on its 55 digital platforms."[9] Equinor is a Norwegian semi-state-owned multinational energy company headquartered in Stavanger, Norway, Arcangel's new place of residence. It is among the largest petroleum and energy companies in the world, operating in thirty-six countries, including participation in Canada's controversial extraction of large deposits of bitumen on the Athabasca oil sands. Environmental activists argue that this practice poses risks to the cultural, social, and economic way of life of Canada's Indigenous populations.[10] Equinox Holdings is an American luxury fitness company which operates several lifestyle brands. It caused controversy after reports that trainers often worked long hours, sometimes as many as eighty hours a week, forcing some to sleep in employee locker rooms. In 2019, Equinox gyms faced prominent calls for a boycott and protests, after one of their major investors also organized a widely publicized fundraiser for then-president Donald J. Trump.[11] E-Trade Financial Corporation offers an electronic trading platform to trade financial assets. It specializes in algorithmic high-frequency trading technology, which can enable a firm to make tens of thousands of trades per second. The company is a subsidiary of Morgan Stanley, the bank that borrowed $107.3 billion from the Fed, the most of any bank, during the 2008 financial crisis.[12] These super corporations, their controversies and brand-building, bring in the interdependence between energy, finance, and platform infrastructures and business and marketing flows, rarely, if ever, seen in Arcangel's art before.

During the last decade, big corporations have invaded social media for marketing purposes, and to build brand reputation and loyalty. Sprout Social reports:

While only 58.4 % [4.65 billion] of the world's population (e.g., 85% in Scandinavia, 8% in Middle Africa) is on social media, 91% of businesses in the US are, and the latter are increasing at a fast rate. [. . .] In January of 2022, the average Internet user spent an average of 2 hours and 27 minutes between messaging apps and social media.[13]

The use of social media in branding has become big business, targeting especially cell phone users, since "social media users spend almost 80% of their social media time using the platform's mobile versions."[14] According to the article "The Importance of Social Media Marketing: 7 Stats that Prove Social's Role in Business Success," capturing and fostering the customer flow are key tasks. It elaborates on the need to "gain a better understanding of customers," to "inform stronger, more customer-centric business strategies," and to monitor and mine social data using AI-powered business intelligence supplied by the same consultant.[15]

Arcangel's scrolling and clicking bots foreground with diligence the overwhelming amount of redundant information they want their customers to share, like, and comment on. The experience is not silent. Many of the posts contain music, short videos, oral presentations, and texts. It becomes a grand multimedia composition based on found feeds as raw material. However, the thoughtless and mechanical bot remains disinterested; its movements are executed with mathematical precision and

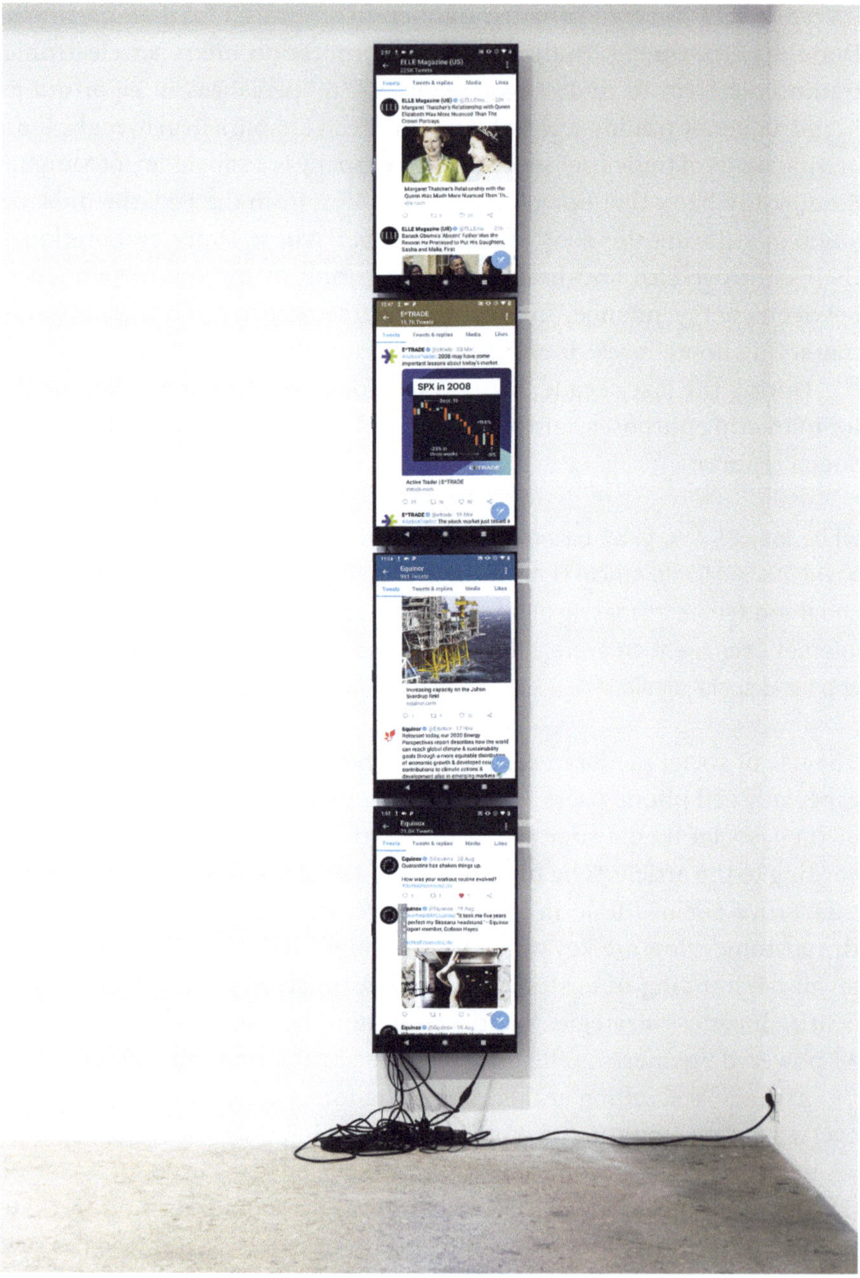
ELLE Magazine (US)
E*TRADE
SPX in 2008
Equinor
Equinox

the rhythm of a surveillance tool akin to an absurd archival machine that harvests and likes everything. Arcangel arranges the flows according to Steve Reich's compositional technique of the phased loop. Reich's technique is not traditionally counterpoint in the classical sense but can be viewed as an evolution of counterpoint concepts applied to rhythmic and harmonic processes. Arcangel applies it to the random flows of found feeds. The bot stays with each post for three seconds, as if glancing at the post, before it clicks "like," leaving a shiny red heart below the post. Each video contains about 800 likes. The four videos are of unequal length (*elleusa* (37:28), *equinor* (44:24), *equinox* (40:12), and *etrade_financial* (41:25)). They are looped, but the loops are not synced. Therefore, the piece is infinitely phasing, erecting an inhuman monument, a totem, to the glorious reign of social media (figure 4.1).

Marketing manager at Nike, Kate Ruda, reveals that it is all about "love." Her viral slogan reads: "I love when brands engage with you on social. A simple 'like' can go a long way in building brand love. Never underestimate the power of social listening and community management."[16] Social media marketing budgets are on the rise across the board to develop the like-economy. "90% of executives agree social will soon become the primary communications channel for connecting with customers," and "over half of the executives surveyed anticipate that their social marketing budgets will increase by over 50% by 2024."[17] The regular user is no longer, if they ever were, dominant on social media.

According to the media scholars Carolin Gerlitz and Anne Helmond, the like-economy transforms the flow of affects, beliefs, and desires into quantifiable data flows with the help of the like button.[18] Platforms use

4.1

Cory Arcangel, *elleusa, equinor, equinox, etrade_financial*, 2020. (Installation view: *Century 21*, Greene Naftali Gallery, New York, March 2021–April 2021.) 4-channel video recordings of a live bot performance on Twitter, November 30, 2020. Photo by Zeshan Ahmed, courtesy of the artist and Greene Naftali.

the rhetoric of sociality and connectivity to create a recentralized, data-intensive infrastructure in which social interactivity and user affects are instantly turned into valuable data and enter cycles of multiplication and exchange. This aspect of pulling users unknowingly into a large and super-profitable economy, has been foregrounded by many critics of "platform capitalism." Shoshana Zuboff calls it "surveillance capitalism" which "integrate[s] 'society' as a 'first class object' for rendition, computation, modification, monetization, and control."[19] With platform capitalism, social engineering gets a new instrument. While Zuboff investigates the techniques of "surveillance capitalism" as revolutionary inventions, German media scholar Erich Hörl explores it rather as a continuation of cybernetics applied on the entire population. He calls it a general "cyberneticization of society."[20] With Big Tech, "the public . . . has fallen under the control of social-engineering cybernetics . . . a cybernetic totality," Diedrich Diederichson concludes.[21] Several of Arcangel's works at *Century 21*, add an element of subversive affirmation to what Diederichson calls a "cybernetics of the poor." What does this do to the topics of subjectivation, new technology, and critical documentation?

SUBVERSIVE AFFIRMATION

All systems want their subjects to adapt to their commands, which are either explicit, as in terms of agreement, or a combination of the explicit and the implicit, as in actual platform affordances. This makes the topic of subjectivation complex. Analysis and artistic interventions can untangle aspects of this. In *Century 21*, Arcangel replaces subjects with social bots and documents their actions. Some of the bots, like in *elleusa, equinor, equinox, etrade_financial*, behave in a hyperadapted manner. They do what they are supposed to do, but too excessively. They accelerate obedience to an absurd maximum. The bots divert from the way a "normal" subject would act; they click on every post with a machinelike rhythm, slow but consistent, creating an atmosphere of artificiality and meditation. They do not surf like a human being would, jumping, pausing, reversing again, pausing, and jumping back; they *scan* the feeds with scientific precision. Like alien archaeologists, they browse across the remains of a human world, seemingly blissful, friendly, and optimistic posts. The bots are unaffectionate, but still click "like," as if to test the humans' "hottest" invention, the like button. At the same time, the bots' behavior preempts what humans have become. The corporate feeds are molar machines grinding users into groupthink, addictions, and new investments. The monotonous, slave-like obedience of liking every post brings out, not a human, but a machinic connection to the machine. Rather than resisting the feed's flow, Arcangel's bots follow the flow helplessly, or rather, with a more-than-human obedience. This creates a surplus meaning. The bots reflect not only on how both Big Tech, businesses, platforms, and affordances work together to shape a subject needed to make the like-economy work, but on how this system can fail.

The artistic tactic of appropriating the stupidest aspects of a culture was used by many avant-garde art movements such as the Lettrists and the Situationist International but was also widespread among artists and musicians in the former Soviet Union. Starting in the 1960s, they developed a strange artform, sometimes called socialist surrealism.[22] During the totalitarian Soviet era, outright resistance was impossible. Instead, they would follow the flow and adhere to the commandments of communist propaganda and planning, and repeat, say, sing, write, paint, and perform what was expected of them, but do it with a difference, in an eagerly exaggerated manner. The tactic has been named "subversive affirmation" or "overidentification."[23] It is a kind of pastiche or parody that makes fun of a situation by accelerating its effect on the subjects. Philosopher Slavoj Žižek concludes that these artists were not fascists but that their strategic overidentification with the ideology of a totalitarian regime "frustrates the system" and "suspends its efficiency," and he goes on, "[it] does not function as an answer but a question."[24]

According to Inke Arns and Sylvia Sasse subversive affirmation "could only have taken place in the face of a totalitarian machine."[25] However, they see these tactics becoming important also in the West and in the digital age:

While in the context of openly repressive systems there were very narrow limits on what could and what could not be said, today we are confronted with a situation where everything (and thus nothing) can be said. The culture industry manages to co-opt and appropriate even the most critical viewpoints and render them ineffective. In both contexts, critical distance (an "outside") proves to be an impossible or inadequate position. In this situation brought about by the strategy of total recovery and appropriation of critical viewpoints by the dominant political and economic system is rather the viral stealth tactics of subversive affirmation that still seem to hold a potential for resistance.[26]

Their initial description of the situation in the West as a place "where everything (and thus nothing) can be said" is paranoid and collapses the distinction between dictatorships and democracies. However, the general gist of their argument makes sense. Social media platforms have led to an information overload challenging the impact of opinions and critique in a waning public sphere.

As marketing language and the mechanisms of social media become hegemonic and naturalized, the awareness of and attention to their manipulative effects and affordances may weaken; the tactic of subversive affirmation becomes useful. How does it work? Arns and Sasse take inspiration from Michel de Certeau's influential book *The Practice of Everyday Life*. De Certeau discusses how the reuse of already-existing forms, practices, and utterances, may allow for critical, deviating, or oppositional statements. The movements of this "different production" happen entirely inside the enemy's field of vision, in a space controlled by the "enemy."[27] However, despite the use of the same linguistic and social material, these tactics manage, according to de Certeau, "to stay heterogeneous (or alien) to the system they invade," but once inside, they "wittily manage to deploy and formulate *different* interests and wishes."[28] Arns and Sasse go on to discuss the *Nike Ground* prank installation from 2003, by 0100101110101101.org (aka Eva and Franco Mattes), which was set up in Vienna to inform its citizens that Karlsplatz would soon be rebaptized "Nikeplatz"; and the culture jammers The Yes Man, who have repeatedly irritated internet users with fake websites that look confusingly similar to the official websites of politicians and corporations. Arcangel have done similar stunts like *Dooogle* (2004) and *Punk Rock 101* (2006), which are prank websites that lure the logic and affordances of Google to bring out unintended consequences.

Subversive affirmation was developed in many ways depending on the medium, style, technique, and perspective taken. Traditionally, the tactic was deployed at concerts or art performances. It may camouflage itself as "tactics of explicit consent" before becoming "different" and "critical," for instance, through a foregrounding of the practice as a *style* evolving into a process of alienation and estrangement (e.g., through magnifying something). *Elleusa, equinor, equinox, etrade_financial* starts out as a tactic of explicit consent—click "like"!—but is soon ridiculed through mindless repetitions. This type of subversive affirmation is therefore at first, a "parasitical" practice that employs the methods of "imitation, simulation, mimicry, and camouflage in the sense of 'becoming invisible' by disappearing into the background."[29] These tactics create "a psychic/physical experience of what is being criticized."[30] Again, at first, Arcangel's video may seem normal, as if he is just showing what "we all do," a kind of invisible habit. Early in his career, he saw his art as a coevolution with the technical environment; "as an artist I always think of my work being filtered through all these levels of censors."[31] These censors are the standard operating procedures governing flow-arrangements. He *seems* to collaborate with these procedures but actually produces another flow, a minor flow, or a potential flow, a becoming-imperceptible which, according to Deleuze, is an "imperceptible that can only be sensed," not measured.[32] After a short while, as Arcangel's bot repeats the same gesture again and again, the "different production" becomes visible or apparent. The viewer realizes that the bot's rhythm or flow is so mechanical that it must be nonhuman. What seemed animate becomes inanimate.

The way Arcangel stages an ambiguity between human and nonhuman operations resonates with a debate and aesthetic experience which was intensified with the invention of cinema. From its beginning, the uncanny relationship between the still and the moving, the dead and the living, became an attraction, according to film historian Tom Gunning.[33] Arcangel translates this ambiguity into contemporary media life, where this confusion has become domesticated into the new normal. Is it a bot or a human one interacts with? Users seem not to ask this question anymore. Arcangel intensifies the normal human's subservient and obedient platform behavior to a point where it becomes uncanny, and it becomes a gesture of revolt—or a new aesthetic based on surfing and clicking. This is "uncanny" in a way Ernst Jentsch or Sigmund Freud could not have foreseen. A perception that wavers between the animate and the inanimate, the living and the dead, defines the uncanny. However, once the object is stabilized as inanimate, traditional psychoanalysis would view this as a relief: it is not the walking dead or a robot capable of deceiving me. In Arcangel's version, it gets more complex because it deals with media *life*. Seeing *with* the bot's insistent rhythm of clicks and likes creates, perhaps, a moment of humor.

Another classic reference to this issue is Henri Bergson on laughter. Bergson analyzed the perceptual shift from the organic to the mechanical as a cause for humor because it implies a transition from human elegance to the mechanical. To him, the mechanical represented nonhuman clumsiness. Today, technologies like AI and bots are no longer seen as clumsy; they typically perform tasks as instructed—sometimes even better than humans. The humor in Arcangel's work lies in the collapse of the distinction between being a bot and being human as entities "experiencing" the world. Platform capitalism attempts to hold this collapse at bay by occasionally asking the user, "Are you a robot?" Similarly, the algorithms driving these platforms amalgamate thousands of media flows into repetitive patterns and, furthermore, use precise measurements of the user's desires and beliefs to transform this repetition into something perceived as a personalized and enjoyable experience. The confinement of the subject into an autonomous loop reduces the human to an obsessive click-machine. While most movies depict the nonhuman takeover as a dramatic and violent shift, Arcangel portrays the apocalypse as a boring, seamless, and barely perceptible conflation of bots and humans.

Seen from the platform owner's standpoint, clicks are money in the bank, because it helps them create reliable social data. But if the user is mad or just a machine clicking thousands of random clicks, the data becomes unreliable. Moreover, influencers and companies rely on online traffic, and this demand has spawned an entire industry of bot traffic. Influencers and companies can buy clicks by the thousands generated by bot farms. Arcangel's bots are made according to the same principles as bot farms. He has appropriated the techniques of the attention hungry for other purposes. The work of bot farms is invisible and secret. *Elleusa, equinor, equinox, etrade_financial* makes the work of bots visible, debatable, and experienceable.

While *elleusa, equinor, equinox, etrade_financial* plays the game of platform capitalism through the tactic of subversive affirmation, *we deliver / the king checked by the queen* (Dual-channel screen recording of a live bot performance on Instagram, February 26, 2020), is an example of soft subversion. It uses the same hacking technique as in the former work but instead of clicking likes, the algorithm plays chess. It is a recording of two social bots that post cryptic messages like "_7881 mentioned you in a comment @_kxd._8691 e6" on seemingly random profiles on Instagram, ranging from celebrities to brands, big corporations, fast food restaurants, and state power companies, etc. The profile manager would wonder, what the heck is this, a troll, lurkers from the dark web, a hoax, a conspiracy—a hack, a virus, a spam? It demands a bit of decryption skills to decode the scam. "kxd.7881" represents black chess pieces and "kxd.8691" represents the whites. The profile name, "kxd," is chess lingo for "the king checked by the queen" (k = king, x = checked, d = dame/queen); the numbers 7881 and 8691 are Duchamp's birth and death years spelled out backward (1887–1968); and "e6" indicates the piece's coordinate move on the chess board. Figure 4.2 shows the white bot, "kxd.8691," about to make a move. The compositional technique behind these flow-cut arrangements is more random, abstract, and uncanny than that of *elleusa, equinor, equinox, etrade_financial* because the bots' algorithms and instructions are more complex, constructing players rather than merely clickers. Additionally, its intervention appears to intrude into a more intimate area of the found feed—the commentary fields, which often contain personal sentiments and utterances from users—staging a clash with digital diary art.

This Instagram prank is also a homage to Duchamp's archival artwork, *The Box of 1932*, which collects his works on chess and chess theory. After becoming a delegate to the World Chess Federation (FIDE) in 1931, Duchamp collaborated with the French chess player and theorist Vitaly Halberstadt on *Opposition and Sister Squares Are Reconciled*, a book that studied endgame strategies. In his recycled cardboard box from 1932, Duchamp assembled the manuscripts, proofs, diagrams, drawings, and notes produced in the process of the book's publication with other

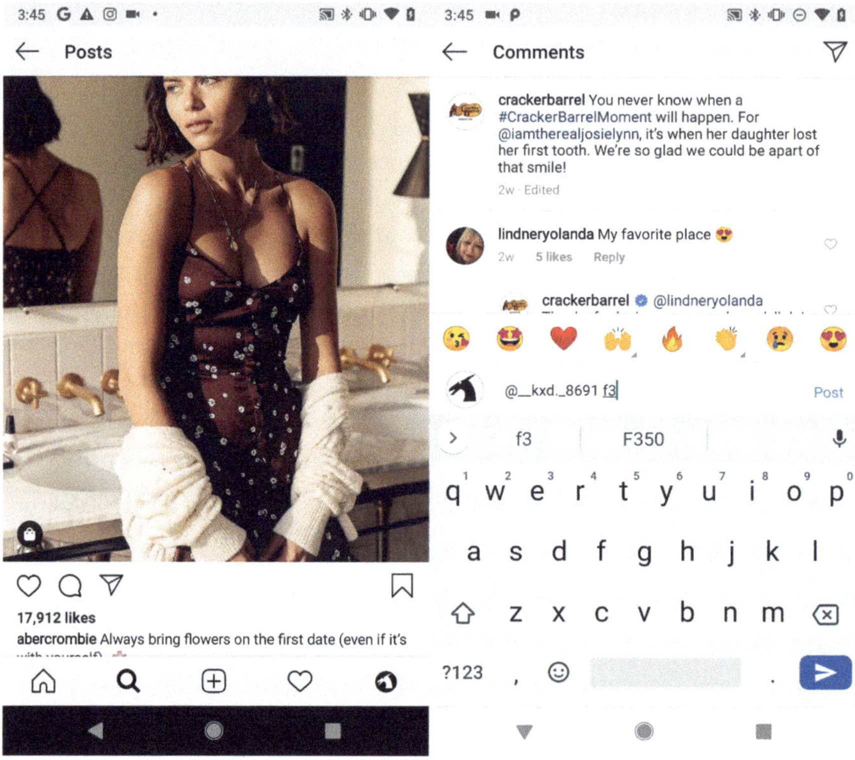

4.2

Cory Arcangel, *we deliver / the king checked by the queen*, 2020. Dual-channel screen recording of a live bot performance on Instagram, February 26, 2020. Photo by Cory Arcangel, courtesy of the artist.

chess-related records. One of his drawings in the box was entitled "The king checked by the queen."

Arcangel "delivers" Duchamp's endgame in an updated version, to be played by two AI bots on Instagram. Their profiles' logo used Duchamp's chess piece design, perhaps inspired by artist Scott Kildall's reconstruction in digital 3D of Duchamp's seventy-two chess game designs in the *Box of 1932*.[34] Arcangel's endgame reconstruction uses an entire social media environment as a playing field and creates a wild deterritorialization of the platform. It is more than an appropriation, it is an ob-scene event. Every chess move turns the feed of a random profile into a flow-break. The profile owners have no choice but to suddenly become an audience to an endgame they cannot overview or participate in. Can the chess-flow and the profiles' gossip-flow ever connect and intermingle? One gets the feeling the stretch between the two will eventually short-circuit the platform and snap it into a silent apocalypse. Perhaps it is the endgame of platform capitalism as a joke.

"LEADERSHIP-CLASS COMPUTING SYSTEMS"

Whereas the two bot-based works discussed previously use smartphone profiles to game and *ungame* social media, the next work uses a smartphone profile connected to a gigantic machine learning system to play a simple role-playing game. Implicitly, it comments on the hype after an AI, Deep Blue, beat the best chess player, and AlfaGo beat the best Go player. Before ChatGPT, Arcangel's game-playing bot spent several years in the making and would have been almost impossible to do without the help of a team of programmers at Arcangel's studio in Brooklyn. As an art installation it is manifold. The game is shown on a large LED-screen which dominates the gallery room, but it also contains a large supercomputer rig (figure 4.3), a "custom built Deep-Q Learning RPG playing software bot with system sounds by Daniel Lopatin" surrounded by an air-cooling system and two smaller computer screens constituting a control room for the system, on a table next to the screen.[35]

The installation set-up, containing a large media ensemble, testifies to the enormous amount of resources and energy invested in its creation,

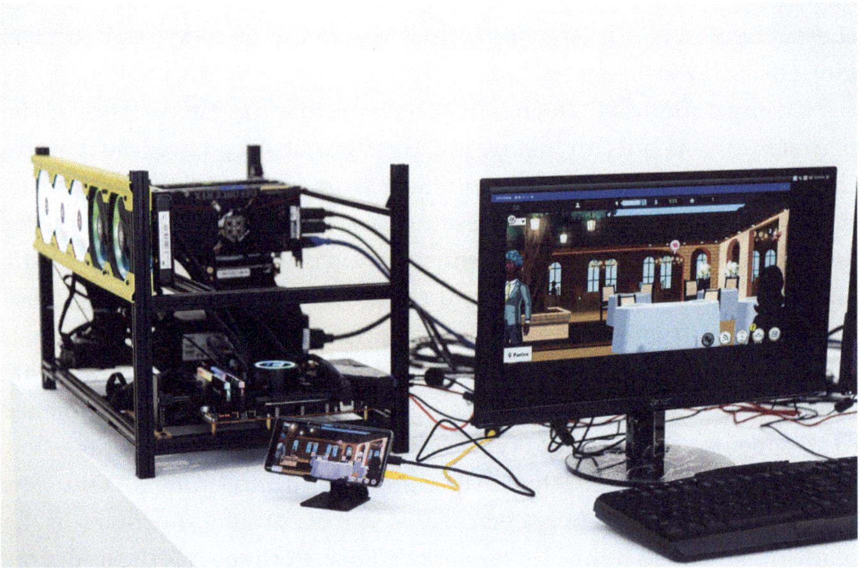

4.3

Cory Arcangel, */roʊˈdeɪoʊ/ Let's Play: HOLLYWOOD*, 2017–2021. Custom built high performance computer rig (AMD Ryzen 9 5950X 16-core 32-Thread Unlocked Desktop Processor central processing unit, Rog Crosshair Viii Dark Hero motherboard, G. SKILL 64GB (2 x 32GB) Trident Z Neo Series DDR4 PC4–21300 2666 MHz 288-Pin Desktop Memory Model F4–2666C18D-64GTZN random access memory, (x2) EVGA 24G-P5–3975-KR GeForce RTX 3090 XC3 Ultra Gaming graphics processing units' & Corsair Professional Series AX 1200 Watt Digital ATX/EPS Modular 80 PLUS Platinum (AX1200i) power supply, various peripherals), custom built Deep-Q Learning RPG playing software bot with system sounds by Daniel Lopatin (Oneohtrix Point Never), Kim Kardashian: Hollywood casual free-to-play role-playing Android game, Android phone, amplifier & speakers, various cables. (*Century 21*, Greene Naftali Gallery, New York, March–April 2021.) Photo by Zeshan Ahmed, courtesy of the artist and Greene Naftali.

systems development, and operation comes to the fore. Furthermore, the four elements—fire (electricity), earth (the metals constituting the motherboards and chips), water (imagine the amount of water used to produce the metals), and air—are a part of the equation. Additionally, the game rig is equipped with a Twitter account logging the system's status and tracing the protagonist's success and failures. Finally, there is an online catalogue text containing a tech spec sheet satirizing the language and rhetoric of the AI industry.

The work is called */roʊ ˈdeɪoʊ/ Let's Play: HOLLYWOOD* (2021). The title is based on audio script, not programming code, and it should be pronounced "Rodeo" as in the street "Rodeo Drive," where Kim Kardashian lives her red-carpet adventures IRL. Normally, the audio script explains the pronunciation but should not replace the written title, as is done here. The comic use of audio script as primary, reverse engineers the order of written language and prefigures Arcangel's reversal of what is shown on the screen. It contains a live transmission of an AI bot struggling to learn the role-playing game *Kim Kardashian: Hollywood*, made for iOS and Android phones. However, what dominates the screen is not the hero's actions but various data flows and operational images, superimposed on the gameplay, depicting the computational processes at work "behind the scenes." Lopatin's soundtrack, called "system sounds," underscores the events of the AI, its calculations and image recognitions, rather than the gameplay. The visible and audible flows of the AI's machine acts undermine and defer immersion in the game flow.

The original game was an instant hit, earning over $1.6 million in revenue in its first five days and over $74 million in its first six months. "At its peak, Kim Kardashian: Hollywood was generating over $700,000 per day in revenue. It revolutionized the celebrity mobile gaming space and inspired numerous copycat games," according to one source.[36] The game's goal is to become an A-list celebrity like Kim K. The player starts at the lowest level as an E-list celebrity. If the player takes assignments as a model, actor, or club guest, dresses up in designer fashions, or goes out on a date to boost the fan base, the chances of getting to the next level will increase. The surprise is that the AI-driven protagonist fails a lot and has a hard time getting beyond level E. This makes the player's "intelligence" the real protagonist of the art installation. The narrative game flow is literally halted while the robot's flow of sensations, thoughts, and actions is hyperactive—but dumb—and for long periods of time takes the game flow nowhere. The robot's "thought flow" is shown in real time as operational images or visible signs overlaying the game flow. The juxtaposition of both flows creates an odd montage displayed on a single large LED wall. A cluster of cables connecting the LED wall to the "custom built high performance computer rig" is visible on the floor, enhancing the presence of a Giant Brain, the real protagonist, AI (figure 4.4).

Typically, Arcangel includes all the trash that comes with engaging with commercial media. This enhances the quality of archiving and documenting contemporary media life in art. Since this is a live stream of a free-to-play game, it comes with the occasional industry-standard interruptions of commercials delaying the game. Many of these commercials are from TikTok and Google Play, but others are more oblique, such as "Starshop." Does it belong to the real world or the game world? A strangely mixed segment of a contemporary business and media ecology arises. Furthermore, since artificial intelligence is foregrounded through its failures rather than successes, the web catalogue presentation of the AI system becomes an important part of the artwork. The presentation mimics the rhetoric of the AI industry's quasi-intellectual and boastful sales pitch. The game's brain is based on cutting-edge tech

> the next leap in leadership-class computing systems for "end of civilisation" style durational moving image experiences. With /roʊˈdeɪoʊ/ we hope to be able to address, with greater complexity and higher fidelity, questions concerning who we are, our place on earth, and in our universe.[37]

Arcangel's attention to language and rhetoric gets more prominent in comparison to the early works. Contrary to the colloquialisms of another work at the show, *Inspos*, this is corporate language, an optimized presentation of custom narrative packaging and offering. The baseless rhetoric serves more as a whip than information; it is a sovereign's call for loyalty and order. In sardonic fashion, the text's "we," presenting the video game installation, belongs to a business leader's royal "we," rather than a subcultural "we," as in his earlier works. We have moved from Duchamp's endgame to another collapse, a twist on AI as a marker of

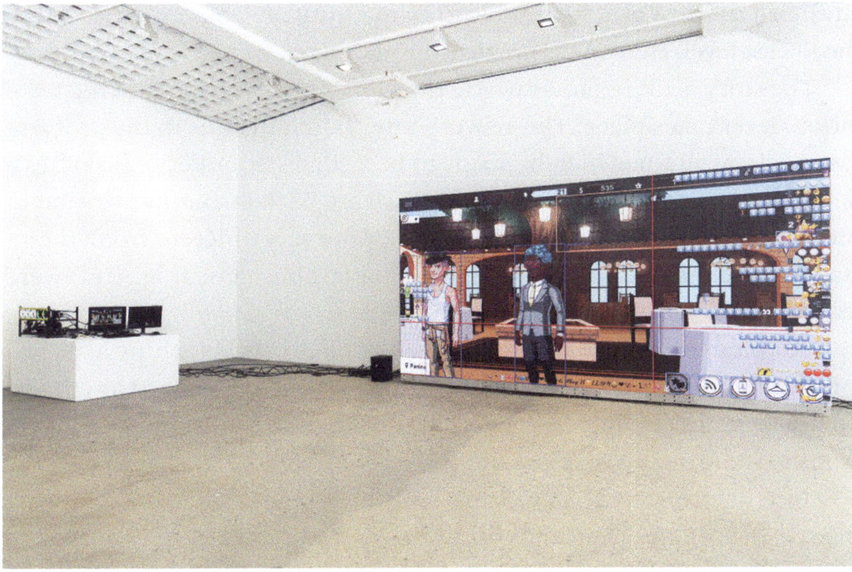

not triumph, but societal collapse. Anthropologists have theorized that collapsed societies essentially exhausted their own designs and technologies, becoming unable to adapt to the naturally diminishing returns of the survival methods they once relied on.[38] Arcangel's installation conjures forth both AI- and the Kim K-hype as two versions of the same apocalypse.

Indeed, AI is supposed to make life and business alike easier and more effective, but its grandiose promises are not always fulfilled. Nevertheless, the sales rhetoric just gets juicier and bolder with each invention. While an AI-critical documentary movie, like for instance *iHuman*, will *talk about* AI through interviews with engineers and critics, Arcangel's installation *engineers and demonstrates* AI in real life.[39] He challenges AI to play one of the simplest and most popular RPGs, but despite running on

4.4

Cory Arcangel, */roʊˈdeɪoʊ/ Let's Play: HOLLYWOOD*, 2017–2021. (Installation view: *Century 21*, Greene Naftali Gallery, New York, March–April 2021.) Photo by Zeshan Ahmed, courtesy of the artist and Greene Naftali.

advanced AI, the bot is never able to round the game, nor even rise above the lowest level. Here, AI is an ultraslow learner. Comical.

The story is like a movie where the plot or goal is given, but the resolution never takes place. The viewer's attention moves from the protagonist to player-brain, which happens to be a supercomputer. It becomes a movie about a sloppy machine. Again, we are back at another version of the schiz-image, but the flow and montage are very different from, for instance, *Super Mario Clouds*, where only unplayable game fragments were looped. *Super Mario Clouds* was minimalism; */roʊˈdeɪoʊ/* is maximalism, as it supplements the real game acts with equally real machine acts, juxtaposed on top of each other. The machine acts are visualized as emojis, numbers, and a rectangle target reticle moving across various people and items to indicate the AI's focus at any given time.

To reiterate, */roʊˈdeɪoʊ/* resonates ironically with the hype following the AI, Deep Blue, beating World Chess Champion Garry Kasparov in 1997 and after Google's artificial intelligence program AlphaGo beat the professional Go player Lee Sedol, during the Google DeepMind Challenge Match in Seoul on March 13, 2016. Arcangel started working on */roʊˈdeɪoʊ/* after the latter event, but this AI, even with the help of "the next leap in leadership-class computing systems," is not able to beat a simple RPG about how to become a celebrity. On the one hand, this speaks to the stupidity of AI at understanding social games, but on the other, it speaks to the complexity of celebrity trends as less graspable for state-of-the-art AI; the social cannot be striated or translated into mathematical terms as easily as chess. This could be one of the reasons the thoughts of */roʊˈdeɪoʊ/*, the AI's acts, are displayed as derogatory emojis superimposed on top of the game image as an "operational image."

Operational image, a term used by the filmmaker Harun Farocki, designates images that transmit a flow of information about information (metadata) within a technical process. These images are usually abstract calculations tracking the process, but in Arcangel's rendition they also contain emojis, and the operational image is not located as a framed image within the screen but spread out as information on the frame's right side, along with a target reticle moving across the screen, making the operational elements a key "player" in the experience of the work. The recursive dynamic between the game image (diegesis or game acts) and the operational image (machine values or machine acts) breaks through on the image plane and disturbs the game flow. It follows a WYSIWYG ("what you see is what you get") logic, but as the player is very slow at solving puzzles, most of the time the action takes place at the level of the machine thinking (operational elements at play). As the game acts are paused—and the game's protagonist just stands there scratching his head to indicate he is "thinking"—the viewer's attention is drawn to the machine's calculations. The game schizzes more than it plays. It becomes an installation about a machine, a stupid machine. AI deterritorialized as emojis.

ORDER-WORDS AND TRAPS

In *Century 21*, certain digital explorations are redirected toward decidedly analog outcomes, such as in the parody of a promotional catalogue-text on AI tech developments accompanying */roʊˈdeɪoʊ/*. Other works reflect on how social media has changed language use. These are not hacks proper but cuts foregrounding web-induced speech. The so-called *Inspos* are a series of works on paper made on a Hewlett-Packard home office LaserJet on found airsickness bags from Scandinavian Airlines and Virgin Atlantic (figure 4.5).

They contain banal phrases like "I don't know who needs to know this," "Let's be clear now," and "Let me explain." An "inspo" is slang for "an inspiring influence; a motivator." Merriam-Webster.com's example goes to the core: "We may not have pockets as deep as them and would max out our credit cards if we even tried to re-create their outfits, but we'll always look to celebrities for fashion inspo." Arcangel's inspos are far from heartening; in fact, they may not be inspirations at all but rather contribute to the enshittification of the web. According to Facebook whistleblower Francis Haugen's testimony from 2021, Facebook's algorithms are set up to incite misinformation, hate speech, and even ethnic violence, simply to increase engagement with the platform.[40] Knowyourmeme.com notes that phrases such as "I don't know who needs to hear this" or "Let's be clear," often employed to preface advice, opinions, or suggestions, are occasionally utilized in tweets to build anticipation and emphasize the

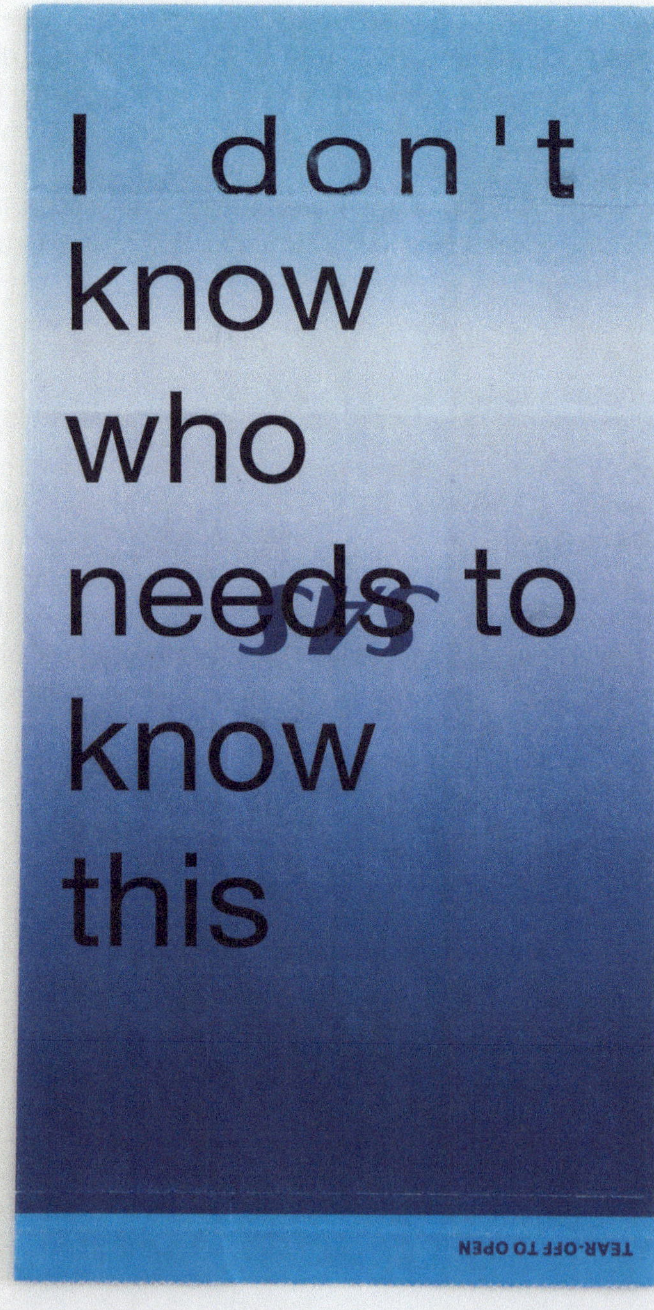
I don't know who needs to know this
TEAR-OFF TO OPEN

significance of the message to someone's well-being.[41] They go back to religious inspirational messages but are today part of a widely used word flow on social media, especially by the messianic Trump cult. Cults, Facebook, and X seem to rely on the use of incendiary language to stoke the algorithms of their feeds.

The phrases—"Let's be clear," etc.—can be suggestive, hypnotic, and encouraging for people to do or believe in something, usually without evidence. They are like the "order-words" analyzed by Deleuze and Guattari. They call them "insigns" or badges of authority that imply a command in disguise.[42] Order-words are tools for making cults or armies, they contend and go on: "Every order-word [. . .] carries a little death sentence." Order-words belong to an "education machine" and are "expression[s] of obedience [. . .] very short phrases that command life and are inseparable from enterprises and large projects," such as election campaigns.[43] Steve Bannon was part of Trump's first presidential election campaign, and his philosophy was laid out in an interview with the writer Michael Lewis: "The Democrats don't matter. The real opposition is the media. And the way to deal with them is to flood the zone with shit."[44] No wonder Arcangel needed vomit bags. These prints stand out as the chorus of this exhibition's drama. They sing the senseless mantras of the paranoid.

DOCUMENTING THE WEB

Arcangel has always been interested in the cultural and expressive flows of media and how they tend to in part be determined by tech innovations and their specific flow-paths. These paths are dotted with affordances or so-called options which discipline the user's expressive capacities. The user-subject becomes part of larger flow-arrangements. Arcangel is good

4.5

Cory Arcangel, *I don't know who needs to know this*, 2020. Hewlett Packard home office LaserJet on found Scandinavian Airlines airsickness bag. Photo by Zeshan Ahmed, courtesy of the artist and Greene Naftali.

at detaching elements from these arrangements to set up new ones, but in other works, he follows the flow-path of a specific medium or website as minutely as possible, as seen in many of the works at *Century 21*. These works also recall his so-called web-episodes or surfing series done ten years earlier. They document a particular business's website by surfing through its options. *So Shines A Good Deed in a Weary World (dunkindonuts.com)* (2014), *Ideas in Action* (*starbucks.com*) (2014), *Max Perch* (*officemax.com*) (2014), and *FRESHBUZZ* (*subway.com*) (2014) are movie-length (60–90 minute) documentaries of dunkindonuts.com, starbucks.com, officemax.com, and subway.com.

He uses screen-capture video tools to record himself or Gil Gentile, his assistant at the time, surfing a website. These "boring" captures of the design or "life" of a website may resemble aspects of documentary photography, like Bernd and Hilla Becher's "archival art." While those artists created photographic typologies of industrial buildings, Arcangel maps the system behavior of specific postindustrial and informatic worlds online. Furthermore, just as their photography followed a carefully planned set of views, Arcangel's surfing series is based on detailed instructions to his assistant on how to proceed. The handwritten "score" or instruction sheet for the work *Freshbuzz* looks like a musical score where each move and click is carefully ordered in a sequence of layered views of the layout, designs, options, and affordances of the website. It indicates which flow-paths to follow and where to stop and move on—if possible (figure 4.7). One would perhaps think that surfing a website is a random act; Arcangel's "composition" is a detailed plan that demonstrates the opposite. What once was thought of as a wonderland of innovation and multiple choices is, just around the next corner, viewed as extremely inflexible. The web-episodes are like comedies as they follow a protagonist surfing across a landscape of menus, clicks, and scrolls, revealing the poverty of every option and in retrospect, as is often the case with technological innovation, it appears as strangely dull and awkward.

4.6

Cory Arcangel, *Freshbuzz (www.subway.com)*, 2014. Single-channel video. Photo by Arcangel Studio, courtesy of the artist.

4.7

Cory Arcangel, *Freshbuzz (www.subway.com)*, 2014. Handwritten score. Photo by Arcangel Studio, courtesy of the artist.

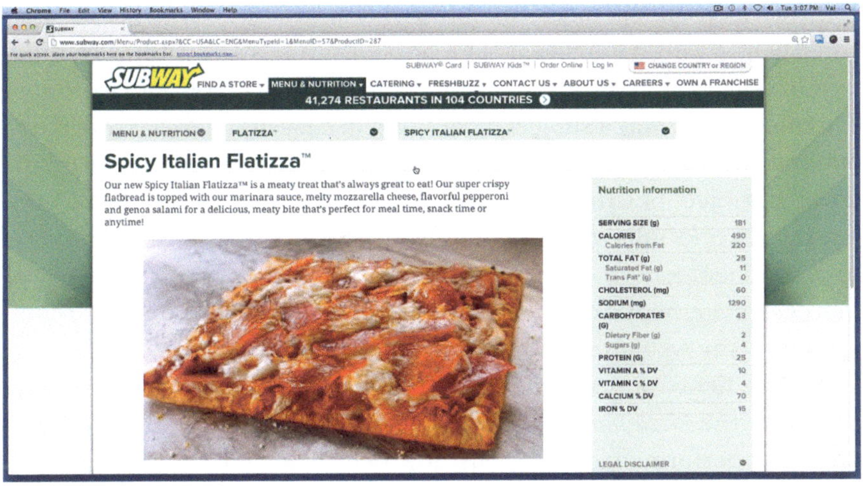
SUBWAY® Card | SUBWAY Kids™ | Order Online | Log In
CHANGE COUNTRY or REGION
SUBWAY
FIND A STORE
MENU & NUTRITION
CATERING
FRESHBUZZ
CONTACT US
ABOUT US
CAREERS
OWN A FRANCHISE
41,274 RESTAURANTS IN 104 COUNTRIES
MENU & NUTRITION
FLATIZZA™
SPICY ITALIAN FLATIZZA™
Spicy Italian Flatizza™
Our new Spicy Italian Flatizza™ is a meaty treat that's always great to eat! Our super crispy flatbread is topped with our marinara sauce, melty mozzarella cheese, flavorful pepperoni and genoa salami for a delicious, meaty bite that's perfect for meal time, snack time or anytime!
Nutrition information
SERVING SIZE (g) 181
CALORIES 490
Calories from Fat 220
TOTAL FAT (g) 25
Saturated Fat (g) 11
Trans Fat (g) 0
CHOLESTEROL (mg) 60
SODIUM (mg) 1290
CARBOHYDRATES (G) 43
Dietary Fiber (g) 2
Sugars (g) 4
PROTEIN (G) 25
VITAMIN A % DV 10
VITAMIN C % DV 4
CALCIUM % DV 70
IRON % DV 15
LEGAL DISCLAIMER

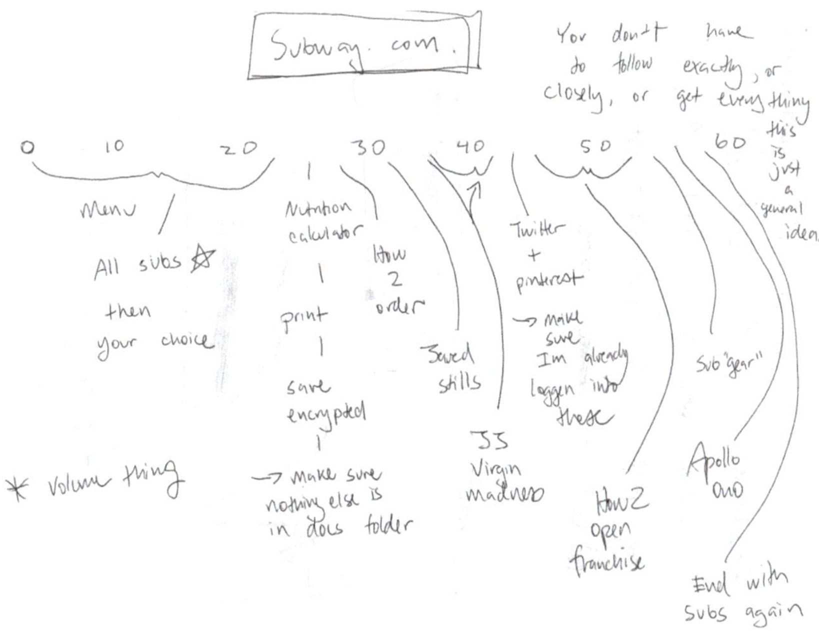
Subway.com
You don't have to follow exactly, or closely, or get everything this is just a general idea.
0
10
20
30
40
50
60
Menu
All subs ☆ then your choice
Nutrition calculator
print
save encrypted
→ make sure nothing else is in docs folder
How 2 order
Saved stills
JJ Virgin madness
Twitter + pinterest
→ make sure I'm already loggen into these
How 2 open franchise
Sub "gear"
Apollo ono
End with subs again
* volume thing

The early web-episodes and many of the works at *Century 21* are governed by an archival impulse. They micropolitically map an infrastructural terrain of affordances and flow-paths online. The web-episodes from 2014 demonstrate the way a subject is captured in a layered maze of ridiculous options; *elleusa, equinor, equinox, etrade_financial* effectively foregrounds how the subject-position is reduced to only one option, click "like." The way these works follow a given or universal flow-path, capturing millions of users, documents the acts of freedom and attention inspiring an age of web design. Perhaps we can call it the age of compression—of everything.

While the web-episodes and certain works at *Century 21* outline circles of obedience or the absurdity of dutifully adopting a given path, early hacks like the *Pizza Party* performance invest in a circle of disobedience. The latter performance was, as already mentioned, an exploration of the interface technology being used in the early 2000s and how to subvert it. Arcangel did a command-line hack of the new website of Domino's Pizza in New York. He tried to order pizzas for the entire audience at the Kitchen theater and succeeded. There are no known recordings of this hack, but the code used is available on his website. However, since this website is no longer in use, the code is useless. They are but archival remains of a hack. The archival and critical dimensions of Arcangel's work give them a special status as artworks. They are somehow less like art and more like messages in a bottle for the future.

Arcangel is modernistic in the sense that he works minutely and credulously with the media-specific qualities of given media and apparatuses, but his media specificity is unlike the media specificity hailed by modernistic critics such as Clement Greenberg. Arcangel's media specificity is linked to technological media and their language: code and programming, software and hardware, and gestures like scrolling, clicking, finger presses, and swipes. The characteristics of new media are in themselves an offense to the poetics of modernism, as new media inherently can remediate any old media without losing its own media specificity. New media destratifies the characteristics of old media without losing its own characteristics. Arcangel's mastery of hybridity and "theater," to use Greenberg and Michael Fried's derogative term for "the projection and hypostatization of literalness and duration" in minimalist and conceptual art, is in Arcangel's case perhaps strategically and tactically borrowed from new media's own penchant for remixing older formats into one plane.[45] "What lies *between* the arts is theater," Fried wrote, and that is exactly where Arcangel's art is: between. If the formalist-modernist art, hailed by Greenberg and Fried, sought to seek the essential of a given medium, the postconceptual art of Arcangel does indeed seek the essential of a new medium, but only to discover that it allows for a permanent being in-between all media and conventions. This may at first sight look like postmodernism, as a free-wheeling play with conventions, but it is not as simple as that. The works reveal the conditional, but in unexpected ways.

His practices embrace the constraints of digital media, such as the language of code and the problem of coded space. They index not only the media of their time but their social and spatial ramifications, their modes of subjectivation, what a subject can do, express, or be. Both implicitly and explicitly, they capture the social facets of computation and the internet. Given the swift pace of digital technological advancements, often driven by substantial scientific funding and the economy of artificial obsolescence, some of his works have an instantaneous archival value, evoking the essence of fossils. If postmodernism is archival art that explores the shifting technicity of new media, his art is indeed postmodern.

The term "postmodernism," however, is so overused that it has lost all specificity. For example, to Fredric Jameson, postmodernism seems to signify an anything-goes of styles or what he calls "blank parody."[46] This does not fit with Arcangel's reuse of styles, because it is often done specially to designate the historicity of technology. Here, aesthetic styles speak to or about a fleeting moment determined by a specific machinic milieu, or the milieu of an earlier decade as with *Super Mario Clouds*. For this reason, the temptation to read Arcangel according to Jameson fails in most cases. To Jameson, postmodernism or "blank parody" is a "blind" reuse of old styles. He writes:

Modernist styles thereby become postmodernist codes. [. . .] In this situation parody finds itself without a vocation; it has lived, and that strange new thing pastiche slowly comes to take its place. Pastiche is, like parody, the imitation of a peculiar or unique, idiosyncratic style, the wearing of a linguistic mask, speech in a dead language. But it is a neutral practice of such mimicry, without any of parody's ulterior motives, amputated of the satiric impulse, devoid of laughter and of any conviction that alongside the abnormal tongue you have momentarily borrowed, some healthy linguistic normality still exists. Pastiche is thus blank parody, a statue with blind eyeballs.[47]

Indeed, there are elements of this type of freewheeling eclecticism in Arcangel's art, but again, Arcangel's modernist quotes are never accidental; they are critical. Furthermore, quoting and recording a social media machine with all its affordances up and running, is a media-specific operation needing the skills of a programmer or hacker. It is very different from the strategies of the postmodern novel, which, regardless of style, belongs to the age of the printing press. Arcangel works *with* specific platforms and modes of subject-production. These environments are themselves ridden with the masquerade of skeuomorphisms, meaning in GUI design, interface objects mimic their real-world counterparts in how they appear or how the user can interact with them, (e.g., a sheet of paper indicates "documents," a floppy disk "save," and a garbage can "delete"). While remediating an analogue world on the surface to comfort its users, the new media system hides subtle mechanisms of capture. "Quoting" traits of the new machinic milieu along with its affordances of clicks and comment spaces, is not "speech in a dead language" but an exploration in the conditional and a warning, pointing at how new media milieus suture the user into a somnambulist attitude, which streamlines both language, creativity, and critique.

Furthermore, Jameson criticizes postmodern art for staying at the surface, circulating without being able to reach any depths. This description does not match the level of complexity at play in the Cory Arcangel hack; digital media have displaced and complicated the surface/depth opposition. Arcangel's media archaeological sensitivity, his ability to dig into various layers of computation, speaks directly to the manifold interconnections between surface and depth in digital media. The political unconscious of digital media is a technological unconscious. It is invisible but affects all. Below the flow of images, there is a flow of data and protocols, and below the media flows of entertainment, there is a reversed data flow of information feeding user activity back to the platform owners before it is fed back to the user. Arcangel's topic is the strangeness of this machinic milieu as an arena where we are supposed to "express ourselves."

Deleuze and Guattari's model of machinic unconscious, even though it was developed long before platform capitalism, supplements Jameson's critique of the postmodern and the political unconscious. Deleuze and Guattari argue that visible cultural flows are in part actualizations of elements of deeper flows at the society's machinic unconscious. To them, society takes shape, is stratified and segmented into separate flows, through modes of capture and actualization where flows become visible as social signs and symbols that citizens can follow, understand, or identify with. These modes of stratification are named *molar*, they create *molar flows*, meaning flows defined and delimited according to cultural and political forms of patterning, programming, or management done by powerful groups and institutions. The opposite movement, which liberates flows from determinations and codifications, they call *molecular flows*. The latter capacitates the remains of, or fragments left untouched by, molar flows. Artistic tactics such as subversive affirmation are the micropolitics of molecular flows for the purpose of critique and creativity. The Cory Arcangel hack does not produce "authentic" archival documents, but hyphenated documents, never simply indexing what was, but exploring the unthought of its times. Perhaps his bots as they crawl across websites, are like Walter Benjamin's Angel of History, who flies backward, blown by the winds of progress, seeing "the pile of debris before him [grow] skyward."[48] As one critic wrote: "Only from this vantage can we develop an intuitive understanding of our existence within history, and hope to recognize a fertile substrate for new art and new ideas."[49]

BOTS, OR DECENTRALIZED ARTIFICIAL STUPIDITY

While many of Arcangel's works document games or the web, the protagonist of these documentations has never been a bot. Foregrounding the nonhuman agency of bots, makes *Century 21* somewhat apocalyptic. Supercomputers with artificial intelligence constitute the heart and infrastructure of most large companies and states, but they are utterly stupid when trying to understand a simple RPG about the red-carpet lives of wannabe celebs. Bots generate untrustworthy news and social profiles. They increase traffic, likes, and revenue. A participatory culture nurtured by click farms and social robots reaches a stalemate. Social media has become antisocial media. Or does the exhibition document a condition that will soon be over? Is it really that calm before the storm? *Art in America* editor Brian Droitcour, wrote:

> The show's grim mood could be a sign of artistic maturity. Or maybe it is just the inevitable outcome of a new media artist working with an increasingly flat and corporatized mediascape, overrun by marketers and bots. Arcangel's art isn't getting worse; the world is.[50]

Today, it is estimated that 15% of the web's activity is generated by nonhuman software agents. Over the next decade, researchers estimate that the absolute number of bots will multiply.[51] In fact, the Big Tech consultant firm, Gartner, predicts that soon "the average person will have more conversations with bots than with their spouse."[52] Bots are robots or nonhuman software agents, sometimes built with AI and ML. They are the virus and bacteria of the web, but like in modern biomedicine, they can also be helpful. They run automated tasks anywhere on the body of the internet, invisibly and much faster than a person can. Hence, both cyberterrorists and businesses are fond of them and invent new tasks for them every day. Hito Steyerl describes the phenomenon as "decentralized artificial stupidity": "Today's real existing proto- and para-fascisms, however, rely on decentralized artificial stupidity. Bot armies, like farms and filter bubbles, form the gut brains of political sentiment, manufacturing shitstorms that pose as popular passion."[53] Indeed, bots can be malicious, like the Russian social bots securing Trump's win in the presidential election of 2016, and biased, like in predictive policing algorithms or in applicant tracking systems filtering job seekers, but they can also be helpful, like the 2,707 bot tasks approved for use on the English Wikipedia that can carry out edits and other tasks on the platform.[54]

Arcangel's bot experiments create a new kind of time-based media art. These artworks merge with their technical environment but, as mentioned, in a hyphenated sense, as they also sidetrack media. Like their machinic milieu, these artworks are programmed time/space entities that in principle can run endlessly across the mediascape. They foreground the character of social media; how social media has become an environment and an infrastructure for the production of subjects.

Big Tech has become a quasiorganism interacting with and controlling its environment through feedback mechanisms, deploying a new type of power technique, philosopher Erich Hörl calls "environmentalitarian."[55] It consists of a global network of intelligent media that monitor and regulate a machinic milieu which offers users a "free" way to connect via smartphones and social media. Citizens are programmed by the logic of the strict market-oriented rationality of "cybernetic capitalism" where users can play and "like" uninhibitedly on a sexy application surface.[56] Arcangel's bots merge with this flow-environment, but it is never a complete amalgamation. They get entangled in it, but without sharing its path; they sidetrack it or walk along a side path, like a "burlesque poem," a *parōidia*, from *para-* "beside" (expressing alteration) and *ōidē* "ode"; they are flow-parodies. A parody is a work or performance that imitates another work or performance with ridicule or irony. As artworks they sing a strange song of detachment and withdrawal, breaching the rules of the game or playing chess where one is not supposed to play chess. They gamify to *ungamify* the platforms, wild bots, trackable but without profitable meaning. They denude the web's enchantment and can knock down its modes of capture. Implicitly, they ask a series of unpleasant questions that make the dream of the perfect connection to the machine appear both stupid and undesirable.

CONCLUSION

The Hack as Social Invention

"You always hope there is more but maybe even I sometimes hope there is less, because if there is nothing, there is even more. Do you understand what I mean?"
—Cory Arcangel[1]

The Cory Arcangel hack examines the forces, flows, and rhythms operating within a machinic milieu. It is precise, targeting just a fragment of a larger eco-operational territory. In the introduction, I called Arcangel the "mechanologist," envisioned by Gilbert Simondon, who explores how humans and machines converge and individuate into new technical milieus. However, unlike Simondon, who focuses on evolution, resolution, and adoption, Arcangel's work instigates anomalies, failures, disequilibrium, and maladaptation. His hack draws upon the energy of confrontation, contempt, and humor inherited from Duchamp and the avant-garde tradition, to explore a diverse array of flow-cut arrangements within a new machinic milieu.

Arcangel reconnects the art world to a contemporary condition that is often ignored or avoided in mainstream art. However, instead of ridiculing the art world as a "white cube" isolated from broader realities, he maintains faith in the art exhibition as an "other place" or heterotopia, a space that offers a unique vantage point from which to interrogate and engage with the world in novel and transformative ways.[2] The exhibition space becomes a site for dissecting and isolating flows lifted from their eco-operational environment governed by the laws of Big Tech, to reexamine them. Arcangel revitalizes the question: What can art do to a body of flows? While similar explorations have been undertaken by many artists before him, Arcangel employs different methods, "sculpting" videos with bots, code, and graphics ripped from a toxic media ecology. Drawing on the avant-garde tradition as a toolbox, his flow-cut arrangements liberate matters of expression—often in fun and gimmicky ways—where the forces and energies between media systems and the art world are renegotiated.

RESISTANCE

Arcangel's art engages with the habitual ways in which human expressions and sense-perceptions (*aisthesis*) are facilitated, shaped, and captured by processes of infrastructuration implemented in interfaces, affordances, software, algorithms, and larger systems. He challenges the efficacy of media systems. His cuts and modifications playfully de-express expressions, de-control control, and de-participate participation. They create meaning through non-sense, in the double meaning of "sense," which encompasses both the exploration of new sensory compositions and the development of novel forms of knowledge with and through machines.[3] Sense perception, and sense-ability takes place with machines and the machinic. The Cory Arcangel hack creates fuzzy aggregates, introducing unpredictability and ambiguity into elements from a system, not seamless extensions of human capabilities where a rational unity, a human being, somehow stands outside the extension and controls it, but an arrangement where every part of it, whether it is a human or nonhuman component, redefines both what is inside and outside the arrangement. Is this also a wild withdrawal from any system?

In their essay "Compression in Philosophy," Alexander R. Galloway and Jason R. LaRivière view Arcangel's work as both a withdrawal and as a critical intervention in the contemporary mode of production:

By putting a conceptual frame around the readymade processes of digital production so prevalent today, by simply leaving be, Arcangel is able to effectively represent the informatic milieu of post-Internet art, rendering a critical intervention into contemporary modes of production—critical in its very withdrawal from expression.[4]

What kind of withdrawal is this? They associate Arcangel's withdrawal from expression with the attitude of Herman Melville's fictional antihero in the short story "Bartleby, the Scrivener" (1853). When asked by his superior to execute a task, Bartleby always answers, "I would prefer not to." His withdrawal from carrying out orders is interpreted by Galloway and LaRivière as a "productive unworking," "a positive tactic."[5] They compare his strategy to the "No demands!" strategy of the global Occupy movement.[6] From the command-and-control imperative of state bureaucracy, Big Tech platforms, and commodity capitalism, Bartleby's response, like Arcangel's one thousand minor machines, appear dysfunctional. Their opacity leaves no clear identity markers for the system. However, their attitude also "reveals the basic insufficiency and indistinction of the real phenomena of everyday life."[7] The media of big corporations want everybody to "express themselves" through processes of sharing and liking, but the expressive affordances they offer only allows for an extremely limited and reduced version of life to be expressed, unable to capture what living is like for most people.

As capitalism is extremely adept at subsuming nearly all criticisms of its machinations into the logic of capital itself, "what remains irrecuperable is the 'absolute indifference' of unemployed negativity," write Galloway and LaRivière.[8] Bartleby's and Arcangel's micropolitical withdrawal implicitly *unworks* or challenges systems of power not through direct opposition but by stepping outside the rules of engagement. Their resistance is a tactical response in need of interpretation. Galloway and LaRivière rely on philosopher Giorgio Agamben's reading of Bartleby. "Bartleby's opaque indifference to work and his refusal to order the real make him an ideal model for withdrawal from the representational contract. Through a kind of productive unworking, Bartleby gestures toward new forms of life and revitalized potentials for living in community," Agamben writes.[9] To him, withdrawal and unworking may imply a new beginning, the "potentiality" to become something new, and to claim "impotentiality" with regards to a working system that tries to control and benefit from the work of its members.[10]

Arcangel's "simply *leaving be*," inherited from Bartleby, erects "inexpressible" machines, disconnected and stupid. They turn the striated spaces of cybernetic capitalism into a folly. He consistently redirects the flows of industrial media into the dysfunctional and unplayable (computer games), the useless (as in his search engine *Dooogle*), the crash (*Permanent Vacation*), a reassembled collectivity (*Paganini Caprice No. 5* and *Working on My Novel*), and the uncanny (*Century 21*). The works are not just relics but decomposed matter, a vast fallow land where potential resides in its impotentiality. The withdrawal of expression throws sand in the gears of the cybernetic machine.

A THOUSAND MINOR ECOLOGIES

Perhaps Arcangel's "dysfunctional" machines are reserves put on hold, awaiting an alternative sociality to come? A withdrawal of one type of expression is also an affirmative opening toward another; it can "take anything and make it into a matter of expression."[11] I paraphrase Deleuze and Guattari's vitalist approach to intervention from *A Thousand Plateaus*. Any withdrawal, any unworking, produces a matter of expression. Typically, it can invert qualities, make content a form or form a content, as the Cory Arcangel hack does in the schiz-image. Deleuze and Guattari explore this in relation to how interventions create a new milieu in a territory, where "expressive qualities or matters of expression enter into shifting relations with one another that 'express' the relation of the territory they draw to the interior milieu of impulses and exterior milieu of circumstances."[12] The intervention produces new movements in the world that builds a territory through hacks. The hacks are like "refrains" or building blocks that deterritorialize to build a new territory. Arcangel's aesthetics of breakthroughs and schizzes highlight the possibility of a techno-aesthetic heterogenesis where an unknown agency or matter-function begins to speak, to gather, to fathom.

The Cory Arcangel hack tampers with the flow-paths of electricity, not only in games and social media but in the playing subject itself and its relation to agency and change. It can replace an action- and goal-oriented instrumental attention that only wants to beat the game with a new social ontology, an open collective of modified agents which, in their nonstandard use, can be "object-comrades or coworkers of an emergent social order of human–thing relationality."[13] The hack shows what a host of tools and micromedia—microchips, EPROMs, ROM hacks, RAM hacks, API hacks, the Android Debug Bridge, Gould Pro tools, monkeyrunner tools, a TIVO-tool, coding, mods, platform hacks, stuttering affordances and feeds, and wild bots—can do. They introduce a swarm of reticular middles, changing our notions of mediation and bifurcation, and create so many "infuriation events," producing a new collectivity, a sociality, acephalous and energetic.[14] These are social inventions teaching us to reassemble and think the social in new ways.

Allied to the hacker ethic of sharing, Arcangel explores flow-cut arrangements that can open new and potentially collective flow-paths. Here's how I do it; here's my code: spread the word, change the subjects. This networking practice lays the foundation for new experiments and alternatives, new models of thought and imagination and, not the least, for a swarm of new hacks. The sharing of codes is both based on and creates a community of hackers, do-it-yourself carpenters, and artists. His hacks gain a potential life in other networks and on other premises outside the art world. The sharing culture of hackers is a countercultural gift economy in which gifts are shared in a "coming community," according to Wark's *A Hacker Manifesto*.[15] Arcangel's new flow-cut arrangements introduce new movements, sensations, and collectives, transcending the homogenizing effects of platform capitalism. A thousand minor ecologies multiply through a politics of distribution and sharing—and critique.[16]

His attention to the fact that the technology around us can be reprogrammed has urgency in an age where the protected mode of computer systems "guards the operating system from users."[17] We do not program anymore, we are programmed. Protected mode and black-boxed systems become habitual new media. "It is through habits that users become like their machines," claims media researcher Wendy Hui Kyong Chun.[18] The naturalization of media as something unprogrammable is a make-believe trap that can be circumvented through programming skills, can be changed, defunctionalized, short-circuited, and refunctionalized. The Cory Arcangel hack cracks the image of the "perfect" human/machine connection and suspends or interrupts the immediate sensorimotor

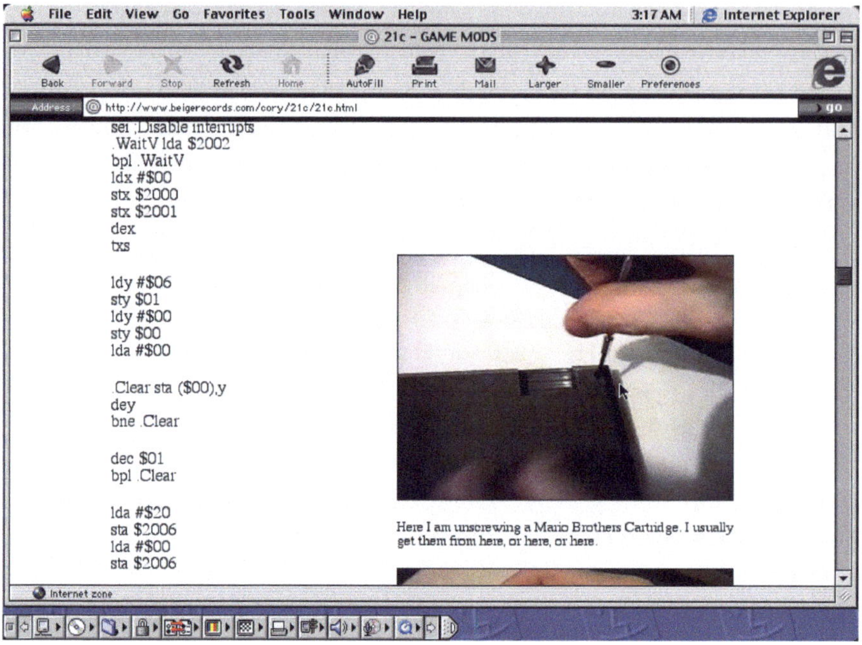

5.1

Cory Arcangel, *Super Mario Clouds* (Tutorial), 2002. Website tutorial. Photo by Cory Arcangel, courtesy of the artist. Historically accurate screenshot created using bwFLA, Emulation as a Service, University of Freiburg.

stimuli that locks the subject into a given flow-path. The deferral of action bifurcates the subject and puts it into a mode seeking out different actions challenging the narrow, efficiency-driven perspective of Big Tech. This can foster a more collective and collaborative rethinking of shared resources, spaces, and experiences. By cutting into and repurposing flows, the hack points to other arrangements beyond the docility of instrumentarian utilitarianism. Such reworkings of the commons could involve reimagining how we share and manage resources, how we build and sustain communities, and how we resist commodification and enclosure by focusing on collective and creative engagement.

The Cory Arcangel hack is an attempt at creating sites for thinking about and making alternative becomings. Critics and curators Tim Griffin and Lumi Tan write that Arcangel's radical do-it-yourself mix of old and new technologies "allows for an escape from and a distance to the totalizing and normalizing forces of any technological regime."[19] The hack, however minute, can enact a necessary alchemy—like homeopathy, altering a path just enough. Within the vast machinic milieu of cybernetic capitalism, there is always a remainder, an unused matter-function that the hack can leverage. In doing so, it can forge new alliances and connections, bringing forth visibilities and socialities that might otherwise remain unsensed, unseen, or unarticulated.

NOTES

INTRODUCTION

1. M. Wark, *A Hacker Manifesto* (Harvard University Press, 2004), paragraph 4.
2. While writing this book, I had a dozen conversations with Cory Arcangel, in person in both New York and Stavanger, Norway, and online, from 2019 to 2023. These conversations have been recorded and are collectively referred to as C. Arcangel in conversation with the author (digital recordings), 2019–2023.
3. Michele Thursz was director at the Moving Image Gallery, one of the first galleries to show contemporary artists using electronic and computer-based mediums.
4. Arcangel in conversation, 2019–2023.
5. They were artist Mark Napier; artist Yael Kanarek; Jacob Ciocci from Paper Rad; early new media sculptor, Michael Rees; artist and computer scientist at Harvard, Martin Wattenberg; artist-engineer Golan Levin, then an MIT graduate student; artist and critic Joseph Nechvatal; Ray Sweeten aka Carrier81; artist Andy Deck; composer Eve Beglarian (Arcangel was her assistant at the time); artist David Crawford; critic and founder of Art F City, Paddy Johnson; Public Lab aka Danny Comer; and artist Gearóid Dolan.
6. G. Deleuze and F. Guattari, *A Thousand Plateaus: Capitalism and Schizophrenia*, trans. B. Massumi (Les Éditions de Minuit, 1980; University of Minnesota Press, 1987). Citations refer to the University of Minnesota Press edition; B. Latour, *Reassembling the Social: An Introduction to Actor-Network-Theory* (Oxford University Press, 2005).
7. See Latour, *Reassembling the Social*, 150.
8. G. Simondon, *On the Mode of Existence of Technical Objects*, trans. C. Malaspina and J. Rogove (Editions Montaigne, 1958; University of Minnesota Press, 2017), 19. Citations refer to the University of Minnesota Press edition. Simondon writes, ". . . one must be capable of reintroducing an awareness of the nature of machines, of their mutual relations and of their relations with man, and of the values implied in these relations. This awareness requires the existence of a technologist or *mechanologist*." (Italics in original.)
9. O. Lialina, "Net Art Generations," from Lialina's website, *art.teleportacia.org*, 2007, updated November 19, 2013, http://art.teleportacia.org/observation/net_art_generations/.
10. C. Paul in conversation with the author (digital recording), New York, 2019.

11. Paper Rad was Jacob Ciocci, Ben Jones, and Jessica Ciocci.
12. C. Arcangel, "WTF," in *Seth Price: Social Synthetic*, edited by B. Ruf, A. Hochdörfer, and E. Banks (Walther Koenig Books, 2017).
13. At Migros Museum, Zurich in 2005.
14. Arcangel in conversation, 2019–2023.
15. Mugaas interview, quoted in D. Quaranta, *Beyond New Media Art* (Link Editions, 2013).
16. See W. Vasulka and P. Weibel, eds., *Buffalo Heads: Media Study, Media Practice, Media Pioneers, 1973–1990* (MIT Press, 2008).
17. Beige, "A Brief History of BEIGE," *Beige Records*, n.d., http://beigerecords.com/aboutus.html.
18. Beige, *Beige [Programming Ensemble]*, website, 2003, https://web.archive.org/web/20100106083300/post-data.org/beige.
19. Beige, "8-bit Construction Set," *Beige Records*, n.d., http://www.beigerecords.com/products/beg-004.html.
20. D. Quaranta, *In Your Computer* (Link Editions, 2010), 125–126.
21. C. Arcangel, "The Making of *Super Mario Clouds*," in *Cory Arcangel (Beige)*, ed. R. Gygax (Migros Museum für Gegenwartskunst and JRP Ringier, 2005).
22. Beige, *Deadtech*, website, June 4, 2001, http://www.epidemic.ws/biennale_press/deadtech.htm.
23. Radical Software Group, "Carnivore. Version 9," *RSG*, March 2024, http://r-s-g.org/carnivore/.
24. Radical Software Group and Beige Records, "Low Level All-Stars," *Rhizome Archive*, n.d., http://archive.rhizome.org/exhibition/Low_Level_All_Stars/.
25. C. Arcangel, "Recent Experiments in Modern Composition, Software, and Stand-Up Comedy," *The Art, Technology, and Culture Colloquium: UC Berkeley's Centre for New Media*, October 16, 2006, https://www.ghostriderrobot.com/bio/Cory_Arcangel/.
26. *Net Art Anthology* (Rhizome, 2019), https://anthology.rhizome.org/.
27. Arcangel explains and shows *Data Diaries* in C. Arcangel, "Digital Media Arts," lecture, Center for New Media Teaching and Learning, Columbia University, posted March 24, 2009 by Columbia University, YouTube, 1 hr., 10 min., 16 sec., https://www.youtube.com/watch?v=ZzHq7PzQWEE.
28. Arcangel, "Digital Media Arts."
29. A. R. Galloway, "*Data Diaries*: Description," Rhizome ArtBase, June 3, 2005, https://artbase.rhizome.org/wiki/Q4007.
30. N. Thrift, "Remembering the Technological Unconscious by Foregrounding Knowledges of Position." *Environment and Planning D: Society and Space* 22, no. 1 (2004): 176, https://doi.org/10.1068/d321t.
31. Thrift, "Remembering the Technological Unconscious," 176.

32. Thrift, "Remembering the Technological Unconscious," 176.

33. Thrift, "Remembering the Technological Unconscious," 176.

34. S. Price, *Dispersion* (Seth Price, 2002), https://anthology.rhizome.org/dispersion and http://sethpricestudio.com/writingarchive/DIspersion.pdf.

35. Deleuze and Guattari, *A Thousand Plateaus*, 105 (and Deleuze and Guattari 1980: 133). On the term "minor" and "outsystem": B. W. Joseph, *Beyond the Dream Syndicate: Tony Conrad and the Arts after Cage* (Zone Books, 2008), 50, connects "minor history" to avant-garde movements from the 1960s and Tony Conrad's work, in particular. It is explicitly inspired by Mike Kelley's use of the term "minor history" in M. Kelley, *Minor Histories: Statements, Conversations, Proposals* (MIT, 2004), alongside Deleuze and Guattari's "minor science" and "minor literature", as a framework to situate Conrad's various art collaborations during the 1960s. Deleuze and Guattari's special use of the term "minor" is developed in G. Deleuze and F. Guattari, *Kafka: Toward a Minor Literature*, trans. D. Polan (Les Éditions de Minuit, 1975; University of Minnesota Press, 1986) and *A Thousand Plateaus*. The notion of minor and minoritization has also been used extensively to describe hacking, see M. Fuller, *Media Ecologies: Materialist Energies in Art and Technoculture* (MIT Press, 2005) and media archaeologist J. Parikka, "Ethologies of Software Art: What Can a Digital Body of Code Do?" in *Deleuze and Contemporary Art*, ed. S. Zepke and S. O'Sullivan (Edinburgh University Press, 2010). Art historian and curator Andreas Broeckmann developed the term "minor media" in his discussion of several types of new media art in A. Broeckmann, "Minor Media—Heterogenic Machines: Heterogenic Machines: Notes on Félix Guattari's Conceptions of Art and New Media," *M/C Journal* 2, no. 6 (1999): https://doi.org/10.5204/mcj.1788.

36. C. Arcangel, "coming soon: ebay paypal blogs the internet," in *Mass Effect: Art and the Internet in the Twenty-First Century*, ed. L. Cornell and E. Halter (MIT Press, 2015), 17.

37. See https://rhizome.org/community/25381/ and https://en.wikipedia.org/wiki/2003_New_York_Underground_Film_Festival.

38. L. Cornell and E. Halter, "Hard Reboot: An Introduction to *Mass Effect*," in *Mass Effect: Art and the Internet in the Twenty-First Century*, ed. L. Cornell and E. Halter (MIT Press, 2015), xix.

39. On B. W. Joseph, see note 35. With regards to Halter, I am thinking of his extensive activity as a film festival programmer, critic, curator, writer, and editor in New York, and especially Halter's interviews and conversations with Arcangel. See E. Halter, "Get It? An Interview with Cory Arcangel on Comedy," *Rhizome*, December 24, 2008, https://rhizome.org/editorial/2008/dec/24/get-it-an-interview-with-cory-arcangel-on-comedy/; L. Cornell and E. Halter, "Hard Reboot: An Introduction to Mass Effect"; and C. Arcangel, in conversation with E. Halter on Arcangel's work in connection with the release of *Source*, no. 10, Arcangel's studio, Stavanger, Norway, 2018, recorded, with permission, by A. Sunnanå.

40. A. Broeckmann, *The Machine Art in the Twentieth Century* (MIT Press, 2016).

41. C. A. Jones, *Machine in the Studio: Constructing the Postwar American Artist* (University of Chicago Press, 1996), 58.

42. C. Jones, "Trajectories of the Studio after the Factory," lecture, Museum of Contemporary Art, Chicago, February 16, 2010, audio recording, 1 hr., 4 min., 4 sec., https://mcachicago.org/Publications/Audio/2010/Caroline-Jones-Trajectories-Of-The-Studio-After-The-Factory.

43. I. Blom, *The Autobiography of Video: The Life and Times of a Memory Technology* (Sternberg Press, 2016), 28.

44. Blom, *The Autobiography of Video*, 10, 13, 16, 24.

45. On how media harnesses and dissolves memory, see also E. Røssaak, "Capturing Life: Biopolitics, Social Media, and Romantic Irony," in *Writing and Unwriting (Media) Art History: Erkki Kurenniemi in 2048*, ed. J. Krysa and J. Parikka (MIT Press, 2015); and I. Blom, T. Lundemo, and E. Røssaak, eds., *Memory in Motion: Archives, Technology, and the Social* (Amsterdam University Press, 2017), http://library.oapen.org/handle/20.500.12657/32015.

46. Blom, *The Autobiography of Video*, 12, 13, 15.

47. Blom, *The Autobiography of Video*, 14.

48. M. Lazzarato, *Videophilosophy: The Perception of Time in Post-Fordism*, ed. and trans. J. Hetrick (Columbia University Press, 2019).

49. Lazzarato, *Videophilosophy*, 15.

50. Lazzarato, *Videophilosophy*, 16.

51. Lazzarato, *Videophilosophy*, 10, 13, 16, and 24.

52. Arcangel in conversation, 2019–2023.

53. D. Gigliotti, "About Us," *Radical Software*, n.d., https://www.radicalsoftware.org/e/about.html.

54. "The Alternate Television Movement" was the title of their first special issue; see *Radical Software* 1, no. 1 (1970). On the "ability to self-cybernate," see P. Ryan, "Three Pieces: Some Explication," *Radical Software* 1, no. 1 (1970): 13.

55. From the "Editorial" of *Radical Software* 1, no. 1 (1970).

56. A. R. Galloway in conversation with the author (digital recordings), New York, 2022.

57. T. Kukielski, "Doing Assembly: The Art of Cory Arcangel," in *Mass Effect: Art and the Internet in the Twenty-First Century*, ed. L. Cornell and E. Halter (MIT Press, 2015).

58. D. Birnbaum and C. Arcangel, "In Conversation," *ArtForum* 47, no. 7 (2009). https://www.artforum.com/print/200903/in-conversation-dara-birnbaum-and-cory-arcangel-22117.

59. Birnbaum and Arcangel, "In Conversation."

60. Deleuze and Guattari, *A Thousand Plateaus*; W. Ernst, *Digital Memory and the Archive*, ed. J. Parikka (University of Minnesota Press, 2012). More on this relationship in chapter 1.

61. The term "eco-operational" is inspired by Aurora Hoel's readings of Gilbert Simondon; see A. S. A. Hoel, "Technicity and the Virtual," *Humanities* 11, no. 6 (2022): 135, https://doi.org/10.3390/h11060135.

CHAPTER 1

1. G. Deleuze, "Sur Leibniz," lecture, University of Paris 8, Vincennes-Saint-Denis, April 15, 1980, posted April 25, 2019, by Webdeleuze, Web Deleuze and YouTube, 2 hr., 3 min., 40 sec., https://www.webdeleuze.com/textes/50.
2. M. Castells, *The Rise of the Network Society*, 2nd ed. (Wiley Blackwell, 2010), 442.
3. N. Bourriaud, *Postproduction: Culture as Screenplay: How Art Reprograms the World*, 2nd ed., trans. J. Herman (Lukas & Sternberg, 2005), 9, 13, 76.
4. Bourriaud, *Postproduction*, 69.
5. P. LeMieux, "Aftermarket, a Game Design Philosophy" (PhD diss., Duke University, 2015), 104, 115, https://hdl.handle.net/10161/10520.
6. P. LeMieux, "Everything but the Clouds," Platform Games at Babycastles, video essay, posted November 8, 2017, Vimeo, 19 min., 44 sec., https://vimeo.com/241966869. This controversy will be discussed more fully in chapter 2.
7. In C. Arcangel, *Drei Klavierstücke op. 11*, 2009, three YouTube videos, https://coryarcangel.com/things-i-made/2009-003-dreiklavierstucke-op-11.
8. B. Sterling, *The Hacker Crackdown: Law and Disorder on the Electronic Frontier* (Bantam, 1992), 51.
9. S. Levy, *Hackers: Heroes of the Computer Revolution* (Penguin, 1994), 7.
10. A. R. Galloway, "Two Statements on Carnivore," in *Mass Effect: Art and the Internet in the Twenty-First Century*, ed. L. Cornell and E. Halter (MIT Press, 2015), 70.
11. M. Mehta, "White Hat Hacker vs Black Hat Hacker—What's the Difference?," *InfoSec Insights*, December 17, 2020, https://sectigostore.com/blog/white-hat-hacker-vs-black-hat-hacker/.
12. See Levy, *Hackers*.
13. Times Square Arts, "Cory Arcangel: Another Romp Thru the IP (Times Square Edit)," *Times Square Official Website*, 2022, https://www.timessquarenyc.org/tsq-arts-projects/another-romp-thru-the-ip-times-square-edit 2022.
14. Arcangel and Oliana published a joint catalogue of their tour, and the exhibition with Jodi was at Lisson Gallery: https://www.lissongallery.com/news/cory-arcangel-and-jodi-s-feedback-loop-independent. See C. Jones, ed., *Cory Arcangel & Olia Lialina: Asymmetrical Response* (Walther Koenig Books, 2018).
15. C. Arcangel, "coming soon: ebay paypal blogs the internet," in *Mass Effect: Art and the Internet in the Twenty-First Century*, ed. L. Cornell and E. Halter (MIT Press, 2015).
16. O. Lialina and D. Espenschied, "Net Art Anthology: *One Terrabyte of Kilobyte Age*," *Net Art Anthology* and *Rhizome*, 2019, 295, also available online at https://anthology.rhizome.org/one-terabyte-of-kilobyte-age.

17. Archive Team, "GeoCities," last modified April 25, 2024, 00:08 (UTC), https://wiki.archiveteam.org/index.php/GeoCities.

18. Here, "interactivity" refers to the playability of a video game, and not to Stuart Card and T. P. Moran's human processor model where all human and machinic symbolic information-processing, and all rational goal-directed behavior, is "interactive."

19. A. R. Galloway, *Gaming: Essays on Algorithmic Culture* (University of Minnesota Press, 2006).

20. In C. Arcangel, "Cory Arcangel Doesn't Even Like Super Mario Brothers," interview by E. Salvaggio, *Turbulence.org*, April 2003, https://web.archive.org/web/20220303103319/http://turbulence.org/Works/curators/salvaggio/arcangel.html.

21. Cf. J. Huizinga, *Homo Ludens: A Study of the Play-Element of Culture* (Wolters-Noordhoff, 1938; Routledge & Kegan Paul, 1949).

22. C. Pias, "Computer Spiel Welten" (PhD diss., Bauhaus-Universität Weimar, 2000), 6, https://e-pub.uni-weimar.de/opus4/frontdoor/index/index/docId/35, my translation. Pias refers to Max Bense, "Kybernetik oder Die Metatechnik einer Maschine", in *Ausgewählte Schriften* 2 (1998): 429–446.

23. Pias, "Computer Spiel Welten," 6, my translation.

24. Games as tools for testing computer systems is discussed by many. See Levy, *Hackers*, 61; Pias, "Computer Spiel Welten"; C. Pias, "The Game Player's Duty: The User as the Gestalt of the Ports," in *Media Archaeology: Approaches, Applications, and Implications*, ed. E. Huhtamo and J. Parikka (University of California Press, 2011); M. Fuller, *Behind the Blip: Essays on the Culture of Software* (Autonomedia, 2003), 13; and P. Crogan, *Gameplay Mode: War, Simulation, and Technoculture* (University of Minnesota Press, 2011). Pias's argument is related to cybernetics; he edited the papers from the Macy Conferences (1946–1953) https://www.diaphanes.com/titel/cybernetics-3301. Patrick Crogan's argument is related to video games as a war technology.

25. Fuller, *Behind the Blip*, 13.

26. Levy, *Hackers*.

27. D. Diederichsen and O. Etxeberria, "Cybernetics of the Poor," in *Cybernetics of the Poor*, eds. D. Diederichsen and O. Etxeberria (Sternberg Press, 2020), 208.

28. A. R. Galloway, "The Cybernetic Hypothesis," *Differences* 25, no. 1 (2014): 111, https://doi.org/10.1215/10407391-2420021.

29. Tiqqun, "L'Hypothèse cybernétique," *Tiqqun* 2 (October 2001): 44.

30. E. Hörl and N. F. Schott, "The Environmentalitarian Situation: Reflections on the Becoming-Environmental of Thinking, Power, and Capital," *Cultural Politics* 14, no. 2 (2018): https://doi.org/10.1215/17432197-6609046.

31. Tiqqun, "L'Hypothèse cybernétique," 42.

32. A. R. Galloway and E. Thacker, *The Exploit: A Theory of Networks* (University of Minnesota Press, 2007), 124. From a cybernetics perspective, systems are about controlling flows in an environment through recursive feedback mechanisms

based on the premise that to be in the world is to be interactive—life is interactive. "There is no such thing as a subject free from [environmental] interactions." (L. Busbea, *The Responsive Environment: Design, Aesthetics, and the Human in the 1970s* (University of Minnesota Press, 2020), 239).

33. Arcangel, *Drei Klavierstücke op. 11*.
34. D. Espenschied, "The Storage is You," preface to C. Arcangel, *The Source Digest* (Arcangel Surfware, 2016).
35. C. Arcangel, *The Source Digest* (Arcangel Surfware, 2016), 92.
36. G. Deleuze, *Difference and Repetition*, trans. P. Patton (Presses Universitaires de France, 1968; Columbia University Press, 1994), 208–209.
37. Many critics have commented upon this aspect in his art. Jacob Gaboury ("Tool Time: Cory Arcangel at The Whitney," *Rhizome*, June 21, 2011, https://rhizome.org/editorial/2011/jun/21/tool-time-cory-arcangel-whitney/) writes about how "the failure of art and technology" as a key topic in Arcangel's art gives a particular flavor to his aesthetics: "If the purpose of technology, broadly speaking, lies in its use-value, then it is his decided refusal of the kind of productive functionality that one expects from technical objects that makes many of the pieces on view [at Whitney, 2011] so frustrating."
38. M. Fuller and E. Weizman, *Investigative Aesthetics: Conflicts and Commons in the Politics of Truth* (Verso, 2021), 110–111.
39. Fuller and Weizman, *Investigative Aesthetics*, 110.
40. L. Manovich, *The Language of New Media* (MIT Press, 2001), 30.
41. T. D. Sampson, *Virality: Contagion Theory in the Age of Networks* (University of Minnesota Press, 2012), 40.
42. For instance, Tiqqun, "L'Hypothèse cybernétique"; Galloway and Thacker, *The Exploit*; and S. Zuboff, *The Age of Surveillance Capitalism: The Fight for a Human Future at the New Frontier of Power* (PublicAffairs, 2019).
43. Shannon Mattern addresses "infrastructural aesthetics" in art as a process to "make sense-able." (S. Mattern, "Sense-able Structures—Infrastructural Aesthetics," lecture, Poetics of Infrastructure conference, Vienna, December 13, 2014, posted June 18, 2015, by *Genealogy+Critique* (blog), G+C, 15 min., 59 sec., https://blog.genealogy-critique.net/essays/100/shannon-mattern-senseable-structures.) The connection between aesthetics and infrastructure is a long-standing topic in architecture and design history with roots in Vitruvius's *De Architectura* and extending through John Ruskin's writings on the built environment, culminating in key modern works like Henri Lefebvre's *The Production of Space* from 1974.
44. M. Lazzarato, *Puissances de L'invention: La Psychologie Économique de Gabriel Tarde contre L'économie Politique* (Les Empêcheurs de Penser en Rond, 2002) and T. Terranova, "Another Life: Social Cooperation and A-Organic Life," *Digithum*, no. 12 (May 2010), https://openaccess.uoc.edu/bitstream/10609/8817/1/n12-terranova eng.pdf, combine a microsociological and biotechnological approach to the power of social invention.

45. F. A. Kittler, *The Truth of the Technological World: Essays on the Genealogy of Presence*, trans. E. Butler (Stanford University Press, 2014), 212.

46. D. A. Norman, "Why Interfaces Don't Work," in *The Art of Human–Computer Interface Design*, ed. B. Laurel (Addison-Wesley, 1990), 218.

47. O. Lialina, "Asymmetrical Response Reader," in *Cory Arcangel & Olia Lialina: Asymmetrical Response*, ed. C. Jones, text by T. Griffin, C. Jones, and L. Tan (Walther Koenig Books, 2018).

48. R. Williams, *Television: Technology and Cultural Form.* 3rd ed. Routledge, 2003.

49. Hacks play with what military systems manuals call the C3I (command, control, communication, and intelligence).

50. M. Wark, *A Hacker Manifesto* (Harvard University Press, 2004), paragraph 4.

51. Manovich, *The Language of New Media*, and M. B. N. Hansen, *New Philosophy for New Media* (MIT Press, 2004).

52. Galloway, *Gaming*; M. Fuller, *Behind the Blip*; Fuller, *Media Ecologies: Materialist Energies in Art and Technoculture* (MIT Press, 2005); Wark, *A Hacker Manifesto*; W. Ernst, *Medium Foucault: Weimarer Vorlesungen über Archive, Archäologie, Monumente und Medien* (VDG, 2000); W. Ernst, *Das Rumoren der Archive: Ordnung aus Unordnung* (Merve, 2002); Lazzarato, *Puissances de L'invention* (Les Empêcheurs de penser en rond, 2002); T. Terranova, *Network Culture: Politics for the Information Age* (Pluto Press, 2004); I. Blom, *On the Style Site: Art, Sociality, and Media Culture* (Sternberg Press, 2007); and B. Latour, *Reassembling the Social: An Introduction to Actor-Network-Theory* (Oxford University Press, 2005). During most of these early years, I was an active participant in the research projects *Media Aesthetics* and *The Archive in Motion*, which included a semester at NYU in 2007 as a visiting scholar. The projects were based out of the University of Oslo between 2003–2015 and involved, among others, art historian Ina Blom and media scholars Trond Lundemo and Susanne Østby Sæther. I worked in particular on speed relations in moving image works; see E. Røssaak, "Negotiating Immobility: The Moving Image and the Arts" (PhD diss., Department of Media and Communication, University of Oslo, 2008); and E. Røssaak, *The Still/Moving Image: Cinema and the Arts* (Lambert Academic Publishing, 2010). Our joint anthologies—E. Røssaak, ed., *Between Stillness and Motion: Film, Photography, Algorithms* (Amsterdam University Press, 2011), https://library.oapen.org/bitstream/handle/20.500.12657/34455/1/431802.pdf; L. Hausken, ed., *Thinking Media Aesthetics: Media Studies, Film Studies and the Arts* (Peter Lang, 2013); and I. Blom, T. Lundemo, and E. Røssaak, eds., *Memory in Motion: Archives, Technology, and the Social* (Amsterdam University Press, 2017) http://library.oapen.org/handle/20.500.12657/32015—featured contributions from, among others, Alexander Galloway, Wolfgang Ernst, W. J. T. Mitchell, Samuel Weber, D. N. Rodowick, Mary Ann Doane, Tom Gunning, Mark B. N. Hansen, George Baker, Thomas Elsaesser, Matthew Fuller, Jussi Parikka, Tiziana Terranova, and Yuk Hui, and sought to bridge the gaps between media philosophy, media aesthetics, and media archaeology through attentive readings of contemporary art and media strategies, not unlike the current book.

53. G. Deleuze and F. Guattari, *Anti-Oedipus: Capitalism and Schizophrenia*, Eng. ed. (University of Minnesota Press, 1983); G. Deleuze and F. Guattari, *A Thousand Plateaus: Capitalism and Schizophrenia*, trans. B. Massumi (Les Éditions de Minuit, 1980; University of Minnesota Press, 1987). Citations refer to the University of Minnesota Press edition.

54. Deleuze and Guattari, *Anti-Oedipus*, 262. Deleuze and Guattari's "generalized theory of flows" is most explicit in Deleuze and Guattari, *Anti-Oedipus*, and continued in Deleuze and Guattari, *A Thousand Plateaus*; F. Guattari, *The Anti-Oedipus Papers*, ed. S. Nadaud, trans. K. Gotman (Semiotext(e), 2006); and in several of Deleuze's lectures. Only a few scholars have highlighted "flow" as a key notion in their assemblage theory, but they have largely disregarded its artistic and aesthetic applications; see D. W. Smith, "Flow, Code and Stock: A Note on Deleuze's Political Philosophy," suppl., *Deleuze Studies* 5 (November 2011): 36–55, https://doi.org/10.3366/dls.2011.0036; and I. Buchanan, "Flow and Resistance," lecture at the Seminar of Aesthetics, University of Oslo, April 13, 2023

55. D. N. Smith, "What is Called Rhythm?," in *Critical Rhythm: The Poetics of a Literary Life Form*, ed. B. Glaser and J. Culler (Fordham University Press, 2019), 44. Here, rhythm also means "articulating, impressing, structuring, and forming," which again resonates with Deleuze and Guattari's notion of *agencement*, assemblage, and arrangement.

56. This is a topic across their work, see Deleuze and Guattari, *Anti-Oedipus*; G. Deleuze and F. Guattari, *Kafka: Toward a Minor Literature*, trans. D. Polan (Les Éditions de Minuit, 1975; University of Minnesota Press, 1986). Citations refer to the University of Minnesota Press edition; Deleuze and Guattari, *A Thousand Plateaus*; and G. Deleuze, *Foucault*, trans. S. Hand (Les Éditions de Minuit, 1986; University of Minnesota Press, 1988). Citations refer to the University of Minnesota Press edition; G. Deleuze, *Cinema 2: The Time-Image*, trans. H. Tomlinson and R. Galeta (Les Éditions de Minuit, 1986; University of Minnesota Press, 1989). Citations refer to the University of Minnesota Press edition; and G. Deleuze, "Postscript on Control Societies," in *Negotiations, 1972–1990*, trans. M. Joughin (*L'Autre Journal* 1 (May 1990); Columbia University Press, 1995).

57. These art strategies are discussed in Deleuze and Guattari, *Anti-Oedipus*. The disagreements between M. Carrouges (*Les machines célibataires* (Arcanes, 1954; Chêne 1976)) and Deleuze on these art forms is a key topic in A. Larue, *Le Surréalisme de Duchamp à Deleuze* (Éditions Talus d'approche, 2003). The term "artmachine" is not from Deleuze and Guattari but rather is a term Anne Sauvagnargues, *Artmachines: Deleuze, Guattari, Simondon*, trans. S. Verderber and E. W. Holland (Edinburgh University Press, 2016), uses to describe their approach.

58. Deleuze and Guattari, *A Thousand Plateaus*, 411.

59. P. Pisters, "Deleuze's Metallurgic Machines," *Los Angeles Review of Books*, November 8, 2015, https://lareviewofbooks.org/article/deleuzes-metallurgic-machines/.

60. M. de Landa, "The Machinic Phylum," *V2*, 1997, https://v2.nl/articles/the-machinic-phylum.

61. G. Deleuze and T. Negri, "Control and Becoming," in *Negotiations, 1972–1990*, trans. M. Joughin (Columbia University Press, 1995), 175.

62. G. Deleuze and T. Negri, "Control and Becoming," 175.

63. Deleuze and Guattari mention several times how flows such as desire should be viewed as part of infrastructure, see Deleuze and Guattari, *Anti-Oedipus*, 63, 104, 118, 345, 348, 361, 379, 385n11.

64. I. Buchanan, *The Incomplete Project of Schizoanalysis: Collected Essays on Deleuze and Guattari* (Edinburgh University Press, 2021), 14. Many have viewed assemblage theory as a "machine theory," see H. Schmidgen, *Das Unbewußte der Maschinen. Konzeptionen des Psychischen bei Guattari, Deleuze und Lacan* (Wilhelm Fink Verlag, 1997); G. Raunig, *A Thousand Machines: A Concise Philosophy of the Machine as Social Movement*, trans. A. Derieg (Semiotext(e), 2010); M. Lazzarato, *Signs and Machines: Capitalism and the Production of Subjectivity*, trans. J. D. Jordan (Semiotext(e), 2014); and M. Fuller in conversation with the author (digital recording), web, 2023.

65. This is also a key topic in W. Ernst, *Technológos in Being: Radical Media Archaeology and the Computational Machine* (Bloomsbury, 2021) and J. Parikka, *A Geology of Media* (University of Minnesota Press, 2015).

66. Such as in books with titles like *The Art of Finding FLOW: How to Get in the Zone, Maintain Razor-Sharp Focus, and Improve Your Productivity and Performance at Will!*

67. M. Csikszentmihalyi, *Flow: The Psychology of Optimal Experience* (Harper Collins, 1990; Harper Perennial Modern Classics, 2008), 4. Citations refer to the Harper Perennial edition.

68. Csikszentmihalyi, *Flow*, 64.

69. Csikszentmihalyi, *Flow*, 91–92.

70. B. Soderman, *Against Flow: Video Games and the Flowing Subject* (MIT Press, 2021), 5–6.

71. Deleuze and Guattari, *A Thousand Plateaus*, 22–23.

72. F. Guattari, "In Flux: An Interview with Deleuze and Guattari," in *Chaosophy: Texts and Interviews 1972–1977*, new ed., ed. S. Lotringer (Semiotext(e), 2009), 73; Lazzarato, *Puissances de L'invention*.

73. Deleuze and Guattari, *A Thousand Plateaus*.

74. Several scholars have sought to establish a Deleuzian aesthetic from Deleuze and Guattari's machine theory (see S. Zepke and S. O'Sullivan, eds. *Deleuze and Contemporary Art* (Edinburgh University Press, 2010); J. H. Faris, *Uncommon Goods: Global Dimensions of the Readymade* (Intellect Books, 2013); Sauvagnargues, *Artmachines*). I tend to see their early machine theoretical aesthetics as different from the model they deploy in *What is Philosophy?* (1994), which is less machinic and more post-Kantian. In the latter work, an aesthetic domain is separated from science and philosophy to exclusively question sensations, percepts, and affects. This "boxing" of art and aesthetics is not present in their first three collaborative books.

75. Deleuze and Guattari, *Kafka*, 87, 81.

76. É. Alliez and A. Goffey, "Introduction," in *The Guattari Effect*, edited by E. Alliez and A. Goffey (Continuum, 2011), 11.

77. I. Buchanan, *Assemblage Theory and Method: An Introduction and Guide* (Bloomsbury, 2021), 27.

78. Deleuze and Guattari (*Anti-Oedipus*, *Kafka*, and *A Thousand Plateaus*) use the examples of Chaplin and Keaton's comedies, Kafka's narratives, Messiaen's music, and many others as examples of the minoritarian mode. Also, Deleuze's approach to Godard's cinema (*Cinema 2*) is similar.

79. In Deleuze and Guattari's work (*A Thousand Plateaus*), the term "vector" typically refers to a direction or trajectory of movement, often in a conceptual or abstract sense. It can represent the flow or movement of ideas, forces, or intensities within a system or across different domains. Vectors are used to describe the dynamic and nonlinear nature of processes, emphasizing the directional movement of change or transformation. They employ the concept of vectors to analyze various phenomena, including social dynamics, artistic creation, and philosophical concepts, highlighting the interconnectedness and flux inherent in complex systems.

80. The crucial French sentence—(G. Deleuze and F. Guattari, *L'Anti-Œdipe: Capitalisme et schizophrénie 1* (Les Éditions de Minuit, 1972): 45–46.)—is transformed in the English translation which disregards the cuts' medical connotation. "Elle fonctionne comme machine à couper le jambon: les coupures opèrent des prélèvements sur le flux associatif."—"It functions like a ham-slicing machine, removing portions from the associative flow" (Deleuze and Guattari, *Anti-Oedipus*, 36).

81. Deleuze and Guattari, *Kafka*.

82. Galloway writes, on Arcangel and Paper Rad's work, *Super Mario Movie* (2005), that "computer art is more like sculpture than like painting or video. In making the work computer artists actually fabricate the substrate of the medium, they don't apply things to surfaces or use prefab tools to move images on a screen. The code is the medium. So in writing code, and running it, the computer artist builds the work from the ground up. It's all math and electricity. To engineer the soundtrack, Cory pokes the audio registers on the NES's chip in specific frequencies. [. . .] To get the video, he writes hundreds of lines of code [. . .]. What appears on the screen is the image of pure data. It is, in a manner of speaking, what numbers look like (if they could). Translation: this is not video art. Maybe call it math art, geek art, whatever. The Mario Movie makes tedium profound, and the other way around." This text was published in a small book which was available at the *Super Mario Movie* show at Deitch Projects: https://deitch.com/archive/deitch-projects/exhibitions/super-mario-movie. The book also contained the source code of the work. A. R. Galloway, "Cory Arcangel (Beige) and Paper Rad," text from booklet/exhibition guide, *Super Mario Movie* show, Deitch Projects, text-file, C. Arcangel's private archive, 2005.

83. Deleuze and Guattari, *Anti-Oedipus*, 36 (italics in original).

84. Deleuze takes this from Henri Bergson and explains it in Deleuze, *Cinema 2*, and G. Deleuze, *Cinema 1: The Movement-Image*, trans. H. Tomlinson and B. Habberjam (Les Éditions de Minuit, 1983; University of Minnesota Press, 1986). Citations refer to the University of Minnesota Press edition.

85. Deleuze and Guattari, *Anti-Oedipus*, 36–41.

86. Arcangel's lecture performances are often about hacking, explicitly or implicitly. *Sans Simon* (2004) is a shadow play performance done in front of a projection of a Simon and Garfunkel video, where Arcangel uses his physical hands and body as an erasure tool or a default algorithm to erase Paul Simon from the screen. *Friendster Suicide* (2005) is a flow-break hack by proxy. He literally cancels his Friendster account during a performance happening at PS1 Contemporary Art Center in New York.

87. Williams, *Television*. For McLuhan's notion of media flow as an extension of man, see his *Understanding Media: The Extensions of Man* (McGraw-Hill, 1964).

88. Parikka, *A Geology of Media*.

89. Williams, *Television*, 89

90. Williams, *Television*, 86.

91. Cf. Manovich, *The Language of New Media*.

92. S. Zepke, *Art as Abstract Machine: Ontology and Aesthetics in Deleuze and Guattari* (Routledge, 2005), 125.

93. Deleuze and Guattari, *Anti-Oedipus*, 32.

94. Deleuze and Guattari (*A Thousand Plateaus*) discuss connections between these terms in chapter 10: "Becoming-Intense, Becoming-Animal, Becoming-Imperceptible." "Machinic-becomings" are discussed as strategies of liberation in F. Guattari, *The Three Ecologies*, trans. I. Pindar and P. Sutton (*New Formation*, no. 8, 1989; Athlone Press, 2000), 38. Citations refer to the Athlone Press edition.

95. Guattari, *The Three Ecologies*, 38.

96. In the chapter "1837: Of the Refrain" (Deleuze and Guattari, *A Thousand Plateaus*), the authors establish an ecological and ethological approach to transgressions and deterritorialization. It is an *ethology* (a branch of knowledge dealing with the human character) which here includes the formation and evolution of conditions and processes that give rise to different forms of organization and thoughts, such as the formation and evolution of concepts, especially in relation to media, technology, and culture. On ethologies of software, see J. Parikka, "Ethologies of Software Art: What Can a Digital Body of Code Do?" in *Deleuze and Contemporary Art*, ed. S. Zepke and S. O'Sullivan (Edinburgh University Press, 2010).

97. F. A. Kittler, *Gramophone, Film, Typewriter*, trans. G. Winthrop-Young and M. Wutz (Brinkmann & Bose, 1986; Stanford University Press, 1999), 5. Citations refer to the Stanford edition; and Ernst *Medium Foucault* and *Das Rumoren der Archive*.

98. Deleuze (*Foucault*) explicitly aligns his own theory with a version of Foucault's archaeology of knowledge. However, Deleuze and Guattari would never call "driving forces" the "arché" of culture. To them, forces are always multiple.

Nevertheless, it is fair to say that they did not approach technology with the finesse demonstrated in media archaeology.

99. Ernst discusses the notion of *arché* in *Das Rumoren der Archive* and *Technológos in Being*.

100. See Ernst, *Technológos in Being*; R. W. Gehl, *Reverse Engineering Social Media: Software, Culture, and Political Economy in New Media Capitalism* (Temple University Press, 2014).

101. Gehl, *Reverse Engineering Social Media*, 10.

102. Latour, *Reassembling the Social*, 71; Latour, *Reassembling the Social*, 11–12.

103. Latour, *Reassembling the Social*, 11–12.

104. Latour, *Reassembling the Social*, 159.

105. G. Simondon, *On the Mode of Existence of Technical Objects*, trans. C. Malaspina and J. Rogove (Editions Montaigne, 1958; University of Minnesota Press, 2017), 15. Citations refer to the University of Minnesota Press edition.

106. C. Bishop, "The Digital Divide: Contemporary Art and New Media," *ArtForum* (September 2012): 436, https://www.artforum.com/print/201207/digital-divide-contemporary-art-and-new-media-31944.

107. S. Cubitt and P. Thomas, "The New Materialism in Media Art History," in *Media Art: Towards a New Definition of Arts in the Age of Technology*, ed. V. Catricalà (Fondazione Mondo Digitale, 2015).

108. D. Quaranta, *Beyond New Media Art* (Link Editions, 2013), 237.

109. Quoted in S. Ngai, *Theory of the Gimmick: Aesthetic Judgment and Capitalist Form* (Harvard University Press, 2020), 47.

110. Ngai, *Theory of the Gimmick*, 47 (italics in original).

111. In Ngai *Theory of the Gimmick*, 47.

112. To be discussed in chapter 3.

113. C. Arcangel, *Personal Film*, 2008, 16mm film, 6 min., 15 sec., https://coryarcangel.com/things-i-made/2008-004-personal-film.

114. Ngai, *Theory of the Gimmick*, 1.

115. Ngai, *Theory of the Gimmick*, 3.

116. Explained in C. Arcangel, "Cory Arcangel," interview by M. Heilmann, *Interview*, March 21, 2011, https://www.interviewmagazine.com/art/cory-arcangel.

117. Ngai, *Theory of the Gimmick*, 3.

118. E. Halter, "Get It? An Interview with Cory Arcangel on Comedy," *Rhizome*, December 24, 2008, https://rhizome.org/editorial/2008/dec/24/get-it-an-interview-with-cory-arcangel-on-comedy/.

119. T. McCormack, "Cory Arcangel and New Media One-Liners," *Art21 Magazine*, June 10, 2011, https://magazine.art21.org/2011/06/10/cory-arcangel-and-new-media-one-liners/.

120. In McCormack, "Cory Arcangel and New Media One-Liners."

121. C. Arcangel, *Continuous Partial Awareness*, November 14, 2008, lecture-performance, 44 min., 4 sec., New Museum, Rhizome, New York, https://video.rhizome.org/w/dcf9D9ESAnSdJqicZNpx9K.

122. Arcangel, *Continuous Partial Awareness*.

123. Halter, "Get It?"

124. Halter, "Get It?"

125. The perspective is elaborated on in J. Zdebik, "Celluloid Film as Digital Art: Aesthetics of Translation, Information and Intermediality in the Works of Cory Arcangel," special issue, *Semiotic Review*, no. 3 (August 2017), https://web.archive.org/web/20190516231342/https://www.semioticreview.com/ojs/index.php/sr/article/view/36.

126. Quoted in Zdebik, "Celluloid Film as Digital Art."

127. Arcangel, *The Source Digest*, 46.

128. Thanks to Matthew Fuller for inspiring me to investigate what he called "misapplied transcoding" in one of our conversations.

129. Fuller, *Behind the Blip*, 43.

130. T. Gunning, "Buster Keaton: or The Work of Comedy in the Age of Mechanical Reproduction," *Cinéaste* 21, no. 3 (1995): 14, https://www.jstor.org/stable/41687377.

131. Gunning, "Buster Keaton," 14.

132. Fuller, *Behind the Blip*, 48.

133. Fuller, *Behind the Blip*, 48.

134. Fuller, *Behind the Blip*, 48.

135. Fuller, *Behind the Blip*, 48.

136. J. Sharp, *Works of Game: On the Aesthetics of Games and Art* (MIT Press, 2015).

137. It is a returning phrase in my conversations with C. Arcangel, 2019–2023.

138. Arcangel in conversation, 2019–2023.

CHAPTER 2

1. In C. Arcangel, "Cory Arcangel Doesn't Even Like Super Mario Brothers," interview by E. Salvaggio, *Turbulence.org*, April 2003, https://web.archive.org/web/20220303103319/http://turbulence.org/Works/curators/salvaggio/arcangel.html.

2. C. Arcangel, "Super Mario Clouds Online," *Cory's Web LOG*, 2002, https://web.archive.org/web/20021219121037/http://www.beigerecords.com/cory/21c/21c.html.

3. C. Arcangel, "The Making of *Super Mario Clouds*," in *Cory Arcangel (Beige)*, ed. R. Gygax (Migros Museum für Gegenwartskunst and JRP Ringier, 2005), 106.

4. Arcangel, "The Making of *Super Mario Clouds*," 106.

5. Arcangel, "Super Mario Clouds Online"; C. Arcangel, *Super Mario Clouds*, 2002, modded *Super Mario Bros.* cartridge, dimensions variable, https://coryarcangel.com/things-i-made/2002-001-super-mario-clouds.
6. The catalog for the show at Migros, München. See Arcangel, "The Making of *Super Mario Clouds*," 107.
7. P. LeMieux, "Everything but the Clouds," Platform Games at Babycastles, video essay, posted November 8, 2017, Vimeo, 19 min., 44 sec., https://vimeo.com/241966869.
8. C. Arcangel in conversation with the author (digital recordings), 2019–2023.
9. Arcangel in conversation, 2019–2023.
10. Arcangel, "The Making of *Super Mario Clouds*," 112.
11. Arcangel in conversation, 2019–2023.
12. Today, instructions on how to modify these games are more easily accessible: https://wiki.nesdev.com/w/index.php/Nesdev#6502 and https://wiki.nesdev.com/w/index.php/CHR_ROM_vs._CHR_RAM.
13. Arcangel's *I Shot Andy Warhol* (2002) was a graphics hack that left the program chip untouched. It kept the game's interactivity intact and is therefore a playable artwork. It is a mod of the one-shooter game Hogan's Alley, where the gangster characters were replaced with known figures such as Andy Warhol. *I Shot Andy Warhol* is installed as an interactive game with a gun. Players rack up points for zapping Warhol's mug while avoiding hits on the Pope, Flavor Flav, and Colonel Sanders.
14. A. Blance, "An Introduction to 6502 Assembly and Low-Level Programming!," *Medium*, July 21, 2020, https://codeburst.io/an-introduction-to-6502-assembly-and-low-level-programming-7c11fa6b9cb9.
15. Arcangel, "The Making of *Super Mario Clouds*," 110.
16. Arcangel, "The Making of *Super Mario Clouds*," 107.
17. Arcangel in conversation, 2019–2023.
18. Arcangel, "The Making of *Super Mario Clouds*," 109.
19. Arcangel, "The Making of *Super Mario Clouds*," 110.
20. Arcangel, "The Making of *Super Mario Clouds*," 109.
21. N. Altice, "The Art of Erasure: *Super Mario Clouds*," *Memory Insufficient: The Games History E-Zine*, no. 5 (August 2013), https://issuu.com/zoyastreet/docs/memory-insufficient-hardware; P. LeMieux, "Aftermarket, a Game Design Philosophy" (PhD diss., Duke University, 2015), https://hdl.handle.net/10161/10520; LeMieux, "Everything but the Clouds."
22. LeMieux, "Everything but the Clouds."
23. M. B. N. Hansen, *New Philosophy for New Media* (MIT Press, 2004), 8. Hansen's quote is in part a quote from the French engineer and media artist Edmond Couchot.
24. P. LeMieux, *Coin Heaven*, 2013, hacked ROM, custom cartridge, Nintendo Entertainment System, CRT TV, dimensions variable, http://patrick-lemieux.com/projects/Aftermarket/04.php.

25. LeMieux, "Everything but the Clouds."
26. LeMieux, "Everything but the Clouds."
27. LeMieux "Aftermarket, a Game Design Philosophy" and "Everything but the Clouds."
28. LeMieux, "Everything but the Clouds."
29. LeMieux, "Everything but the Clouds."
30. Arcangel in conversation, 2019–2023.
31. Arcangel in conversation, 2019–2023.
32. Arcangel in conversation, 2019–2023.
33. However, Tom Moody mistakenly writes in the same blog post (T. Moody, "Erasing the Clouds (and the Collective)," *Tom Moody* (blog), January 6, 2018, https://www.tommoody.us/archives/2018/01/06/erasing-the-clouds-and-the-collective/.) that Arcangel and his gallery at the time, Team Gallery, have "erased" Paul B. Davis as a possible cocreator of the work. This is not the case, as proven with Davis's failed legal complaint in 2021; see *Davis v. Arcangel, Civil Action No.: 1:21-cv-03663 United States District Court for the Eastern District of New York*. The matter has been solved amicably.
34. C. Fino-Radin, "Code, Conservation, and Truth," *Medium*, November 17, 2017, https://medium.com/@benfinoradin/code-conservation-and-truth-10cd5b59e0be.
35. Davis is quoted from *Davis v. Arcangel, Civil Action No.: 1:21-cv-03663 United States District Court for the Eastern District of New York.*
36. Davis quoted in *Davis v. Arcangel.*
37. B. W. Joseph, *Beyond the Dream Syndicate: Tony Conrad and the Arts after Cage* (Zone Books, 2008), 35–36.
38. E. L. Lohmeyer, "Unstable Aesthetics: The Game Engine and Art Modifications" (PhD diss., North Carolina State University, 2018), 14, http://www.lib.ncsu.edu/resolver/1840.20/35313. Lohmeyer claims that design historian John Sharp (*Works of Game: On the Aesthetics of Games and Art* (MIT Press, 2015)) wrote this, but since I cannot find the quote in Sharp's book, the claim is presumably Lohmeyer's.
39. Lohmeyer, "Unstable Aesthetics," 14.
40. J. Roberts, *The Intangibilities of Form: Skill and Deskilling in Art After the Readymade* (Verso, 2007), 181.
41. N. Bourriaud, *Relational Aesthetics* (Les presses du réel, 2002), 18, 19.
42. Roberts, *The Intangibilities of Form*, 165.
43. Roberts, *The Intangibilities of Form*, 184 (italics in original).
44. Roberts, *The Intangibilities of Form*, 184.
45. W. H. K. Chun, *Programmed Visions: Software and Memory* (MIT Press, 2011), 4.
46. Roberts, *The Intangibilities of Form*, 81–82; S. Ngai, *Theory of the Gimmick: Aesthetic Judgment and Capitalist Form* (Harvard University Press, 2020).

47. A. Royer, "The Urgent Need for Regulating Global Ghost Work." *Brookings* (February 9, 2021). https://www.brookings.edu/articles/the-urgent-need-for-regulating-global-ghost-work/.

48. M. Wark, *A Hacker Manifesto* (Harvard University Press, 2004), paragraphs 18, 137, 151, 296, 340.

49. G. Deleuze, *Cinema 2: The Time-Image*, trans. H. Tomlinson and R. Galeta (Les Éditions de Minuit, 1986; University of Minnesota Press, 1989). Citations refer to the University of Minnesota Press edition.

50. The term "a-signifying particles" is developed in Guattari's theory of the "machinic unconsciousness" and related to "machinic enunciation." The a-signifying particles operate as a "technological unconsciousness" and act directly on "infra-sensible, non-individuated qualities" and "components of subjectivity." See F. Guattari, *The Machinic Unconscious: Essays in Schizoanalysis*, trans. T. Adkins (Semiotext(e), 2010); M. Lazzarato, *Signs and Machines: Capitalism and the Production of Subjectivity*, trans. J. D. Jordan (Semiotext(e), 2014; and T. P. Keating, "On the Technological Unconscious: Thinking the (A)signifying Production of Subjects and Bodies with Sonographic Imaging," *Social & Cultural Geography* 24, no. 9 (2023): 1481–1500, https://doi.org/10.1080/14649365.2022.2083665.

51. See note 50.

52. Deleuze, *Cinema 2*, 23.

53. G. Deleuze, *Cinema 1: The Movement-Image*, trans. H. Tomlinson and B. Habberjam (Les Éditions de Minuit, 1983; University of Minnesota Press, 1986), iix. Citations refer to the University of Minnesota Press edition.

54. Deleuze, *Cinema 2*.

55. The three aspects of the time-image are summarized in Deleuze, *Cinema 2*, 22.

56. Deleuze, *Cinema 2*, 21.

57. G. Deleuze and F. Guattari, *Anti-Oedipus: Capitalism and Schizophrenia*, Eng. ed. (University of Minnesota Press, 1983).

58. Deleuze, *Cinema 1*, 109.

59. My term is also different from Stephen Zepke's term "schizo-image," which he uses once, to designate a "schizophrenic image" as a specific aspect of the affection-image happening outside "the sensorimotor interval in any-space-whatever" (S. Zepke, *Art as Abstract Machine: Ontology and Aesthetics in Deleuze and Guattari* (Routledge, 2005), 94). Furthermore, Zepke characterizes Deleuze's aesthetic as a search for a different time, "an ontogenetic vision of duration's construction/expression" and concludes: "Art would therefore share mysticism's task of finding new forms to express the fundamentally creative energy of life itself" (Zepke, *Art as Abstract Machine*, 97). My term, *schiz-image*, is primarily focused on techno-aesthetic concerns and does not delve into what Zepke describes as Deleuze's "materialist mysticism," (Zepke, *Art as Abstract Machine*, 54).

60. Deleuze, *Cinema 2*, 19.

61. C. Arcangel, in conversation with E. Halter on Arcangel's work in connection with the release of *Source*, no. 10, Arcangel's studio, Stavanger, Norway, 2018, recorded, with permission, by A. Sunnanå.

62. Described in M. Tribe and R. Grosenick, "Art in the Age of Digital Distribution," in *New Media Art*, ed. M. Tribe and U. Grosenick (Taschen, 2009), 28.

63. J. H. Faris, *Uncommon Goods: Global Dimensions of the Readymade* (Intellect Books, 2013).

64. Faris, *Uncommon Goods*, 8.

65. A term Ernst uses to describe artworks committed to media archaeology in practice: W. Ernst, *Technológos in Being: Radical Media Archaeology and the Computational Machine* (Bloomsbury, 2021).

66. Deleuze, *Cinema 2*, 173.

67. See Faris, *Uncommon Goods*; Hansen, *New Philosophy for New Media*; Wark, *A Hacker Manifesto*; W. Ernst, *Digital Memory and the Archive*, ed. J. Parikka (University of Minnesota Press, 2012); and Ernst, *Technológos in Being*.

68. D. J. Haraway, *Staying with the Trouble: Making Kin in the Chthulucene* (Duke University Press, 2016).

69. Hansen, *New Philosophy for New Media*, 254.

70. Hansen, *New Philosophy for New Media*, 260. I have proposed a different reading of Viola in E. Røssaak, "Affects and Medium: Re-imagining Media Differences Through Bill Viola's *The Quintet of the Astonished*," *New Review of Film and Television Studies* 7, no. 3 (2009): 339–352, https://doi.org/10.1080/17400300903047086.

71. Ernst, *Technológos in Being*, 3.

72. Ernst, *Technológos in Being*, 3.

73. Ernst, *Technológos in Being*, 22.

74. Wiener's notion of the time of nonreality is discussed in Ernst, *Technológos in Being*, 10 and C. Pias, "Time of Non-Reality: Miszellen zum Thema Zeit und Auflösung," in *Zeitkritische Medien*, ed. A. Volmar (Kulturverlag Kadmos, 2009).

75. Deleuze discusses "noosigns" as an image which goes beyond itself toward something that can only be thought, such as when confronting conjunctions of incommensurable images or sequences, and I add, incommensurable conjunctions of computational and cultural layers in works like *SMC*. See Deleuze, *Cinema 2*, 24, 278, 334.

76. Deleuze, *Cinema 2*, 181–182.

77. Deleuze, *Cinema 2*, 4.

78. Deleuze, *Cinema 2*, 181–182.

79. D. N. Rodowick, *Gilles Deleuze's Time Machine* (Duke University Press, 1997); K. Thiele, "'To Believe In This World, As It Is': Immanence and the Quest for Political Activism," suppl., *Deleuze Studies* 4 (November 2010): 28–45, https://doi.org/10.3366/dls.2010.0204.

80. Rodowick, *Gilles Deleuze's Time Machine*, 5. It is at this point where I disagree with Hansen's reading (*New Philosophy for New Media*) of Deleuze's time-image as simply pure disembodiment. It is not, and this is most visible where Deleuze connects the time-image with a belief in the world, which Rodowick develops as a production of new "cultural strategies for imagining and imaging the world." This implies the creation of a more complex body-assemblage with the visions and skills of, say, a hack.

81. Deleuze, *Cinema 2*, 5.

82. Deleuze, *Cinema 2*, 4.

83. See Harun Farocki's essay film, *Eye/Machine I-II* (Harun Farocki Filmproduktion, Berlin, 2001–2002).

84. E.g., as in works like *Boo-Yaa Counter: Carnivore Client* and the superimposed graphics in */roʊ ˈdeɪoʊ/ Let's Play: HOLLYWOOD.*

85. A. R. Galloway, *Gaming: Essays on Algorithmic Culture* (University of Minnesota Press, 2006), 112.

CHAPTER 3

1. P. Morley, "Reproduction," 3.

2. B. Raftery, "I'm Not Here to Make Friends: The Rise and Fall of the Supercut Video," *Wired*, August 30, 2018, https://www.wired.com/story/supercut-video-rise-and-fall/.

3. C. Arcangel, "Euro-Trance," *Artforum* 49, no. 10 (2011): https://www.artforum.com/columns/euro-trance-197652/.

4. The term "supercut" was coined by writer and net-culture observer Andy Baio in 2008. See Raftery, "I'm Not Here to Make Friends."

5. J. van Dijck, *The Culture of Connectivity: A Critical History of Social Media* (Oxford University Press, 2013), 110, https://doi.org/10.1093/acprof:oso/9780199970773.001.0001.

6. van Dijck, *The Culture of Connectivity*, 196 n1.

7. T. O'Reilly, "What Is Web 2.0," O'Reilly.com, September 30, 2005. https://www.oreilly.com/pub/a/web2/archive/what-is-web-20.html.

8. L. Manovich, "Remix Strategies in Social Media," in *The Routledge Companion to Remix Studies*, ed. E. Navas, O. Gallagher, and x. burrough (Routledge, 2015), 148.

9. Manovich, "Remix Strategies in Social Media," 136.

10. G. Gould, "The Prospects of Recording," in *Audio Culture: Reading in Modern Music*, ed. C. Cox and D. Warner (Continuum, 2004), 117.

11. Gould quoted in P. Morley, "Reproduction," in *A Couple Thousand Short Films About Glenn Gould: A Book in Relation to a Project of the Same Name by Cory Arcangel*, ed. S. Bode (Film and Video Umbrella, 2008), 214.

12. C. Shirky, *Here Comes Everybody: The Power of Organizing Without Organizations* (Penguin, 2008), xi.

13. A. Merrifield, "Here Comes Everybody: Joyce's Urban Chaosmos," *Antipode Online*, December 18, 2013, https://antipodeonline.org/2013/12/18/here-comes-everybody/.

14. His affirmative attitude would change later (more on this in the next chapter).

15. C. Arcangel, "Everybody Else," in *Digital Folklore: To Computer Users with Love and Respect*, ed. O. Lialina and D. Espenschied (Merz Akademie, 2009), 7.

16. Gould, "The Prospects of Recording," 125–126.

17. O. Lialina and D. Espenschied, "Do You Believe in Users?" in *Digital Folklore: To Computer Users with Love and Respect*, ed. O. Lialina and D. Espenschied (Merz Akademie, 2009), 11.

18. van Dijck, *The Culture of Connectivity*, 10.

19. D. Birnbaum and C. Arcangel, "In Conversation," *ArtForum* 47, no. 7 (2009). https://www.artforum.com/print/200903/in-conversation-dara-birnbaum-and-cory-arcangel-22117.

20. B. Latour, *Reassembling the Social: An Introduction to Actor-Network-Theory* (Oxford University Press, 2005).

21. Latour, *Reassembling the Social*, 257.

22. Web mining, text mining, and data mining have now become a standard operating procedure within digital humanities. The practices of net and computer artists can be viewed as both a supplement and perhaps an inspiration for certain techniques of visualization, cf. Galloway's early piece *StarryNight* (2000) which mapped the use and content of an online archive, Rhizome.org.

23. C. Arcangel in conversation with the author (digital recordings), 2019–2023.

24. Arcangel in conversation, 2019–2023.

25. A. Rice, "Does BuzzFeed Know the Secret?" *New York Magazine*, April 5, 2013, https://nymag.com/news/features/buzzfeed-2013-4/; T. Wu, *The Attention Merchants: The Epic Scramble to Get Inside Our Heads* (Knopf Doubleday, 2016).

26. See Wu, *The Attention Merchants* and Wikipedia, "Reblogging," last modified January 17, 2025, 07:52 (UTC), https://en.wikipedia.org/wiki/Reblogging.

27. Wu, *The Attention Merchants*, 281.

28. M. Fuller, *Media Ecologies: Materialist Energies in Art and Technoculture* (MIT Press, 2005), 174.

29. reBlog became a very popular tool among artists and bloggers. "One fundamental aspect that separates reBlog from other software that is used to simply steal peoples' [sic] content is that it always automatically attributes the original publisher with language and with hyperlinks," Eyebeam technical director Michael Frumin said (in M. Frumin, "Interview of Michael Frumin," interview by Regine, *We Mak$ $$ney Not Art* (blog), August 18, 2006, https://we-make-money-not-art.com/in_the_past_you/.). About the tool: http://www.reblog.org/.

30. In Frumin, "Interview of Michael Frumin."
31. J. Peretti, "My Nike Media Adventure," *The Nation*, March 22, 2001, https://www.thenation.com/article/archive/my-nike-media-adventure/.
32. J. Peretti, "Notes on Contagious Media," in *Structures of Participation in Digital Culture*, ed. J. Karaganis (Social Science Research Council, 2007); see also Wu, *The Attention Merchants*, 281.
33. Peretti, "Notes on Contagious Media."
34. Wikipedia, "BuzzFeed," last modified December 13, 2024, 08:33 (UTC), https://en.wikipedia.org/wiki/BuzzFeed.
35. Rice, "Does BuzzFeed Know the Secret?"
36. S. Houpt, "FrankenArt: The Mix and Mash Future," *The Globe and Mail*, May 15, 2004, https://www.theglobeandmail.com/arts/frankenart-the-mix-and-mash-future/article25679322/.
37. S. Campion, "Kurt Cobain's Suicide Letter vs. Google AdSense," *FutureLab*, November 2, 2006, https://www.futurelab.net/blog/2006/11/kurt-cobains-suicide-letter-vs-google-adsense/.
38. C. Arcangel, *Punk Rock 101*, 2006, website, https://coryarcangel.com/things-i-made/2006-012-punkrock-101.
39. A. W. Baker, "Punk Rock 101: An Example of Digital Art," *[av]brey winona*, October 4, 2017, https://aubreywbaker.wordpress.com/2017/10/04/punk-rock-101-an-example-of-digital-art/.
40. M. Olson, "Best of the Web 2006," *Rhizome Editorial*, January 3, 2007, https://rhizome.org/editorial/2007/jan/03/the-best-of-the-web-2006/.
41. Olson, "Best of the Web 2006."
42. Arcangel in conversation, 2019–2023.
43. Raftery, "I'm Not Here to Make Friends."
44. L. Dormehl, "YouTube Poop is Punk Rock for the Internet Age, and You Probably Don't Get It," *DigitalTrends.com*, March 30, 2019, https://www.digitaltrends.com/cool-tech/youtube-poop-worthy-respect/.
45. Dormehl, "YouTube Poop." Link to *TROLLOLOLOL*: https://www.youtube.com/watch?v=gwH8vo2H2ZY.
46. C. Arcangel, *A Couple Thousand Short Films About Glenn Gould*, 2007, dual channel video, https://coryarcangel.com/things-i-made/2007-006-a-couple-thousand-short-films-about-glenn-gould.
47. O. Goriunova, "Introduction," in *Fun and Software: Exploring Pleasure, Paradox and Pain in Computing*, ed. O. Goriunova (Bloomsbury, 2014), 3.
48. Goriunova, "Introduction," 4, 6.
49. S. Ngai, *Theory of the Gimmick: Aesthetic Judgment and Capitalist Form* (Harvard University Press, 2020), 3.
50. Ngai, *Theory of the Gimmick*, 2.

51. Ngai, *Theory of the Gimmick*, 4.

52. Ngai, *Theory of the Gimmick*, 3.

53. Ngai, *Theory of the Gimmick*, 1.

54. Ngai, *Theory of the Gimmick*, 1.

55. Ngai, *Theory of the Gimmick*, 90.

56. Ngai, *Theory of the Gimmick*, 4.

57. Ngai, *Theory of the Gimmick*, 4.

58. The score can be seen at MoMA, https://www.moma.org/collection/works/127629.

59. A video of the lecture-performance was borrowed from Arcangel's archive.

60. S. Reich, "Steve Reich Reflects on His Most Significant Works," interview by Shad, posted April 14, 2016, by Q on CBC, YouTube, 36 min., 47 sec., https://www.youtube.com/watch?v=yg7kKJsFpvc.

61. Latour, *Reassembling the Social*, 161.

62. R. Beato, "What Makes a Virtuoso?" video, posted June 12, 2018, by Rick Beato, YouTube, 7 min., 19 sec., https://www.youtube.com/watch?v=C8xhqxI8GHc.

63. S. Levy, *Hackers: Heroes of the Computer Revolution* (Penguin, 1994).

64. coryarcangel, "Gould-Pro," *GitHub*, 2007, https://github.com/coryarcangel/Gould-Pro.

65. coryarcangel, "Gould-Pro."

66. S. Bode, ed., *A Couple Thousand Short Films About Glenn Gould: A Book in Relation to a Project of the Same Name by Cory Arcangel* (Film and Video Umbrella, 2008).

67. Arcangel in M. Connor, "Interview with Cory Arcangel," in *A Couple Thousand Short Films About Glenn Gould: A Book in Relation to a Project of the Same Name by Cory Arcangel*, ed. S. Bode (Film and Video Umbrella, 2008), 245.

68. Gould, "The Prospects of Recording," 125–126.

69. Gould, "The Prospects of Recording," 125–126.

70. Gould quoted in Morley "Reproduction," 214.

71. T. Hecker, "Glenn Gould, the Vanishing Performer and the Ambivalence of the Studio," *Leonardo Music Journal* 18 (December 2008): 78, https://doi.org/10.1162/lmj.2008.18.77.

72. Gould's article "Let's ban applause!" was published in *Musical America* 82 (February 1962).

73. Gould, "The Prospects of Recording."

74. Gould, "The Prospects of Recording."

75. According to Hecker, "Glenn Gould," 77.

76. M. McLuhan, *Understanding Media: The Extensions of Man* (McGraw-Hill, 1964).

77. Quoted in Morley, "Reproduction," 241.

78. Gould cited in Hecker, "Glenn Gould," 78.

79. Interview no longer available online, but quote confirmed in conversation with Arcangel.

80. Morley, "Reproduction," 3.

81. Morley, "Reproduction," 3.

82. Arcangel, *A Couple Thousand Short Films About Glenn Gould*.

83. Jaimie Baron used the term "found collectivity" in this sense in an analysis of *The Mass Ornament* (J. Baron, "Subverted Intentions and the Potential for 'Found' Collectivity in Natalie Bookchin's Mass Ornament," *Maska: Performing Arts Journal* 26, nos. 143–144 (2011): 303–314, https://doi.org/10.17613/x34b-n904.).

84. N. Bookchin and B. Stimson, "Out in Public: Natalie Bookchin in Conversation with Blake Stimson," in *Video Vortex Reader II: Moving Images Beyond YouTube*, ed. G. Lovink and R. S. Miles (Institute of Network Cultures, 2011), 308.

85. N. Bookchin, "Dancing Machines: An Interview with Natalie Bookchin," interview by C. Kane, *Rhizome*, May 27, 2009, https://bookchin.net/wp-content/uploads/2015/09/2interview-Rhizome-Dancing-Machines.pdf.

86. W. H. K. Chun, *Updating to Remain the Same: Habitual New Media* (MIT Press, 2016), 99; Baron, "Subverted Intentions."

87. M. Kawabata, *Paganini: The "Demonic" Virtuoso* (Boydell Press, 2013).

88. The guitarists Yngwie Malmsteen, Jason Becker, and Steve Vai mention their fascination with Paganini in several interviews. See the discussion in Encyclopedia.com, S. Shelton, "Malmsteen, Yngwie," last modified January 8, 2025, https://www.encyclopedia.com/education/news-wires-white-papers-and-books/malmsteen-yngwie.

89. A. R. Galloway in conversation with the author (digital recordings), New York, 2019–2024.

90. However, even before YouTube, difficult-to-find VHS instructional videos by guitarists like Jason Becker, featuring performances of pieces like Caprice No. 5, were available. Becker's recording, released in 1987, is now on YouTube (https://www.youtube.com/watch?v=Zzf9-ruSl2s), but before that, magazines like *Guitar Player* would sell instructions.

91. Wikipedia, "Cross Road Blues," last modified January 9, 2025, 18:42 (UTC), https://en.wikipedia.org/wiki/Cross_Road_Blues.

92. Cf. "Steve Vai vs Ralph Macchio Epic Guitar Battle," https://www.youtube.com/watch?v=CqdL36VKbMQ.

93. Link at C. Arcangel, *Drei Klavierstücke op. 11*, 2009, three YouTube videos, https://coryarcangel.com/things-i-made/2009-003-dreiklavierstucke-op-11.

94. I. Blom, *The Autobiography of Video: The Life and Times of a Memory Technology* (Sternberg Press, 2016), 61. Brion Gysin and Ian Sommerville's *Dreamachine* (1959) is a classic example of an artistic exploration of stroboscopic effects to transform the subconscious into an open system. See https://www.youtube.com/watch?v=rJFgNMVePaQ&t=6s.

95. D. Diederichsen and O. Etxeberria, "Cybernetics of the Poor," in *Cybernetics of the Poor*, eds. D. Diederichsen and O. Etxeberria (Sternberg Press, 2020), 218.

96. G. Deleuze, "Postscript on Control Societies," in *Negotiations, 1972–1990*, trans. M. Joughin (*L'Autre Journal* 1 (May 1990); Columbia University Press, 1995): 180.

97. H. Steyerl, "In Defense of the Poor Image," *e-flux journal* no. 10 (November 2009), https://www.e-flux.com/journal/10/61362/in-defense-of-the-poor-image/.

98. F. Guattari, *The Three Ecologies*, trans. I. Pindar and P. Sutton (*New Formation*, no. 8, 1989; Athlone Press, 2000), 38. Citations refer to the Athlone Press edition.

99. G. Gould, "Glenn Gould on Animals," video, June 22, 2006, by michaeltravis, YouTube, 2 min., 22 sec., https://www.youtube.com/watch?v=57kR6RsV2iA.

100. G. Gould, "Full text of 'The Complete Music for Solo Piano,'" Glenn Gould's liner notes to Drei Klavierstücke, 1968, https://archive.org/stream/lp_the-complete-music-for-solo-piano_glenn-gould-arnold-schoenberg/lp_the-complete-music-for-solo-piano_glenn-gould-arnold-schoenberg_djvu.txt.

101. M. Jay, *The Dialectical Imagination: A History of the Frankfurt School and the Institute of Social Research, 1923–1950* (Little, Brown, 1973), 31.

102. Letter quoted in J. F. Boss, "'Away with Motivic Working?' Not So Fast: Motivic Processes in Schoenberg's op. 11, no. 3," *Music Theory Online* 21, no. 3 (2015), https://mtosmt.org/issues/mto.15.21.3/mto.15.21.3.boss.html.

103. Boss, "'Away with Motivic Working?' Not So Fast."

104. T. Adorno, *Philosophy of Modern Music* (Seabury Press, 1973), 40.

105. Adorno, *Philosophy of Modern Music*, 45.

106. Adorno, *Philosophy of Modern Music*.

107. S. Buck-Morss, *The Origin of Negative Dialetics: Theodor W. Adorno, Walter Benjamin, and the Frankfurt Institute* (Free Press, 1977), 5.

108. However, there is an error in the English translation of Adorno's *Philosophy of New Music* on this point: Drei Klavierstücke op. 11 is replaced with Six Little Piano Pieces op. 19. They are from the same period and both are based on free atonality, but the translation error is nevertheless odd. Cf. T. Adorno, *Philosophie der neuen Musik* (Verlag Ullstein, 1958), 40.

109. Adorno quoted in M. Paddison, *Adorno's Aesthetics of Music* (Cambridge University Press, 1993), 105.

110. Adorno seems, like Deleuze and Guattari, to deploy Freud's notion of the unconscious as not linked to a personal trauma but rather to a social, political, and aesthetic symptomatology, decipherable in art and inscribed with, for Deleuze and Guattari, the force of becomings.

111. Adorno, *Philosophy of Modern Music*, 35.

112. Paddison, *Adorno's Aesthetics of Music*, 75.

113. In Wikipedia, "*Europeras*," last modified August 13, 2019, 04:42 (UTC). https://en.wikipedia.org/wiki/Europeras.

114. Paddison, *Adorno's Aesthetics of Music*, 274.

115. Paddison, *Adorno's Aesthetics of Music*, 274.

116. Paddison, *Adorno's Aesthetics of Music*, 274–275.

117. M. MacDonald, *Schoenberg*, 2nd ed. (Oxford University Press, 2008), 9.

118. D. J. Haraway, *Staying with the Trouble: Making Kin in the Chthulucene* (Duke University Press, 2016).

119. A. Eysteinsson, "'What's the Difference?' Revisiting the Concepts of Modernism and the Avant-Garde." In *Europa! Europa? The Avant-Garde, Modernism and the Fate of a Continent*, edited by S. Bru, J. Baetens, B. Hjartarson, P. Nicholls, T. Ørum, and H. van den Berg (Berling: De Gruyter, 2009), 22.

120. Arcangel, *Drei Klavierstücke op. 11*.

121. Arcangel, *Drei Klavierstücke op. 11*.

122. This is how Arcangel presented his list with algorithmically interconnected links: "The Infinite Cat Project, Cats in Sinks, Cat in Fan, Ninja cat comes closer while not moving!, Smart Cat Open Door, Fat Cat VS Small Box, Pussy versus Printer, Edison's The Boxing Cats (Prof. Welton's), It's been a long day, Panta improvising on the piano featuring my cat (my personal favorite cat video), the Ultimate Canon Rock, Sopranos every profanity, The Big Lebowski—Every Single Fucking Dude, Marclay's "hello" supercut, 50 50s, Check out my new stereo—Extreme Bass! (also see Goldstein's "A Glass of Milk" here), Watching the Paint Dry (also see Burt Barr's Watching The Paint Dry series here), even Andy Eating a Hamburger, & Infinite Warhol (you might have noticed we are back 2 the beginning of this list)." Quoted from Arcangel, *Drei Klavierstücke op. 11*.

123. G. Deleuze and F. Guattari, *Anti-Oedipus: Capitalism and Schizophrenia*, Eng. ed. (University of Minnesota Press, 1983): 36–41.

124. Arcangel, *Drei Klavierstücke op. 11*.

125. Currently at https://www.comparisonics.com/.

126. Ngai, *Theory of the Gimmick*, 3. This argument follows Ngai's analysis of Duchamp's strategy of staging collisions between what is estimated in terms of time, value, and labor.

127. Cf. A. Galloway, "What You See Is What You Get?" in *The Archive in Motion: New Conceptions of the Archive in Contemporary Thought and New Media Practices*, ed. Røssaak (Novus Press, 2010), 174.

128. G. Deleuze and F. Guattari, *A Thousand Plateaus: Capitalism and Schizophrenia*, trans. B. Massumi (Les Éditions de Minuit, 1980; University of Minnesota Press, 1987), 312. Citations refer to the University of Minnesota Press edition.

129. Haraway, *Staying with the Trouble*, 12.

130. As of January 2025. See YouTube link at Arcangel, *Drei Klavierstücke op. 11*.

131. See YouTube link at Arcangel, *Drei Klavierstücke op. 11*.

132. See YouTube link at Arcangel, *Drei Klavierstücke op. 11*.

133. See YouTube link at Arcangel, *Drei Klavierstücke op. 11*.

134. See E. Navas, O. Gallagher, and x. burrough, eds., *Keywords in Remix Studies* (Routledge, 2017).

135. C. Arcangel, *Sorry I Haven't Posted*, 2010, website, https://coryarcangel.com/things-i-made/2010-020-sorry-i-havent-posted.

136. On "paraliterature," see E. Røssaak, *Sic: Fra litteraturens randsone* (Spartacus, 2001), and on "para-graphy," etc., see R. Barthes, *The Preparation of the Novel: Lecture Courses and Seminars at the Collège de France (1978–1979 and 1979–1980)*, trans. K. Briggs (Columbia University Press, 2011), 150.

137. These spiderbots and crawlers are also used by commercial search engines. See https://en.wikipedia.org/wiki/Internet_bot and https://en.wikipedia.org/wiki/Web_crawler.

138. In C. Arcangel, "Cory Arcangel Talks about His Exhibition at the Barbican," interview by A. T. Baker, *Artforum*, March 5, 2011, https://www.artforum.com/columns/cory-arcangel-talks-about-his-exhibition-at-the-barbican-196963/.

139. This intensive and ongoing capture of attention by media entertainment can also lead to what Deleuze and Guattari, *A Thousand Plateaus*, call "machinic enslavement" (*l'asservissement machinique*) and to "desubjectivation" (M. Lazzarato, *Signs and Machines: Capitalism and the Production of Subjectivity*, trans. J. D. Jordan (Semiotext(e), 2014), 12).

140. C. Arcangel, *Working on My Novel* (Penguin, 2014), unpaginated.

141. Sara Ahmed calls affects "sticky." They "sustain specific connections between ideas, values, and objects." S. Ahmed, "Happy Objects," in *The Affect Theory Reader*, edited by M. Gregg and G. J. Seigworth (Duke University Press, 2010), 29.

142. J. Jones, "A Novel about People Who Say They're Working on Novels? How Novel," *The Guardian*, July 31, 2014, https://www.theguardian.com/artanddesign/jonathanjonesblog/2014/jul/31/cory-arcangel-working-on-my-novel-twitter-book.

143. D. Piepenbring, "Working on My Novel," *The Paris Review*, July 28, 2014, https://www.theparisreview.org/blog/2014/07/28/working-on-my-novel/.

144. Arcangel, *Working on My Novel*.

145. Piepenbring, "Working on My Novel."

146. L. Benson, "Cory Arcangel's Monument to Digital Distraction," *Elephant*, October 17, 2019, https://elephant.art/cory-arcangel-working-on-my-novel/.

147. Quoted in F. Cramer and P. Jandrić, "Postdigital: A Term That Sucks but Is Useful," *Postdigital Science and Education* 3 (March 2021): 966–989, https://doi.org/10.1007/s42438-021-00225-9.

CHAPTER 4

1. J. Burnham, "Systems Esthetics," *Artforum* 7, no. 1 (Sep. 1968), https://monoskop.org/images/0/03/Burnham_Jack_1968_Systems_Esthetics_Artforum.pdf.

2. All the works are shown here: https://conifer.rhizome.org/cory_arcangel/century-21-linktree/list/home/b1/20220113134341/https://linktr.ee/century21.

3. Greene Naftali, "Cory Arcangel: Century 21," *Greene Naftali Gallery Viewing Room*, 2021, https://greenenaftaligallery-viewingroom.exhibit-e.art/viewing-room/cory-arcangel#tab:thumbnails.

4. On gamification, see P. Jagoda, *Network Aesthetics* (University of Chicago Press, 2016).

5. C. Arcangel, "Cory Arcangel Doesn't Even Like Super Mario Brothers," interview by E. Salvaggio, *Turbulence.org*, April 2003, https://web.archive.org/web/20220303103319/http://turbulence.org/Works/curators/salvaggio/arcangel.html.

6. On Arcangel's YouTube page: https://www.youtube.com/@coryarcangel

7. "monkeyrunner," *Android Developers*, last modified January 3, 2024, https://developer.android.com/studio/test/monkeyrunner.

8. P. Dockrill, "A Handful of Super-Corporations Control the Fate of the World, Chilling Report Shows," *Science Alert*, September 16, 2019, https://www.sciencealert.com/a-handful-of-super-corporations-controls-the-fate-of-the-world-scientists-warn.

9. Wikipedia, "*Elle* (magazine)," last modified January 5, 2025, 09:49 (UTC), https://en.wikipedia.org/wiki/Elle_(magazine).

10. Wikipedia, "Athabasca Oil Sands," last modified January 8, 2025, 19:07 (UTC), https://en.wikipedia.org/wiki/Athabasca_oil_sands.

11. Wikipedia, "Equinox Group," last modified December 6, 2024, 23:26 (UTC), https://en.wikipedia.org/wiki/Equinox_Group.

12. Wikipedia, "Morgan Stanley," last modified January 10, 2025, 17:39 (UTC), https://en.wikipedia.org/wiki/Morgan_Stanley.

13. R. Gomez, "The Importance of Social Media Marketing: 7 Stats that Prove Social's Role in Business Success," *Sprout Social*, September 18, 2023, https://sproutsocial.com/insights/importance-of-social-media-marketing-in-business/.

14. Gomez, "The Importance of Social Media Marketing."

15. Gomez, "The Importance of Social Media Marketing."

16. L. Cover, "7 Statistics That Prove the Importance of Social Media Marketing in Business," *Sprout Social*, June 17, 2021, http://19tamalvista.com/index-1558.html.

17. *The State of Social Media: After a Year of Transformation, Executives Are All-In on Social*, Sprout Social, 2021, https://sproutsocial.com/insights/data/future-of-business-intelligence/.

18. C. Gerlitz and A. Helmond, "The Like Economy: Social Buttons and the Data-Intensive Web," *New Media & Society* 15, no. 8 (2013): 1348–1365, https://doi.org/10.1177/1461444812472322.

19. S. Zuboff, *The Age of Surveillance Capitalism: The Fight for a Human Future at the New Frontier of Power* (PublicAffairs, 2019), 416.

20. E. Hörl, "A Thousand Ecologies: The Process of Cyberneticization and General Ecology," in *The Whole Earth: California and the Disappearance of the Outside*, ed.

D. Diederichsen and A. Franke (Sternberg Press, 2013). On the problematical absence of cybernetics in Zuboff, *The Age of Surveillance Capitalism*, see E. Røssaak, "Eivind Røssaak reviews The Age of Surveillance Capitalism," *Critical Inquiry* 47, no. 1 (2020), https://criticalinquiry.uchicago.edu/eivind_rssaak_reviews_the_age_of_surveillance_capitalism/.

21. D. Diederichsen and O. Etxeberria, "Cybernetics of the Poor," in *Cybernetics of the Poor*, eds. D. Diederichsen and O. Etxeberria (Sternberg Press, 2020), 208.

22. I. Arns and S. Sasse, "Subversive Affirmation: On Mimesis as a Strategy of Resistance," *Maska*, nos. 98–99 (Winter 2006): 162–181.

23. Arns and Sasse, "Subversive Affirmation."

24. S. Žižek, "Why Are Laibach and Neue Slowenische Kunst Not Fascists?" in *The Universal Exception: Selected Writings, Volume Two*, ed. R. Butler and S. Stephens (Continuum, 2006).

25. Arns and Sasse, "Subversive Affirmation," 444.

26. Arns and Sasse, "Subversive Affirmation," 444.

27. Arns and Sasse, "Subversive Affirmation," 452.

28. Arns and Sasse, "Subversive Affirmation," 452.

29. Arns and Sasse, "Subversive Affirmation," 445.

30. Arns and Sasse, "Subversive Affirmation," 446.

31. In S. Houpt, "FrankenArt: The Mix and Mash Future," *The Globe and Mail*, May 15, 2004, https://www.theglobeandmail.com/arts/frankenart-the-mix-and-mash-future/article25679322/.

32. G. Deleuze, *Difference and Repetition*, trans. P. Patton (Presses Universitaires de France, 1968; Columbia University Press, 1994), 230.

33. T. Gunning, "The Cinema of Attractions: Early Film, Its Spectator and the Avant-Garde," in *Early Cinema: Space, Frame, Narrative*, ed. T. Elsaesser and A. Barker (British Film Institute, 1990).

34. S. Kildall, "Readymake: Duchamp Chess Pieces (3D Recreations From Photographs)," *Autodesk Instructables*, n.d., https://www.instructables.com/Readymake-Duchamp-Chess-Pieces-3D-Recreations-from/.

35. C. Arcangel, */roʊˈdeɪoʊ/ Let's Play: HOLLYWOOD*, 2017–2021. https://coryarcangel.com/things-i-made/2017-006-rodeo-performance.

36. Subscrible, "The Rise and Fall of Kim Kardashian: Hollywood," *Subscrible* on LinkedIn, January 25, 2024, https://www.linkedin.com/pulse/rise-fall-kim-kardashian-hollywood-subscrible-mir4f.

37. C. Arcangel, "/roʊˈdeɪoʊ/," web-doc., */roʊˈdeɪoʊ/*, 2021, https://rodeo.computer/.

38. J. A. Tainter, *The Collapse of Complex Societies* (Cambridge University Press, 1990).

39. T. H. Schei, dir. *iHuman*. UpNorth, 2019.

40. See K. Hao, "The Facebook Whistleblower Says Its Algorithms Are Dangerous. Here's Why," *MIT Technology Review*, October 5, 2021, https://www.technologyreview.com/2021/10/05/1036519/facebook-whistleblower-frances-haugen-algorithms/.

41. Know Your Meme. "I Don't Know Who Needs to Hear This." *Know Your Meme*. Last modified February 22, 2021. https://knowyourmeme.com/memes/i-dont-know-who-needs-to-hear-this.

42. G. Deleuze and F. Guattari, *A Thousand Plateaus: Capitalism and Schizophrenia*, trans. B. Massumi (Les Éditions de Minuit, 1980; University of Minnesota Press, 1987), 75f. Citations refer to the University of Minnesota Press edition.

43. Deleuze and Guattari, *A Thousand Plateaus*, 76.

44. M. Lewis, "Has Anyone Seen the President?," *Bloomberg*, February 9, 2018, https://www.bloomberg.com/opinion/articles/2018-02-09/has-anyone-seen-the-president?leadSource=uverify%20wall.

45. M. Fried, *Art and Objecthood: Essays and Reviews* (University of Chicago Press, 1998), 43, 45.

46. F. Jameson, *Postmodernism, or, the Cultural Logic of Late Capitalism* (Duke University Press, 1991), 17.

47. Jameson, *Postmodernism*, 17.

48. W. Benjamin, "Theses on the Philosophy of History," in *Illuminations*, ed. H. Arendt (Schocken Books, 1968), 258.

49. D. Garfield, "Cory Arcangel's 'So Shines a Good Deed in a Weary World (dunkindonuts.com),'" *Dunkunsthalle Communications*, May 16, 2023, https://dunkunsthalle.substack.com/p/cory-archangels-so-shines-a-good.

50. B. Droitcour, "Artificial Stupidity," *Art in America*, April 9, 2021, https://www.artnews.com/art-in-america/aia-reviews/cory-arcangel-century-21-greene-naftali-1234589266/.

51. R. W. Gehl, *Reverse Engineering Social Media: Software, Culture, and Political Economy in New Media Capitalism* (Temple University Press, 2014).

52. H. P. Levy, "Gartner Predicts a Virtual World of Exponential Change," *Gartner*, October 18, 2016, https://www.gartner.com/smarterwithgartner/gartner-predicts-a-virtual-world-of-exponential-change.

53. H. Steyerl, "Talks: Hito Steyerl," interview by S. Basar, *TANK Magazine* 8, no. 13 (2017), https://tankmagazine.com/tank/2019/talks/hito-steyerl/.

54. Wikipedia, "Wikipedia:Bots," last modified August 14, 2024, 07:27 (UTC), https://en.wikipedia.org/wiki/Wikipedia:Bots.

55. E. Hörl and N. F. Schott. "The Environmentalitarian Situation: Reflections on the Becoming-Environmental of Thinking, Power, and Capital," *Cultural Politics* 14, no. 2 (2018): https://doi.org/10.1215/17432197-6609046.

56. On "cybernetic capitalism," see Hörl and Schott, "The Environmentalitarian Situation"; E. Røssaak "Infrastruktur," in *Medieæstetik: En Introduktion*, ed. J. Lund and U. Schmidt (Samfundslitteratur, 2020); and "Capturing Life: Biopolitics, Social Media, and Romantic Irony," in *Writing and Unwriting (Media) Art History: Erkki Kurenniemi in 2048*, ed. J. Krysa and J. Parikka (MIT Press, 2015); and I. Blom, "Informasjoner, maskiner og estetikk," in *Medieæstetik: en introduction*, ed. J. Lund and U. Schmidt (Samfundslitteratur, 2020); on "cybernetic

machines," see A. Broeckmann, *The Machine Art in the Twentieth Century* (MIT Press, 2016); Tiqqun, "L'Hypothèse cybernétique," *Tiqqun* 2 (October 2001): 40–83; A. R. Galloway, "The Cybernetic Hypothesis," *Differences* 25, no. 1 (2014): 107–131, https://doi.org/10.1215/10407391-2420021; and G. Deleuze and T. Negri, "Control and Becoming," in *Negotiations, 1972–1990*, trans. M. Joughin (Columbia University Press, 1995).

CONCLUSION

1. C. Arcangel, "Introduction to the Weekend at Bernie's performance and screening," lecture, Whitney Museum of American Art, 2011, video, Arcangel's archive.
2. M. Foucault, "Of Other Spaces," *Diacritics* 16, no. 1. (Spring 1986).
3. M. Fuller and E. Weizman, *Investigative Aesthetics: Conflicts and Commons in the Politics of Truth* (Verso, 2021).
4. A. R. Galloway and J. R. LaRivière, "Compression in Philosophy," *Boundary 2* 44, no. 1 (2017): 139 n14, https://doi.org/10.1215/01903659-3725905.
5. Galloway and LaRivière, "Compression in Philosophy": 127.
6. Judith Butler ("For and Against Precarity," *Tidal: Occupy Theory, Occupy Strategy*, no. 1 (December 2011): 12–13, https://monoskop.org/images/8/81/Tidal_Occupy_Theory_Occupy_Strategy_1_2011.pdf.) explains: "The reason it is said that sometimes there are 'no demands' when bodies assemble under the rubric of 'Occupy Wall Street' is that any list of demands would not exhaust the ideal of justice that is being demanded."
7. Galloway and LaRivière, "Compression in Philosophy": 127–128.
8. Galloway and LaRivière, "Compression in Philosophy": 136.
9. G. Agamben, *The Coming Community* (University of Minnesota Press, 1993), 44.
10. Agamben elaborates on potentiality in this way: "What appears for the first time as such in deactivation (in the *Brachliegen*) of possibility, then, is *the very origin of potentiality*—and with it, of Dasein, that is, the being which exists in the form of potentiality-for-being [poter-essere]"; from G. Agamben, *The Open: Man and Animal* (Stanford University Press, 2004), 67. Italics in original.
11. G. Deleuze and F. Guattari, *Mille Plateaux: Capitalisme et schizophrénie 2* (Les Éditions de Minuit, 1980), 316.
12. Deleuze and Guattari, *Mille Plateaux*, 317.
13. I. Blom, *The Autobiography of Video: The Life and Times of a Memory Technology* (Sternberg Press, 2016), 28.
14. On "the infuriation event" of new media, see A. Galloway, "What You See Is What You Get?" in *The Archive in Motion: New Conceptions of the Archive in Contemporary Thought and New Media Practices*, ed. E. Røssaak (Novus Press, 2010), 163.
15. M. Wark, *A Hacker Manifesto* (Harvard University Press, 2004), paragraphs 274 (on the coming community) and 203 (on the gift economy).

16. E. Hörl, "A Thousand Ecologies: The Process of Cyberneticization and General Ecology," in *The Whole Earth: California and the Disappearance of the Outside*, ed. D. Diederichsen and A. Franke (Sternberg Press, 2013), 130.
17. F. A. Kittler, *The Truth of the Technological World: Essays on the Genealogy of Presence*, trans. E. Butler (Stanford University Press, 2014), 212.
18. W. H. K. Chun, *Updating to Remain the Same: Habitual New Media* (MIT Press, 2016), 1.
19. T. Griffin and L. Tan, "After the Fact," in *Cory Arcangel & Olia Lialina: Asymmetrical Response*, ed. C. Jones (Walther Koenig Books, 2018), 53.

BIBLIOGRAPHY

Adorno, T. *Philosophie der neuen Musik*. Verlag Ullstein, 1958.

Adorno, T. *Philosophy of Modern Music*. Seabury Press, 1973.

Agamben, G. *The Coming Community*. University of Minnesota Press, 1993.

Agamben, G. *The Open: Man and Animal*. Stanford University Press, 2003.

Ahmed, S. "Happy Objects." In *The Affect Theory Reader*, edited by M. Gregg and G. J. Seigworth. Duke University Press, 2010.

Alliez, É., and A. Goffey "Introduction." In *The Guattari Effect*, edited by É. Alliez and A. Goffey. Continuum, 2011.

Altice, N. "The Art of Erasure: *Super Mario Clouds*." *Memory Insufficient: The Games History E-Zine*, no. 5 (August 2013). https://issuu.com/zoyastreet/docs/memory-insufficient-hardware.

Arcangel, C. "/roʊˈdeɪoʊ/." Web-Documentation. */roʊˈdeɪoʊ/*, 2021. https://rodeo.computer/.

Arcangel, C. */roʊˈdeɪoʊ/ Let's Play: HOLLYWOOD*. 2017–2021. https://coryarcangel.com/things-i-made/2017-006-rodeo-performance.

Arcangel, C. "Artist talk: Cory Arcangel at Whitechapel Gallery." Lecture, Whitechapel Gallery, London, May 7, 2016. Video by C. McEvoy. Posted June 24, 2016, by Lisson-Gallery. YouTube. 21 min., 1 sec. https://www.lissongallery.com/news/cory-arcangel-in-conversation-at-whitechapel-gallery.

Arcangel, C. "coming soon: ebay paypal blogs the internet." In *Mass Effect: Art and the Internet in the Twenty-First Century*, edited by L. Cornell and E. Halter. MIT Press, 2015.

Arcangel, C. *Continuous Partial Awareness*. November 14, 2008. Lecture-performance, 44 min., 4 sec. New Museum, Rhizome, New York. https://video.rhizome.org/w/dcf9D9ESAnSdJqicZNpx9K.

Arcangel, C. "Cory Arcangel." Interview by M. Heilmann. *Interview*, March 21, 2011. https://www.interviewmagazine.com/art/cory-arcangel.

Arcangel, C. "Cory Arcangel Doesn't Even Like Super Mario Brothers." Interview by E. Salvaggio. *Turbulence.org*, April 2003. https://web.archive.org/web/20220303103319/http://turbulence.org/Works/curators/salvaggio/arcangel.html.

Arcangel, C. "Cory Arcangel Talks about His Exhibition at the Barbican." Interview by A. T. Baker. *Artforum*, March 5, 2011. https://www.artforum.com/columns/cory-arcangel-talks-about-his-exhibition-at-the-barbican-196963/.

Arcangel, C. *A Couple Thousand Short Films About Glenn Gould*. 2007. Dual channel video. https://coryarcangel.com/things-i-made/2007-006-a-couple-thousand-short-films-about-glenn-gould.

Arcangel, C. "Digital Media Arts." Lecture, Center for New Media Teaching and Learning, Columbia University. Posted March 24, 2009, by Columbia University. YouTube. 1 hr., 10 min., 16 sec. https://www.youtube.com/watch?v=ZzHq7PzQWEE.

Arcangel, C. Drei Klavierstücke op. 11. 2009. Three YouTube videos. https://coryarcangel.com/things-i-made/2009-003-dreiklavierstucke-op-11.

Arcangel, C. "Euro-Trance." *Artforum* 49, no. 10 (2011). https://www.artforum.com/columns/euro-trance-197652/.

Arcangel, C. "Everybody Else." In *Digital Folklore: To Computer Users with Love and Respect*, edited by O. Lialina and D. Espenschied. Merz Akademie, 2009.

Arcangel, C. *Gould Pro*. 2007–2011. Code. https://web.archive.org/web/20200217225035/http://www.coryarcangel.com/things-i-made/code-gould-pro.

Arcangel, C. In conversation with E. Halter on Arcangel's work in connection with the release of *Source*, no. 10. Arcangel's studio, Stavanger, Norway, 2018. Recorded with permission of A. Sunnanå.

Arcangel, C. In conversation with E. Røssaak (digital recordings). New York; Stavanger and Oslo, Norway, 2019–2023.

Arcangel, C. "Introduction to the Weekend at Bernie's performance and screening." Lecture, Whitney Museum of American Art, 2011. Video. Arcangel's archive.

Arcangel, C. "The Making of *Super Mario Clouds*." In *Cory Arcangel (Beige)*, edited by R. Gygax. Migros Museum für Gegenwartskunst and JRP Ringier, 2005.

Arcangel, C. *Personal Film*. 2008. 16mm film, 6 min., 15 sec. https://coryarcangel.com/things-i-made/2008-004-personal-film.

Arcangel, C. "On Compression." In *A Couple Thousand Short Films About Glenn Gould: A Book in Relation to a Project of the Same Name by Cory Arcangel*, edited by S. Bode. Film and Video Umbrella, 2008.

Arcangel, C. *Punk Rock 101*. 2006. Website. https://coryarcangel.com/things-i-made/2006-012-punkrock-101.

Arcangel, C. "Raw Materials: Cory Arcangel." Video. Directed by I. Cohen. Posted August 24, 2018, by NOWNESS. YouTube. 4 min., 11 sec. https://www.youtube.com/watch?v=oEieZIeOy4c.

Arcangel, C. "Recent Experiments in Modern Composition, Software, and Stand-Up Comedy." *The Art, Technology, and Culture Colloquium: UC Berkeley's Centre for New Media*, October 16, 2006. https://www.ghostriderrobot.com/bio/Cory_Arcangel/.

Arcangel, C. *Sorry I Haven't Posted*. 2010. Website. https://coryarcangel.com/things-i-made/2010-020-sorry-i-havent-posted.

Arcangel, C. *The Source Digest*. Arcangel Surfware, 2016.

Arcangel, C. *Super Mario Clouds*. 2002. Modded *Super Mario Bros.* cartridge, dimensions variable. https://coryarcangel.com/things-i-made/2002-001-super-mario-clouds.

Arcangel, C. "Super Mario Clouds Online." *Cory's Web LOG*, 2002. https://web.archive.org/web/20021219121037/http://www.beigerecords.com/cory/21c/21c.html.

Arcangel, C. *Working on My Novel*. Penguin, 2014.

Arcangel, C. "WTF." In *Seth Price: Social Synthetic*, edited by B. Ruf, A. Hochdörfer, and E. Banks. Walther Koenig Books, 2017.

Archive Team. "GeoCities." Last modified April 25, 2024, 00:08 (UTC). https://wiki.archiveteam.org/index.php/GeoCities.

Arns, I., and S. Sasse. "Subversive Affirmation. On Mimesis as a Strategy of Resistance." *Maska*, nos. 98–99 (Winter 2006): 162–181.

Baker, A. W. "Punk Rock 101: An Example of Digital Art." *[av]brey winona*, October 4, 2017. https://aubreywbaker.wordpress.com/2017/10/04/punk-rock-101-an-example-of-digital-art/.

Baron, J. "Subverted Intentions and the Potential for 'Found' Collectivity in Natalie Bookchin's Mass Ornament." *Maska: Performing Arts Journal* 26, nos. 143–144 (2011): 303–314. https://doi.org/10.17613/x34b-n904.

Barthes, R. *The Preparation of the Novel: Lecture Courses and Seminars at the Collège de France (1978–1979 and 1979–1980)*. Translated by K. Briggs. Columbia University Press, 2011.

Beato, R. "What Makes a Virtuoso?" Video. Posted June 12, 2018, by Rick Beato. YouTube. 7 min., 19 sec. https://www.youtube.com/watch?v=C8xhqxI8GHc.

Beige. "8-bit Construction Set." *Beige Records*, n.d. http://www.beigerecords.com/products/beg-004.html.

Beige. *Beige [Programming Ensemble]*. Website. 2003. https://web.archive.org/web/20100106083300/post-data.org/beige.

Beige. "A Brief History of BEIGE." *Beige Records*, n.d. http://beigerecords.com/aboutus.html.

Beige. *Deadtech*. Website. June 4, 2001. http://www.epidemic.ws/biennale_press/deadtech.htm.

Benjamin, W. "Theses on the Philosophy of History." In *Illuminations*, edited by H. Arendt. Schocken Books, 1968.

Benson, L. "Cory Arcangel's Monument to Digital Distraction." *Elephant*, October 17, 2019. https://elephant.art/cory-arcangel-working-on-my-novel/.

Berlant, L. "The Commons: Infrastructures for Troubling Times." *Environment and Planning: Society and Space* 34, no. 3 (2016): 393–419. https://doi.org/10.1177/0263775816645989.

Berlant, L. *Cruel Optimism*. Duke University Press, 2011.

Birnbaum, D., and C. Arcangel. "In Conversation." *ArtForum* 47, no. 7 (2009). https://www.artforum.com/print/200903/in-conversation-dara-birnbaum-and-cory-arcangel-22117.

Bishop, C. "The Digital Divide: Contemporary Art and New Media." *ArtForum* (September 2012). https://www.artforum.com/print/201207/digital-divide-contemporary-art-and-new-media-31944.

Blance, A. "An Introduction to 6502 Assembly and Low-Level Programming!" *Medium*, July 21, 2020. https://codeburst.io/an-introduction-to-6502-assembly-and-low-level-programming-7c11fa6b9cb9.

Blom, I. *The Autobiography of Video: The Life and Times of a Memory Technology*. Sternberg Press, 2016.

Blom, I. "Informasjoner, maskiner og estetikk." In *Medieæstetik: en introduction*, edited by J. Lund and U. Schmidt. Samfundslitteratur, 2020.

Blom, I. *On the Style Site: Art, Sociality, and Media Culture*. Sternberg Press, 2007.

Blom, I., T. Lundemo, and E. Røssaak, eds. *Memory in Motion: Archives, Technology, and the Social*. Amsterdam University Press, 2017. http://library.oapen.org/handle/20.500.12657/32015.

Bode, S. ed., *A Couple Thousand Short Films About Glenn Gould: A Book in Relation to a Project of the Same Name by Cory Arcangel*. Film and Video Umbrella, 2008.

Bogost, I. *Persuasive Games: The Expressive Power of Videogames*. MIT Press, 2007.

Bookchin, N. "Dancing Machines: An Interview with Natalie Bookchin." Interview by C. Kane. *Rhizome*, May 27, 2009. https://bookchin.net/wp-content/uploads/2015/09/2interview-Rhizome-Dancing-Machines.pdf.

Bookchin, N., and B. Stimson. "Out in Public: Natalie Bookchin in Conversation with Blake Stimson." In *Video Vortex Reader II: Moving Images Beyond YouTube*, edited by G. Lovink and R. S. Miles. Institute of Network Cultures, 2011.

Boss, J. F. "'Away with Motivic Working?' Not So Fast: Motivic Processes in Schoenberg's op. 11, no. 3." *Music Theory Online* 21, no. 3 (2015). https://mtosmt.org/issues/mto.15.21.3/mto.15.21.3.boss.html.

Bourriaud, N. *Postproduction: Culture as Screenplay: How Art Reprograms the World*. 2nd ed. Translated by J. Herman. Lukas & Sternberg, 2005.

Bourriaud, N. *Relational Aesthetics*. Les presses du réel, 2002.

Bowker, G., and S. L. Star. *Sorting Things Out: Classification and Its Consequences*. MIT Press, 1999.

Broeckmann, A. *The Machine Art in the Twentieth Century*. MIT Press, 2016.

Broeckmann, A. "Minor Media—Heterogenic Machines: Heterogenic Machines: Notes on Félix Guattari's Conceptions of Art and New Media." *M/C Journal* 2, no. 6 (1999). https://doi.org/10.5204/mcj.1788.

Buchanan, I. *Assemblage Theory and Method: An Introduction and Guide*. Bloomsbury, 2021.

Buchanan, I. "Flow and Resistance." Lecture at the Seminar of Aesthetics. University of Oslo, April 13, 2023.

Buchanan, I. *The Incomplete Project of Schizoanalysis: Collected Essays on Deleuze and Guattari*. Edinburgh University Press, 2021.

Buck-Morss, S. *The Origin of Negative Dialetics: Theodor W. Adorno, Walter Benjamin, and the Frankfurt Institute*. Free Press, 1977.

Burnham, J. "Systems Esthetics." *Artforum* 7, no. 1 (1968): 30–35. https://monoskop.org/images/0/03/Burnham_Jack_1968_Systems_Esthetics_Artforum.pdf.

Busbea, L. *The Responsive Environment: Design, Aesthetics, and the Human in the 1970s*. University of Minnesota Press, 2020.

Butler, J. "For and Against Precarity." *Tidal: Occupy Theory, Occupy Strategy*, no. 1 (December 2011): 12–13. https://monoskop.org/images/8/81/Tidal_Occupy_Theory_Occupy_Strategy_1_2011.pdf.

Campion, S. "Kurt Cobain's Suicide Letter vs. Google AdSense." *FutureLab*, November 2, 2006. https://www.futurelab.net/blog/2006/11/kurt-cobains-suicide-letter-vs-google-adsense/.

Carrouges, M. *Les machines célibataires*. New ed. Chêne, 1976. [Original edition Arcanes, 1954.]

Castells, M. *The Rise of the Network Society*. 2nd ed. Wiley Blackwell, 2010.

Chan, D. "Geek Chic." *Artforum*, August 12, 2008. https://www.artforum.com/diary/dawn-chan-at-a-cory-arcangel-concert-20892.

Christoffersen, M. B. "Cory Arcangels Stedlige Arkiv/ The Vernacular Archive of Cory Arcangel." In *Cory Arcangel: All the Small Things*. Exhibition Catalog, HEART—Herning Museum of Contemporary Art. Edited by M. B. Christoffersen. Walther Koenig, 2014.

Chun, W. H. K. *Programmed Visions: Software and Memory*. MIT Press, 2011.

Chun, W. H. K. *Updating to Remain the Same: Habitual New Media*. MIT Press, 2016.

Connor, M. "Interview with Cory Arcangel." In *A Couple Thousand Short Films About Glenn Gould: A Book in Relation to a Project of the Same Name by Cory Arcangel*, edited by S. Bode. Film and Video Umbrella, 2008.

Cornell, L., and E. Halter. "Hard Reboot: An Introduction to *Mass Effect*." In *Mass Effect: Art and the Internet in the Twenty-First Century*, edited by L. Cornell and E. Halter. MIT Press, 2015.

Cover, L. "7 Statistics That Prove the Importance of Social Media Marketing in Business," *Sprout Social*, June 17, 2021. http://19tamalvista.com/index-1558.html.

coryarcangel. "Gould-Pro." *GitHub*, 2007. https://github.com/coryarcangel/Gould-Pro.

Cramer, F., and P. Jandrić. "Postdigital: A Term That Sucks but Is Useful." *Postdigital Science and Education* 3 (March 2021): 966–989. https://doi.org/10.1007/s42438-021-00225-9.

Crogan, P. *Gameplay Mode: War, Simulation, and Technoculture*. University of Minnesota Press, 2011.

Csikszentmihalyi, M. *Flow: The Psychology of Optimal Experience*. Harper Perennial Modern Classics, 2008. [Original edition Harper Collins, 1990.]

Cubitt, S., and P. Thomas. "The New Materialism in Media Art History." In *Media Art: Towards a New Definition of Arts in the Age of Technology*, edited by V. Catricalà. Fondazione Mondo Digitale, 2015.

de Landa, M. "The Machinic Phylum." *V2*. 1997. https://v2.nl/articles/the-machinic-phylum.

Deleuze, G. *Bergsonism*. Translated by H. Tomlinson and B. Habberjam. Zone Books, 1988. [Original edition Presses Universitaires de France, 1966.]

Deleuze, G. *Cinema 1: The Movement-Image*. Translated by H. Tomlinson and B. Habberjam. University of Minnesota Press, 1986. [Original edition Les Éditions de Minuit, 1983.]

Deleuze, G. *Cinema 2: The Time-Image*. Translated by H. Tomlinson and R. Galeta. University of Minnesota Press, 1989. [Original edition Les Éditions de Minuit, 1986.]

Deleuze, G. *Difference and Repetition*. Translated by P. Patton. Columbia University Press, 1994. [Original edition Presses Universitaires de France, 1968.]

Deleuze, G. *Foucault*. Translated by S. Hand. University of Minnesota Press, 1988. [Original edition Les Éditions de Minuit, 1986.]

Deleuze, G. "Postscript on Control Societies." In *Negotiations, 1972–1990*. Translated by M. Joughin. Columbia University Press, 1995. [Original edition *L'Autre Journal* 1 (May 1990).]

Deleuze, G. "Sur Leibniz." Lecture, University of Paris 8, Vincennes-Saint-Denis, April 15, 1980. Posted April 25, 2019, by Webdeleuze. Web Deleuze and YouTube. 2 hr., 3 min., 40 sec. https://www.webdeleuze.com/textes/50.

Deleuze, G., and F. Guattari. *Anti-Oedipus: Capitalism and Schizophrenia*. University of Minnesota Press, 1983. [Original edition Les Éditions de Minuit, 1972.]

Deleuze, G., and F. Guattari. *Kafka: Toward a Minor Literature*. Translated by D. Polan. University of Minnesota Press, 1986. [Original edition Les Éditions de Minuit, 1975.]

Deleuze, G., and F. Guattari. *L'Anti-Œdipe: Capitalisme et schizophrénie 1*. Les Éditions de Minuit, 1972.

Deleuze, G., and F. Guattari. *Mille Plateaux: Capitalisme et schizophrénie 2*. Les Éditions de Minuit, 1980.

Deleuze, G., and F. Guattari. *A Thousand Plateaus: Capitalism and Schizophrenia*. Translated by B. Massumi. University of Minnesota Press, 1987. [Original edition Les Éditions de Minuit, 1980.]

Deleuze, G., and T. Negri. "Control and Becoming." In G. Deleuze, *Negotiations, 1972–1990*. Translated by M. Joughin. Columbia University Press, 1995. [Original edition Les Éditions de Minuit, 1990.]

Diederichsen, D., and O. Etxeberria, "Cybernetics of the Poor." In *Cybernetics of the Poor*. Edited by D. Diederichsen and O. Etxeberria. Sternberg Press, 2020.

Dockrill, P. "A Handful of Super-Corporations Control the Fate of the World, Chilling Report Shows." *Science Alert*, September 16, 2019. https://www.sciencealert.com/a-handful-of-super-corporations-controls-the-fate-of-the-world-scientists-warn.

Dormehl, L. "YouTube Poop is Punk Rock for the Internet Age, and You Probably Don't Get It." *DigitalTrends.com*, March 30, 2019. https://www.digitaltrends.com/cool-tech/youtube-poop-worthy-respect/.

Droitcour, B. "Artificial Stupidity." *Art in America*, April 9, 2021. https://www.artnews.com/art-in-america/aia-reviews/cory-arcangel-century-21-greene-naftali-1234589266/.

Edwards, P. N. "Infrastructure and Modernity: Force, Time, and Social Organization in the History of Sociotechnical Systems." In *Modernity and Technology*, edited by T. J. Misa, P. Brey, and A. Feenberg. MIT Press, 2003. https://doi.org/10.7551/mitpress/4729.003.0011.

Encyclopedia.com. S. Shelton. "Malmsteen, Yngwie." Last modified January 8, 2025. https://www.encyclopedia.com/education/news-wires-white-papers-and-books/malmsteen-yngwie.

Ernst, W. *Das Rumoren der Archive: Ordnung aus Unordnung*. Merve, 2002.

Ernst, W. *Digital Memory and the Archive*. Edited by J. Parikka. University of Minnesota Press, 2012.

Ernst, W. *Medium Foucault: Weimarer Vorlesungen über Archive, Archäologie, Monumente und Medien*. VDG, 2000.

Ernst, W. *Technológos in Being: Radical Media Archaeology and the Computational Machine*. Bloomsbury, 2021.

Espenschied, D. "The Storage is You," preface to *The Source Digest*, by C. Arcangel. Arcangel Surfware, 2016.

Eysteinsson, A. "'What's the Difference?' Revisiting the Concepts of Modernism and the Avant-Garde." In *Europa! Europa? The Avant-Garde, Modernism and the Fate of a Continent*, edited by S. Bru, J. Baetens, B. Hjartarson, P. Nicholls, T. Ørum, and H. van den Berg. De Gruyter, 2009.

Faris, J. H. *Uncommon Goods: Global Dimensions of the Readymade*. Intellect Books, 2013.

Fino-Radin, C. “Code, Conservation, and Truth.” *Medium*, November 17, 2017. https://medium.com/@benfinoradin/code-conservation-and-truth-10cd5b59e0be.

Foucault, M. “Of Other Spaces.” *Diacritics* 16, no. 1 (spring 1986).

Foucault, M. *The Birth of Biopolitics: Lectures at Collège de France, 1978–79*. Edited by M. Senellart. Palgrave Macmillan, 2008.

Frankel, E. “Cory Arcangel: currentmood.” *Time Out: London*, May 25, 2016. https://www.timeout.com/london/art/cory-arcangel-currentmood-1.

Fried, M. *Art and Objecthood: Essays and Reviews*. University of Chicago Press, 1998.

Frumin, M. “Interview of Michael Frumin.” Interview by Regine. *We Mak$ $$ney Not Art* (blog), August 18, 2006. https://we-make-money-not-art.com/in_the_past_you/.

Fuller, M. *Behind the Blip: Essays on the Culture of Software*. Autonomedia, 2003.

Fuller, M. In conversation with E. Røssaak (digital recording). Web. 2023.

Fuller, M. *Media Ecologies: Materialist Energies in Art and Technoculture*. MIT Press, 2005.

Fuller, M., ed. *Software Studies: A Lexicon*. MIT Press, 2008.

Fuller, M., and E. Weizman. *Investigative Aesthetics: Conflicts and Commons in the Politics of Truth*. Verso, 2021.

Gaboury, J. “Tool Time: Cory Arcangel at The Whitney.” *Rhizome*, June 21, 2011. https://rhizome.org/editorial/2011/jun/21/tool-time-cory-arcangel-whitney/.

Gabrys, J. *Program Earth: Environmental Sensing Technology and the Making of a Computational Planet*. University of Minnesota Press, 2016.

Galloway, A. “Cory Arcangel (Beige) and Paper Rad.” Text from booklet/exhibition guide for the *Super Mario Movie* show at Deitch Projects. Text-file from Arcangel’s private archive, 2005.

Galloway, A. “What You See Is What You Get?” In *The Archive in Motion: New Conceptions of the Archive in Contemporary Thought and New Media Practices*, edited by E. Røssaak. Novus Press, 2010.

Galloway, A. R. “The Cybernetic Hypothesis.” *Differences* 25, no. 1 (2014): 107–131. https://doi.org/10.1215/10407391-2420021.

Galloway, A. R. “*Data Diaries*: Description.” Rhizome ArtBase, June 3, 2005. https://artbase.rhizome.org/wiki/Q4007.

Galloway, A. R. *Gaming: Essays on Algorithmic Culture*. University of Minnesota Press, 2006.

Galloway, A. R. In conversation with E. Røssaak (digital recordings). New York, 2019–2024.

Galloway, A. R. “Two Statements on Carnivore.” In *Mass Effect: Art and the Internet in the Twenty-First Century*, edited by L. Cornell and E. Halter. MIT Press, 2015.

Galloway, A. R., and E. Thacker. *The Exploit: A Theory of Networks*. University of Minnesota Press, 2007.

Galloway, A. R., and J. R. LaRivière. "Compression in Philosophy." *Boundary 2* 44, no. 1 (2017): 125–147. https://doi.org/10.1215/01903659-3725905.

Garfield, D. "Cory Arcangel's 'So Shines a Good Deed in a Weary World (dunkindonuts .com).'" *Dunkunsthalle Communications*, May 16, 2023. https://dunkunsthalle.substack .com/p/cory-archangels-so-shines-a-good.

Gehl, R. W. *Reverse Engineering Social Media: Software, Culture, and Political Economy in New Media Capitalism*. Temple University Press, 2014.

Gerlitz, C., and A. Helmond. "The Like Economy: Social Buttons and the Data-Intensive Web." *New Media & Society* 15, no. 8 (2013): 1348–1365. https://doi.org/10.1177 /1461444812472322.

Gigliotti, D. "About Us." *Radical Software*. n.d. https://www.radicalsoftware.org/e /about.html.

Gomez, R. "The Importance of Social Media Marketing: 7 Stats that Prove Social's Role in Business Success." *Sprout Social*, September 18, 2023. https://sproutsocial.com /insights/importance-of-social-media-marketing-in-business/.

Goriunova, O. "Introduction." In *Fun and Software: Exploring Pleasure, Paradox and Pain in Computing*, edited by O. Goriunova. Bloomsbury, 2014.

Gould, G. "Full text of 'The Complete Music for Solo Piano.'" Glenn Gould's liner notes to Drei Klavierstücke. 1968. https://archive.org/stream/lp_the-complete-music -for-solo-piano_glenn-gould-arnold-schoenberg/lp_the-complete-music-for-solo -piano_glenn-gould-arnold-schoenberg_djvu.txt.

Gould, G. "Glenn Gould on Animals." Video. June 22, 2006, by michaeltravis. YouTube. 2 min., 22 sec. https://www.youtube.com/watch?v=57kR6RsV2iA.

Gould, G. "The Prospects of Recording." In *Audio Culture: Reading in Modern Music*, edited by C. Cox and D. Warner. Continuum, 2004: 125–126.

Greene Naftali. "Cory Arcangel: Century 21." *Greene Naftali Gallery Viewing Room*, 2021. https://greenenaftaligallery-viewingroom.exhibit-e.art/viewing-room/cory-arcangel #tab:thumbnails.

Griffin, T. "Compression." *October* 135 (Winter 2011): 3–20. https://doi.org/10.1162 /OCTO_a_00018.

Griffin, T., and L. Tan. "After the Fact." In *Cory Arcangel & Olia Lialina: Asymmetrical Response*, edited by C. Jones. Walther Koenig Books, 2018: 53–54.

Guattari, F. *The Anti-Oedipus Papers*. Edited by S. Nadaud. Translated by K. Gotman. Semiotext(e), 2006.

Guattari, F. "In Flux: An Interview with Deleuze and Guattari." In F. Guattari, *Chaoso phy: Texts and Interviews 1972–1977*, new ed., edited by S. Lotringer. Semiotext(e), 2009: 69–89.

Guattari, F. *The Machinic Unconscious: Essays in Schizoanalysis*. Translated by T. Adkins. Semiotext(e), 2010.

Guattari, F. *The Three Ecologies*. Translated by I. Pindar and P. Sutton. Athlone Press, 2000. [Original edition *New Formation*, no. 8, 1989.]

Gudmundson, I. M. L. "In the Clouds." *Stavanger Art Museum*, 2020. https://www.stavangerkunstmuseum.no/en/events/i-skyene.

Gunning, T. "Buster Keaton: or The Work of Comedy in the Age of Mechanical Reproduction." *Cinéaste* 21, no. 3 (1995): 14–16. https://www.jstor.org/stable/41687377.

Gunning, T. "The Cinema of Attractions: Early Film, Its Spectator and the Avant-Garde." In *Early Cinema: Space, Frame, Narrative*, edited by T. Elsaesser and A. Barker. British Film Institute, 1990.

Gygax, R. "Minimalize Mario: The Work of Cory Arcangel (Beige)." In *Cory Arcangel (Beige)*, edited by R. Gygax. Migros Museum für Gegenwartskunst and JRP Ringier, 2005.

Halter, E. "Get It? An Interview with Cory Arcangel on Comedy." *Rhizome*, December 24, 2008. https://rhizome.org/editorial/2008/dec/24/get-it-an-interview-with-cory-arcangel-on-comedy/.

Hansen, M. B. N. *New Philosophy for New Media*. MIT Press, 2004.

Hao, K. "The Facebook Whistleblower Says Its Algorithms Are Dangerous. Here's Why." *MIT Technology Review*, October 5, 2021. https://www.technologyreview.com/2021/10/05/1036519/facebook-whistleblower-frances-haugen-algorithms/.

Haraway, D. J. *Staying with the Trouble: Making Kin in the Chthulucene*. Duke University Press, 2016.

Hausken, L., ed. *Thinking Media Aesthetics: Media Studies, Film Studies and the Arts*. Peter Lang, 2013.

Hecker, T. "Glenn Gould, the Vanishing Performer and the Ambivalence of the Studio." *Leonardo Music Journal* 18 (December 2008): 77–83. https://doi.org/10.1162/lmj.2008.18.77.

Hoel, A. S. A. "Technicity and the Virtual." *Humanities* 11, no. 6 (2022): 135. https://doi.org/10.3390/h11060135.

Hörl, E. "Becoming Infrastructural—Becoming Environmental." Keynote lecture with L. Parks, moderated by J. Parikka, Transmediale, Berlin, February 3, 2017. Posted February 15, 2017, by transmediale. YouTube. 1 hr., 59 min., 24 sec. https://www.youtube.com/watch?v=yREfIXLdl9M&t=791s.

Hörl, E. "A Thousand Ecologies: The Process of Cyberneticization and General Ecology." In *The Whole Earth: California and the Disappearance of the Outside*, edited by D. Diederichsen and A. Franke. Sternberg Press, 2013.

Hörl, E., and N. F. Schott. "The Environmentalitarian Situation: Reflections on the Becoming-Environmental of Thinking, Power, and Capital." *Cultural Politics* 14, no. 2 (2018): 153–173. https://doi.org/10.1215/17432197-6609046.

Houpt, S. "FrankenArt: The Mix and Mash Future." *The Globe and Mail*, May 15, 2004. https://www.theglobeandmail.com/arts/frankenart-the-mix-and-mash-future/article25679322/.

Jagoda, P. *Network Aesthetics*. University of Chicago Press, 2016.

Jameson, F. *Postmodernism, or, the Cultural Logic of Late Capitalism*. Duke University Press, 1991.

Jay, M. *The Dialectical Imagination: A History of the Frankfurt School and the Institute of Social Research, 1923–1950*. Little, Brown, 1973.

Jones, C. "Trajectories of the Studio after the Factory." Lecture, Museum of Contemporary Art, Chicago, February 16, 2010. Audio recording. 1 hr., 4 min., 4 sec. https://mcachicago.org/Publications/Audio/2010/Caroline-Jones-Trajectories-Of-The-Studio-After-The-Factory.

Jones, C., ed. *Cory Arcangel & Olia Lialina: Asymmetrical Response*. Text by T. Griffin, C. Jones, and L. Tan. Walther Koenig Books, 2018.

Jones, C. A. *Machine in the Studio: Constructing the Postwar American Artist*. University of Chicago Press, 1996.

Jones, J. "A Novel about People Who Say They're Working on Novels? How Novel." *The Guardian*, July 31, 2014. https://www.theguardian.com/artanddesign/jonathanjonesblog/2014/jul/31/cory-arcangel-working-on-my-novel-twitter-book.

Joseph, B. W. *Beyond the Dream Syndicate: Tony Conrad and the Arts after Cage*. Zone Books, 2008.

Kawabata, M. *Paganini: The "Demonic" Virtuoso*. Boydell Press, 2013.

Keating, T. P. "On the Technological Unconscious: Thinking the (A)signifying Production of Subjects and Bodies with Sonographic Imaging." *Social & Cultural Geography* 24, no. 9 (2023): 1481–1500. https://doi.org/10.1080/14649365.2022.2083665.

Kelley, M. *Minor Histories: Statements, Conversations, Proposals*, ed. J. C. Welchman. MIT Press, 2004.

Kildall, S. "Readymake: Duchamp Chess Pieces (3D Recreations From Photographs)." *Autodesk Instructables*. n.d. https://www.instructables.com/Readymake-Duchamp-Chess-Pieces-3D-Recreations-from/.

Kittler, F. A. *Gramophone, Film, Typewriter*. Translated by G. Winthrop-Young and M. Wutz. Stanford University Press, 1999. [Original edition Brinkmann & Bose, 1986.]

Kittler, F. A. *Literature, Media, Information Systems*. Edited by J. Johnston. G+B Arts, 1997.

Kittler, F. A. *The Truth of the Technological World: Essays on the Genealogy of Presence*. Translated by E. Butler. Stanford University Press, 2014.

Know Your Meme. "I Don't Know Who Needs to Hear This." *Know Your Meme*. Last modified February 22, 2021. https://knowyourmeme.com/memes/i-dont-know-who-needs-to-hear-this.

Kukielski, T. "Doing Assembly: The Art of Cory Arcangel." In *Mass Effect: Art and the Internet in the Twenty-First Century*, edited by L. Cornell and E. Halter. MIT Press, 2015.

Larue, A. *Le Surréalisme de Duchamp à Deleuze*. Éditions Talus d'approche, 2003.

Latour, B. *Reassembling the Social: An Introduction to Actor-Network-Theory*. Oxford University Press, 2005.

Lazzarato, M. "The Concepts of Life and the Living in the Societies of Control." In *Deleuze and the Social*, edited by M. Fuglsang and B. M. Sørensen. Edinburgh University Press, 2006.

Lazzarato, M. *Puissances de L'invention: La Psychologie Économique de Gabriel Tarde contre L'économie Politique*. Les Empêcheurs de Penser en Rond, 2002.

Lazzarato, M. *Signs and Machines: Capitalism and the Production of Subjectivity*. Translated by J. D. Jordan. Semiotext(e), 2014.

Lazzarato, M. *Videophilosophy: The Perception of Time in Post-Fordism*. Edited and translated by J. Hetrick. Columbia University Press, 2019.

LeMieux, P. "Aftermarket, a Game Design Philosophy." PhD diss., Department of Art, Art History, and Visual Studies, Duke University, 2015. https://hdl.handle.net/10161/10520.

LeMieux, P. *Coin Heaven*. 2013. Hacked ROM, custom cartridge, Nintendo Entertainment System, CRT TV, dimensions variable. http://patrick-lemieux.com/projects/Aftermarket/04.php.

LeMieux, P. "Everything but the Clouds." Platform Games at Babycastles. Video Essay. Posted November 8, 2017. Vimeo. 19 min., 44 sec. https://vimeo.com/241966869.

Levy, H. P. "Gartner Predicts a Virtual World of Exponential Change." *Gartner*, October 18, 2016. https://www.gartner.com/smarterwithgartner/gartner-predicts-a-virtual-world-of-exponential-change.

Levy, S. *Hackers: Heroes of the Computer Revolution*. Penguin, 1994.

Lewis, M. "Has Anyone Seen the President?" *Bloomberg*, February 9, 2018. https://www.bloomberg.com/opinion/articles/2018-02-09/has-anyone-seen-the-president?leadSource=uverify%20wall.

Lialina, O. "Asymmetrical Response Reader." In *Cory Arcangel & Olia Lialina: Asymmetrical Response*, edited by C. Jones. Text by T. Griffin, C. Jones, and L. Tan. Walther Koenig Books, 2018.

Lialina, O. "Net Art Generations." From Lialina's website. *art.teleportacia.org*, 2007. Updated November 19, 2013. http://art.teleportacia.org/observation/net_art_generations/.

Lialina, O., and D. Espenschied. "Do You Believe in Users?" In *Digital Folklore: To Computer Users with Love and Respect*, edited by O. Lialina and D. Espenschied. Merz Akademie, 2009.

Lialina, O., and D. Espenschied. "Net Art Anthology: *One Terrabyte of Kilobyte Age*." *Net Art Anthology* and *Rhizome*, 2019. https://anthology.rhizome.org/one-terabyte-of-kilobyte-age.

Lohmeyer, E. L. "Unstable Aesthetics: The Game Engine and Art Modifications." PhD diss., North Carolina State University, 2018. http://www.lib.ncsu.edu/resolver/1840.20/35313.

MacDonald, M. *Schoenberg*. 2nd ed. Oxford University Press, 2008.

Manovich, L. *The Language of New Media*. MIT Press, 2001.

Manovich, L. "Remix Strategies in Social Media." In *The Routledge Companion to Remix Studies*, edited by E. Navas, O. Gallagher, and x. burrough. Routledge, 2015.

Massumi, B. "National Enterprise Emergency: Steps Toward an Ecology of Powers." *Theory, Culture & Society* 26, no. 6 (2009): 153–185. https://doi.org/10.1177/0263276409347696.

Mattern, S. "Sense-able Structures—Infrastructural Aesthetics." Lecture, Poetics of Infrastructure conference, Vienna, December 13, 2014. Posted June 18, 2015, by *Genealogy+Critique* (blog). G+C. 15 min., 59 sec. https://blog.genealogy-critique.net/essays/100/shannon-mattern-senseable-structures.

McCormack, T. "Cory Arcangel and New Media One-Liners." *Art21 Magazine*, June 10, 2011. https://magazine.art21.org/2011/06/10/cory-arcangel-and-new-media-one-liners/.

Mehta, M. "White Hat Hacker vs Black Hat Hacker—What's the Difference?" *InfoSec Insights*, December 17, 2020. https://sectigostore.com/blog/white-hat-hacker-vs-black-hat-hacker/.

Merrifield, A. "Here Comes Everybody: Joyce's Urban Chaosmos." *Antipode Online*, December 18, 2013. https://antipodeonline.org/2013/12/18/here-comes-everybody/.

"monkeyrunner." *Android Developers*. Last modified January 3, 2024. https://developer.android.com/studio/test/monkeyrunner.

Moody, T. "Erasing the Clouds (and the Collective)." *Tom Moody* (blog), January 6, 2018. https://www.tommoody.us/archives/2018/01/06/erasing-the-clouds-and-the-collective/.

Morley, P. "Reproduction." In *A Couple Thousand Short Films About Glenn Gould: A Book in Relation to a Project of the Same Name by Cory Arcangel*, edited by S. Bode. Film and Video Umbrella, 2008.

Navas, E., O. Gallagher, and x. burrough, eds. *Keywords in Remix Studies*. Routledge, 2017.

Ngai, S. *Theory of the Gimmick: Aesthetic Judgment and Capitalist Form*. Harvard University Press, 2020.

Norman, D. A. "Why Interfaces Don't Work." In *The Art of Human–Computer Interface Design*, edited by B. Laurel. Addison-Wesley, 1990.

Olson, M. "Best of the Web 2006." *Rhizome Editorial*, January 3, 2007. https://rhizome.org/editorial/2007/jan/03/the-best-of-the-web-2006/.

O'Reilly, T. "What Is Web 2.0," O'Reilly.com, September 30, 2005. https://www.oreilly.com/pub/a/web2/archive/what-is-web-20.html?page=all

Paddison, M. *Adorno's Aesthetics of Music*. Cambridge University Press, 1993.

Parikka, J. "Ethologies of Software Art: What Can a Digital Body of Code Do?" In *Deleuze and Contemporary Art*, edited by S. Zepke and S. O'Sullivan. Edinburgh University Press, 2010.

Parikka, J. *A Geology of Media*. University of Minnesota Press, 2015.

Parikka, J. *What is Media Archaeology?* Polity, 2012.

Paul, C. *Cory Arcangel: Pro Tools*. Whitney Museum of American Art, 2011. Brochure published in conjunction with an exhibition of the same title, organized by and presented at the Whitney, May 26–September 11, 2011. https://whitney.org/Exhibitions/CoryArcangel.

Paul, C. In conversation with E. Røssaak (digital recording). New York, 2019.

Peretti, J. "My Nike Media Adventure." *The Nation*, March 22, 2001. https://www.thenation.com/article/archive/my-nike-media-adventure/.

Peretti, J. "Notes on Contagious Media." In *Structures of Participation in Digital Culture*, edited by J. Karaganis. Social Science Research Council, 2007.

Pias, C. "Computer Spiel Welten." PhD diss., Bauhaus-Universität Weimar, 2000. https://e-pub.uni-weimar.de/opus4/frontdoor/index/index/docId/35.

Pias, C. "The Game Player's Duty: The User as the Gestalt of the Ports." In *Media Archaeology: Approaches, Applications, and Implications*, edited by E. Huhtamo and J. Parikka. University of California Press, 2011.

Pias, C. "Time of Non-Reality: Miszellen zum Thema Zeit und Auflösung." In *Zeitkritische Medien*, edited by A. Volmar. Kulturverlag Kadmos, 2009.

Piepenbring, D. "Working on My Novel." *The Paris Review*, July 28, 2014. https://www.theparisreview.org/blog/2014/07/28/working-on-my-novel/.

Pisters, P. "Deleuze's Metallurgic Machines." *Los Angeles Review of Books*, November 8, 2015. https://lareviewofbooks.org/article/deleuzes-metallurgic-machines/.

Price, S. *Dispersion*. Seth Price, 2002. https://anthology.rhizome.org/dispersion and http://sethpricestudio.com/writingarchive/DIspersion.pdf.

Prytz, Ø. *Litteratur i en digital tid*. Scandinavian Academic Press, 2016.

Quaranta, D. *Beyond New Media Art*. Link Editions, 2013.

Quaranta, D. *In Your Computer*. Link Editions, 2010.

Radical Software. "The Alternate Television Movement." *Radical Software* 1, no. 1 (1970). https://www.radicalsoftware.org/e/volume1nr1.html.

Radical Software Group. "Carnivore. Version 9." *RSG*, March 2024. http://r-s-g.org/carnivore/.

Radical Software Group and Beige Records. "Low Level All-Stars." *Rhizome Archive*, n.d. http://archive.rhizome.org/exhibition/Low_Level_All_Stars/.

Raftery, B. "I'm Not Here to Make Friends: The Rise and Fall of the Supercut Video." *Wired*, August 30, 2018. https://www.wired.com/story/supercut-video-rise-and-fall/.

Raunig, G. *A Thousand Machines: A Concise Philosophy of the Machine as Social Movement*. Translated by A. Derieg. Semiotext(e), 2010.

Reich, S. "Steve Reich Reflects on His Most Significant Works." Interview by Shad. Posted April 14, 2016, by Q on CBC. YouTube. 36 min., 47 sec. https://www.youtube.com/watch?v=yg7kKJsFpvc.

Rice, A. "Does BuzzFeed Know the Secret?" *New York Magazine*, April 5, 2013. https://nymag.com/news/features/buzzfeed-2013-4/.

Roberts, J. *The Intangibilities of Form: Skill and Deskilling in Art After the Readymade*. Verso, 2007.

Roberts, R. "The Beige Programming Ensemble: An Essay." *PEM PlayTime*, 2017. http://playtime.pem.org/the-beige-programming-ensemble-an-essay/.

Rodowick, D. N. *Gilles Deleuze's Time Machine*. Duke University Press, 1997.

Royer, A. "The Urgent Need for Regulating Global Ghost Work." *Brookings*, February 9, 2021. https://www.brookings.edu/articles/the-urgent-need-for-regulating-global-ghost-work/.

Røssaak, E. "Affects and Medium: Re-imagining Media Differences Through Bill Viola's *The Quintet of the Astonished*." *New Review of Film and Television Studies* 7, no. 3 (2009): 339–352. https://doi.org/10.1080/17400300903047086.

Røssaak, E., ed. *Between Stillness and Motion: Film, Photography, Algorithms*. Amsterdam University Press, 2011. https://library.oapen.org/bitstream/handle/20.500.12657/34455/1/431802.pdf.

Røssaak, E. "Capturing Life: Biopolitics, Social Media, and Romantic Irony." In *Writing and Unwriting (Media) Art History: Erkki Kurenniemi in 2048*, edited by J. Krysa and J. Parikka. MIT Press, 2015.

Røssaak, E. "Eivind Røssaak reviews The Age of Surveillance Capitalism." *Critical Inquiry* 47, no. 1 (2020). https://criticalinquiry.uchicago.edu/eivind_rssaak_reviews_the_age_of_surveillance_capitalism/.

Røssaak, E. "Infrastruktur." In *Medieæstetik: En Introduktion*, edited by J. Lund and U. Schmidt. Samfundslitteratur, 2020.

Røssaak, E. "Maskinteori: Om syntesene i *Anti-Ødipus*." In "*Anti-Oedipus*—50 Years After," edited by L. Bugge, H. J. Ohldieck, G. O. Rønning, and G. Selnes. Special issue, *Agora: Journal for Metafysisk Spekulasjon* 41, no. 4 (2023): 71–94. https://doi.org/10.18261/agora.41.4.5.

Røssaak, E. "Negotiating Immobility: The Moving Image and the Arts." PhD diss., Department of Media and Communication, University of Oslo, 2008.

Røssaak, E. *Sic: Fra Litteraturens Randsone*. Spartacus, 2001.

Røssaak, E. *The Still/Moving Image: Cinema and the Arts*. Lambert Academic Publishing, 2010.

Ryan, P. "Three Pieces: Some Explication." *Radical Software* 1, no. 1 (1970): 13. https://www.radicalsoftware.org/volume1nr1/pdf/VOLUME1NR1_0015.pdf.

Sampson, T. D. *Virality: Contagion Theory in the Age of Networks*. University of Minnesota Press, 2012.

Sauvagnargues, A. *Artmachines: Deleuze, Guattari, Simondon*. Translated by S. Verderber and E. W. Holland. Edinburgh University Press, 2016.

Schmidgen, H. *Das Unbewußte der Maschinen. Konzeptionen des Psychischen bei Guattari, Deleuze und Lacan*. Wilhelm Fink Verlag, 1997.

Sharp, J. *Works of Game: On the Aesthetics of Games and Art*. MIT Press, 2015.

Shirky, C. *Here Comes Everybody: The Power of Organizing Without Organizations*. Penguin, 2008.

Simondon, G. *On the Mode of Existence of Technical Objects*. Translated by C. Malaspina and J. Rogove. University of Minnesota Press, 2017. [Original edition Editions Montaigne, 1958.]

Smith, D. N. "What is Called Rhythm?" In *Critical Rhythm: The Poetics of a Literary Life Form*, edited by B. Glaser and J. Culler. Fordham University Press, 2019.

Smith, D. W. "Flow, Code and Stock: A Note on Deleuze's Political Philosophy." Supplement. *Deleuze Studies* 5 (November 2011): 36–55. https://doi.org/10.3366/dls.2011.0036.

Soderman, B. *Against Flow: Video Games and the Flowing Subject*. MIT Press, 2021.

The State of Social Media: After a Year of Transformation, Executives Are All-In on Social. Sprout Social, 2021. https://sproutsocial.com/insights/data/future-of-business-intelligence/.

Sterling, B. *The Hacker Crackdown: Law and Disorder on the Electronic Frontier*. Bantam, 1992.

Sterne, J. *MP3: The Meaning of a Format*. Duke University Press, 2012.

Steyerl, H. "In Defense of the Poor Image," *e-flux journal*, no. 10 (November 2009). https://www.e-flux.com/journal/10/61362/in-defense-of-the-poor-image/

Steyerl, H. "Talks: Hito Steyerl." Interview by S. Basar. *TANK Magazine* 8, no. 13 (2017). https://tankmagazine.com/tank/2019/talks/hito-steyerl/.

Subscrible. "The Rise and Fall of Kim Kardashian: Hollywood." *Subscrible* on LinkedIn. January 25, 2024. https://www.linkedin.com/pulse/rise-fall-kim-kardashian-hollywood-subscrible-mir4f.

Tainter, J. A. *The Collapse of Complex Societies*. Cambridge University Press, 1990.

Terranova, T. "Another Life: Social Cooperation and A-Organic Life." *Digithum*, no. 12 (May 2010): 16. https://openaccess.uoc.edu/bitstream/10609/8817/1/n12-terranova-eng.pdf.

Terranova, T. *Network Culture: Politics for the Information Age*. Pluto Press, 2004.

Thiele, K. "'To Believe in This World, As It Is': Immanence and the Quest for Political Activism." Supplement. *Deleuze Studies* 4 (November 2010): 28–45. https://doi.org/10.3366/dls.2010.0204.

Thrift, N. "Remembering the Technological Unconscious by Foregrounding Knowledges of Position." *Environment and Planning D: Society and Space* 22, no. 1 (2004): 175–190. https://doi.org/10.1068/d321t.

Times Square Arts. "Cory Arcangel: Another Romp Thru the IP (Times Square Edit)." *Times Square Official Website*, 2022. https://www.timessquarenyc.org/tsq-arts-projects/another-romp-thru-the-ip-times-square-edit.

Tiqqun. "L'Hypothèse cybernétique." *Tiqqun* 2 (October 2001): 40–83.

Tribe, M., and R. Jana. "Art in the Age of Digital Distribution." In *New Media Art*, edited by M. Tribe and U. Grosenick. Taschen, 2009.

van Dijck, J. *The Culture of Connectivity: A Critical History of Social Media*. Oxford University Press, 2013. https://doi.org/10.1093/acprof:oso/9780199970773.001.0001.

van Dijck, J., T. Poell, and M. de Waal. *The Platform Society: Public Values in a Connective World*. Oxford University Press, 2018. https://doi.org/10.1093/oso/9780190889760.001.0001.

Vasulka, W., and P. Weibel, eds. *Buffalo Heads: Media Study, Media Practice, Media Pioneers, 1973–1990*. MIT Press, 2008.

Walser, R. "Eruptions: Heavy Metal Appropriations of Classical Virtuosity." *Popular Music* 11, no. 3 (1992): 263–308. https://doi.org/10.1017/S0261143000005158.

Wark, M. *A Hacker Manifesto*. Harvard University Press, 2004.

Wikipedia. "Athabasca Oil Sands." Last modified January 8, 2025, 19:07 (UTC). https://en.wikipedia.org/wiki/Athabasca_oil_sands.

Wikipedia. "BuzzFeed." Last modified December 13, 2024, 08:33 (UTC). https://en.wikipedia.org/wiki/BuzzFeed.

Wikipedia. "Cross Road Blues." Last modified January 9, 2025, 18:42 (UTC). https://en.wikipedia.org/wiki/Cross_Road_Blues.

Wikipedia. "*Elle* (magazine)." Last modified January 5, 2025, 09:49 (UTC). https://en.wikipedia.org/wiki/Elle_(magazine).

Wikipedia. "Equinox Group." Last modified December 6, 2024, 23:26 (UTC). https://en.wikipedia.org/wiki/Equinox_Group.

Wikipedia. "*Europeras*." Last modified August 13, 2019, 04:42 (UTC). https://en.wikipedia.org/wiki/Europeras.

Wikipedia. "Morgan Stanley." Last modified January 10, 2025, 17:39 (UTC). https://en.wikipedia.org/wiki/Morgan_Stanley.

Wikipedia. "Reblogging." Last modified January 17, 2025, 07:52 (UTC). https://en.wikipedia.org/wiki/Reblogging.

Wikipedia. "Side-scrolling video game." Last modified December 22, 2020, 15:34 (UTC). https://en.wikipedia.org/w/index.php?title=Side-scrolling_video_game&oldid=995725143.

Wikipedia. "*Super Mario*." Last modified March 11, 2021, 03:10 (UTC). https://en.wikipedia.org/w/index.php?title=Super_Mario&oldid=1011478454.

Wikipedia. "Tony Conrad." Last modified July 19, 2024, 12:38 (UTC). https://en.wikipedia.org/wiki/Tony_Conrad.

Wikipedia. "Wikipedia:Bots." Last modified August 14, 2024, 07:27 (UTC). https://en.wikipedia.org/wiki/Wikipedia:Bots.

Williams, R. *Television: Technology and Cultural Form*. 3rd ed. Routledge, 2003.

Wu, T. *The Attention Merchants: The Epic Scramble to Get Inside Our Heads*. Knopf Doubleday, 2016.

Zdebik, J. "Celluloid Film as Digital Art: Aesthetics of Translation, Information and Intermediality in the Works of Cory Arcangel." Special issue. *Semiotic Review*, no. 3 (August 2017). https://web.archive.org/web/20190516231342/https://www.semioticreview.com/ojs/index.php/sr/article/view/36.

Zepke, S. *Art as Abstract Machine: Ontology and Aesthetics in Deleuze and Guattari*. Routledge, 2005.

Žižek, S. "Why Are Laibach and Neue Slowenische Kunst Not Fascists?" In *The Universal Exception: Selected Writings, Volume Two*, edited by R. Butler and S. Stephens. Continuum, 2006.

Zuboff, S. *The Age of Surveillance Capitalism: The Fight for a Human Future at the New Frontier of Power*. Public Affairs, 2019.

INDEX

Note: Page numbers in italics denote references to figures.

Publisher contact:
The MIT Press
Massachusetts Institute of Technology
77 Massachusetts Avenue, Cambridge, MA 02139
mitpress.mit.edu

EU Authorised Representative:
Easy Access System Europe, Mustamäe tee 50,
10621 Tallinn, Estonia
gpsr.requests@easproject.com

Printed by Integrated Books International,
United States of America